D1615071

Low Countries (Spanish Netherlands)
1 Douai—1594
2 Antwerp—1600
3 Lille—1610
4 Tournai—1616

Louvain
1 St. Anthony's—1607 (F)
2 Collegium Pastorale—1623
3 Holy Cross—1626 (D)

Other Places on Continent
1 Prague (Bohemia)—1620 (F)
2 Vielun (Poland)—1645 (F)
3 Capranica (Italy)—1656 (F)

Rome
1 St. Isidore's—1625 (F)
2 Irish College—1627
3 St. Metteo Merulana—1656 (A)
4 San Clemente—1677 (D)

F—Franciscan
D—Dominican
C—Capuchin
A—Augustinian
Car—Carmelite

THE IRISH CONTINENTAL COLLEGE MOVEMENT

THE COLLEGES AT BORDEAUX, TOULOUSE, AND LILLE

The Irish Continental College Movement

THE COLLEGES AT BORDEAUX, TOULOUSE, AND LILLE

by

T. J. WALSH, M.A.

GOLDEN EAGLE BOOKS

DUBLIN AND CORK

$3\ 10,\ 184\ /\ 941.56$

GOLDEN EAGLE BOOKS
4 Bridge Street, Cork
25 Lower Abbey Street, Dublin 1
SBN 1 0 85342 380 6

CONTENTS

ACKNOWLEDGMENTS

I owe a deep debt of gratitude to the late Abbé J. B. Pelette, curé, St Germain du Puch, Bordeaux. He guided me through the files of documents in the departmental and municipal archives, Bordeaux. I record my thanks to Canon Delaruelle and Mgr Ducros of the Institut Catholique, Toulouse. M. de Hérbicourt, departmental archives of Aube, Troyes, was most helpful. The late Father Stanislaus Kavanagh, O.F.M.Cap., D.Litt., allowed me to draw on his vast knowledge of Irish Capuchin history. Professor P. MacBride and Miss Nevin, M.A., University college, Dublin, gave me permission to cite the latter's unpublished thesis : *La Colonie Irlandaise à Bordeaux au xviiie Siècle*. Father S. Corkery, M.A., librarian, St Patrick's College, Maynooth, gave me facilities to consult the papers of Dr Paul Long, administrator-general of Irish foundations in France. I am grateful to Professor S. Pender, University college, Cork. He read the manuscript, and made helpful criticisms and suggestions. The library staff with tireless patience and courtesy located some rare French pamphlets.

T. J. WALSH

INTRODUCTION

I

Archdeacon John Lynch's memoir of Francis Kirwan, bishop of Killala, 1645-61, is an instructive piece of Irish biographical writing of the seventeenth century.[1] Kirwan is depicted as an apostolic figure whose pastoral idealism drew its inspiration from the reforming decrees of the council of Trent. His biographer often harks back to St Malachy of Armagh, the proto-figure of Irish religious reform. Like another Malachy, Kirwan wrestled with ignorance, superstition, priestly indifference and worse.

There is astringent comment on the contemporary religious scene in the western dioceses of Ireland. So Francis Kirwan, as vicar general of Tuam, and then as bishop of Killala, journeyed to remote and nigh inaccessible places in search of souls. His unflagging zeal and dauntless courage brought spiritual felicity to a hapless flock.

One point is stressed by Lynch : the priesthood had first claim on the reforming idealism of Kirwan. Spiritual stagnation was countered by regular retreats and other means of pastoral renewal such as the spiritual exercises of St Ignatius. The bishop accepted the responsibility imposed upon him by the Fathers of Trent : his own humble home was the diocesan seminary. With paternal vigilance he supervised the education and training of the young men for the priestly dignity.

The high *motif* of Lynch's biography is clear. Despite the deadly hazards of the Cromwellian régime Kirwan was determined to implement the Tridentine reforms.

It was all in vain. The good bishop suffered ultimate defeat. He died in exile at Rennes in 1661.

Kirwan's pastoral endeavours must be seen as a one-man effort to grapple with a long-standing and perplexing problem. In its simplest terms, the problem was how to implement the clerical reforms declared at the twenty-third session of the council of Trent. The bishop was imprisoned for fourteen months and then driven to exile : he was cast in a heroic mould. But persecution of the Church in Ireland was intermittent. Anti-Catholic legislation by the Dublin parliament never reached the degree of ferocity that

1. *Pii Antistitis Icon* (St Malo, 1669), Ir. MSS. Comm., 1952.

marked the Elizabethan persecution of Catholicism in England. For example, there never was an Irish counterpart of the act of 1585 (27 Eliz. c.2) under which the very presence of a seminary priest within the queen's realm was treason. Nor was the celebration of Mass ever proscribed by Irish penal legislation Nonetheless, by reason of the penal enactments of the Dublin parliament Ireland was a non-Tridentine place. In other words, the Holy See recognised that the various reforms of Trent were impossible of achievement in Ireland. In particular, the difficulties that beset clerical education were insurmountable. Kirwan's challenge, whatever its heroism in the circumstances of the time, had little more than a symbolic meaning.

From the evidence that has so far come to light it is impossible to analyse in depth the system of clerical training and education in Ireland during late medieval times. At best, the system was disorganised and haphazard; at worst, it lacked the exalted standards that must always be integral to the priesthood. An examination of the sources of history dealing with the pre-Tridentine period leaves little room for an assurance that all was well.[2] One finds it easy to understand that in the absence of adequate facilities at home Irish Catholicism soon began to breathe seawards. Even before the Fathers of Trent passed their reforming decrees there was an Irish drift to the continent. As early as 1548 Irish students began to enrol at the university of Louvain.

In England, as in Ireland, Catholicism was under attack during the reign of Elizabeth. The reforming decrees of Trent were sure bulwarks of defence of a Church under siege but the deployment of resources in both countries did not follow the same plan. There was a common threat to continuity of the priesthood but immediate reaction was varied.

William, afterwards, Cardinal, Allen, architect-in-chief of the English college movement, was not primarily committed to supplying pastoral clergy.[3] His college at Douai, founded in 1568, was professedly intended to serve as an academic sanctuary for scholars of Oxford and Cambridge who refused to subscribe to Elizabeth's acts of uniformity and supremacy. In Allen's own words : 'Our first purpose was to establish a college in which our countrymen who

---

2. Cf. Wilson, *The Beginnings of Modern Ireland* (Dublin, 1914), chap. iii.
3. Cf. McClelland, 'From Douai to Dublin; Four Hundred Years of Educational Endeavour', *Studies,* lix, 1970.

were scattered abroad in different places might live and study together.' The first generation at Douai, therefore, was almost entirely composed of university men, expatriates for conscience sake, who were offered some compensation for the loss of their university.[4] Moreover, Allen believed that the schism in England would be of short duration : on the day of national recantation there would be an instant demand for Catholic scholars. So he wrote : 'For we thought it would be an excellent thing to have men of learning always ready outside the realm to restore religion when the proper moment should come.' Soon, however, it became obvious that the day of reconciliation was remote; the national need was priests skilled in controversy, not scholars of the university. Missionaries were trained for work in England. By 1603 some 413 priests had returned, trained at Douai university, an institution 'that had been founded in controversy for controversy'.[5] Persons, on the other hand, from the outset sought only seminary priests to minister to English recusants. He founded two colleges on the soil of the national enemy, at Valladolid in 1589 and at Seville in 1592.

Inevitably, the Irish planners of the college movement turned to Spain. Not only was Philip II the leading protagonist of the counter reform but politically Ireland was moving within the Spanish ambit. In 1569 when James FitzMaurice of Desmond gave shape to his Catholic confederacy his aim was a military alliance with Spain. McGibbon, archbishop of Cashel and envoy to the courts of Europe, was empowered to offer the crown of Ireland to any Catholic prince of Spain or Burgundy whom Philip might nominate. The Geraldine wars which filled the years 1570-80 were seen by the Irish and understood by the Holy See and Philip II as a religious crusade. Fittingly, Gerald, sixteenth earl of Desmond, bore arms as 'dux exercitus Catholicorum in Hibernia'. But apart from two token expeditions to Ireland in 1579-80 Philip was wary of a major military commitment to the Irish cause.

Meanwhile, in Spain John Howling and Thomas White, pioneers of the Irish college movement, made ready to forge an alliance of another kind. From the *diaspora* of the Munster plantations came the nucleus of the first regular foundation, the Irish college at Salamanca in 1592. Within a year another was added at Lisbon. In 1605 a third seminary was established at Seville.

4. Of the Forty Martyrs canonised in 1970 twelve were alumni of the universities; *Oxford*: Sherwin, Briant, Mayne, Boste, Campion, Roberts; *Cambridge* : Reynolds, Walpole, Gwyn, Kirby, Roe, Howard.
5. Cf. Taylor, 'The Douai Defence', *Recusant History*, x, no. 13, 1969.

A hard fact was driven home at Madrid. The failure of the Armada in 1588 and the failure of Hugh O'Neill, despite Spanish support, at Kinsale in 1601, brought a new assessment of the counter reform in terms other than military. Already, the election of Clement VIII in 1592 had meant a change in papal policy. The new pope set small premium on force of arms as an instrument of religious policy. Although O'Neill and O'Donnell protested their religious motives Clement had little enthusiasm for the Nine Years' War. The primary need in Ireland was priests; hence, the spiritual succour offered by the colleges in the peninsula was more enduring. Significantly, in 1616 there were nine Irish foundations in Spain and the Spanish Netherlands. A report, dated 6 April 1613, by Bentivoglio, internuncio at Brussels, stated that there were 800 secular priests in Ireland, the best having been educated in continental seminaries.[6]

Historical factors, therefore, favoured Irish educational expansion in Spain; for political reasons the establishment of colleges in France was less spontaneous. Not until 1615, and then in spite of lay opposition, did the assembly of the French clergy accept the administrative reforms of Trent. Only then was a move made to set up French diocesan seminaries.[7] Nevertheless, in 1603 the first organised group of Irish students was cordially welcomed at Bordeaux. Similarly, in 1659 when Louis XIV issued letters patent in favour of a college at Toulouse the formal act was simply a recognition of an Irish student settlement that already had existed for several years. But the college at Paris, the premier Irish foundation in France, appears in a different light. Patrick Boyle, a former rector, has written a richly-documented survey of the seminary from its origins to modern times.[8] One is made aware of Irish continuity in the French capital. In the ninth century Erick of Auxerre avowed that 'almost all Ireland with a vast train of philosophers had removed to France'.[9] In the seventeenth century when the Irish college achieved legal status in the university of Paris the tradition of Dungal and John Scotus Erigena was given added strength.

The extent to which Irish military units were contributory factors to the establishment of Irish seminaries in the Spanish Nether-

---

6. *Arch. Hib.*, iii, 301.
7. Cf. Parker, 'The Papacy and Catholic Reform', *The New Cambridge Modern History*, vol. iii.
8. *The Irish College in Paris* (Dublin, 1901).
9. *Ware's Writer*, ed. Harris, bk. 1, p. 57.

lands is uncertain. Louvain, Douai, Lille, and Antwerp summon
up the names of Florence Conry, archbishop of Tuam, Peter Lombard, archibshop of Armagh, Christopher Cusack, Francis Nugent,
and Laurence Sedgrave. They moved in scenes where Old Irish and
Anglo-Irish had a continuous military presence after 1586. Documents of the period list the regiments of William Stanley, Henry
and John O'Neill, sons of Hugh O'Neill, earl of Tyrone, Hugh
O'Donnell, son of Rory O'Donnell, earl of Tyrconnell.[10] We may
suspect that many young Irishmen exchanged the camp for the
seminary.

The post-Tridentine entry of Irish students in the continental
universities was in accord with the change of emphasis in educational practice. Medieval universities, formed in the scholastic
mould, were primarily centres of instruction with little concern for
the moral training of students. Spiritual theory was often far
removed from practice. If the Tridentine reforms meant anything
they meant a reinforcement of elevated spiritual standards in the
priestly state. Forthwith, the broad purposes of the seminary legislation in 1563 were put into effect. The Holy See itself set the
headline. In 1565 Pius IV founded a seminary for the diocese of
Rome. St Charles Borromeo, cardinal archbishop of Milan (1560-
84), established three diocesan seminaries. A few years later Gregory
XIII (1572-84) began the *collegium Germanicum* and the *collegium Romanum* for the training and education of students from
all parts of the World. The new emphasis on pastoral competence
was a stimulus to theological thought. At Louvain and at Rome St
Robert Bellarmine was a renowned teacher but the theological
revival reached the highest levels in the universities of Spain :
Salamanca, Alcalá, Valladolid and at Coimbra in Portugal. It was
the age of Suarez, Soto, Vasquez, and Molina. Soon after its re-
constitution in 1560-61 the university of Salamanca attracted
Irish students who won distinction in later years : Florence Conry,
Hugh MacCaughwell, Luke Wadding and Hugh Ward. But before
they appeared in the lecture halls there was an enrolment of young
Irishmen. In 1574 Oliver Eustace and John Philipps applied to
the senate of the university for the means of subsistence. Nothing
more is known of the pioneer Irish students but they traced a
path for the many hundreds who followed.

10. *Wild Geese in Spanish Flanders, 1582-1700,* ed. Jennings, Ir. MSS.
Comm. 1964.

II

In the early years of the seventeenth century the movement of Irish students to the continent gathered momentum. By the middle period there were twenty-five foundations, secular and regular. The absence of a national or co-ordinating authority in Ireland, such as a hierarchy, had enormous disadvantages. Tridentine legislation required that ordination of a student to the diocesan priesthood must be authorised by the bishop of the diocese. In those years many dioceses were without bishops or the bishops were inaccessible in their places of refuge. The anomalous position *vis-à-vis* the law was first experienced at Salamanca. In 1600 Hugh O'Neill petitioned Clement VIII to remove the legal obstacle. Ultimately, the problem was solved by Urban VIII. In 1623 by apostolic indult he authorised the ordination of students in all the Irish continental seminaries on the sole title of a mission in Ireland. Responsibility was vested in the local college superior. In effect, the privilege was an invasion of episcopal duty, and in the long term, was fraught with peril. In 1750 when the Irish hierarchy was fully re-constituted an early effort was made by the bishops to secure a modification of the privilege. The question will be discussed at a later stage.

Scarcely had the college movement got under way when another cause of harassment arose—provincial or regional rivalry. Again, Salamanca was the first scene of the agitation. The dominance of the Munster dioceses was challenged. In 1602 O'Neill and O'Donnell championed the claims of Connacht and Ulster. The Franciscan Florence Conry addressed a memorial to Philip III requesting the reservation of half the enrolment at the college to students from the western and northern dioceses. Apparently, there was little student disturbance at Salamanca but provincial rivalry led to dissensions of a more grievous nature at Douai in 1614, at Antwerp in 1631, and at Bordeaux in 1678. Regional exclusiveness was a first axiom in Lille college : an unassailable reservation in favour of the dioceses of Meath and Leinster, that is of Anglo-Irish students, was enshrined in the terms of its foundation. Francis Nugent, the founder, defended his regionalism against many critics and finally, in the law courts of Flanders. Paradoxically, in 1636, a year after Nugent's death, the Holy See, notwithstanding official disclaimers, approved the Capuchin restriction of entry to Lille college. But the matter was a *question de droit* on many occasions.

Provincial rivalry did not provoke the grave disorders at the college at Toulouse; the reservation in favour of the dioceses of Cork, Cloyne, and Ross was not questioned. Although the documents in the departmental archives at Toulouse highlight the student agitations during 1669-1699 we confess that we are at a loss to discover the heads of the indictment. Beyond doubt, the election of a superior by student vote led to dissensions but we must seek some other reasons to explain the drastic disciplinary actions. There was high drama on 2 May 1669 when the entire Irish community was assembled in the great hall of the archbishop's palace to hear an official complaint of their 'pestilential quarrels'. Three students were removed from the college; two in priests' orders were suspended and a severe communal penance was imposed.

Our generation has learned to be tolerant of student restiveness. In the history of the Irish colleges isolated disturbances which must surely be related to the tangled and confused pattern of our country's story do not deserve unequivocal condemnation. Temptation to censure is repelled when we remember that the students accepted without demur conditions of living that sometimes were but one remove from near-starvation.

Throughout the seventeenth century student life in the colleges in the Spanish dominions was a stern novitiate; a central theme is the constant struggle against poverty. Almost the only assured revenue was the promised state subsidy. A not very reliable estimate of the subvention is the equivalent of an annual grant of a hundred pounds to each foundation. With the slow decline of Spanish power and wealth the appointed subsidies were often withheld. In 1623 Spanish state credit was low : the Infanta Isabella, viceroy of the Low Countries, complained to Philip IV that payments of 157712 crowns had been refused by the bankers at Antwerp.[11] Under such conditions, payments to the colleges fell into deep arrears. In 1627 three Irish bishops appealed to Cardinal Ludovisi, protector of Ireland, to induce the Spanish court to meet Irish claims.

In the Low Countries the economic plight of the colleges was worse. In 1625 the sale of Douai college was imminent to meet the demands of the creditors but there was timely intervention by the bishops of Flanders and the abbots of Benedictine abbeys. There was a temporary closure of the seminary at Antwerp while the Pastoral college at Louvain was rescued by the Holy See. In 1680 Paul van Hamale, archpriest of Antwerp, wrote that the Irish seminary in that city needed a Maecenas of superlative munificence !

11. *Ibid.*, p. 628.

At that period vast political changes affected many Irish foundations. In the expansionist wars of Louis XIV between 1668 and 1678 much of Flanders was incorporated into the kingdom of France. The consequent loss of revenues reduced to destitution the colleges at Lille, Douai, and Tournai. Once again, alms from the Holy See appeared to have ensured survival. While there is little record of initial French subsidies it is clear that under French rule the impact of poverty was greatly reduced.

An important factor in the French foundations may not be overlooked. In contrast to the earlier entry into Spain the Irish arrival in France did not bear a political complexion nor was there any offer of state benevolence. Thus in 1603 when Diarmuid MacCarthy and his students reached Bordeaux the only patronage was that of the archbishop, Cardinal de Sourdis. He explained the purpose of the Irish venture to his clergy then assembled in synod and invoked their co-operation. There was a ready response : a house, the property of the diocesan chapter, was handed over to MacCarthy and his group. More than once in the succeeding years Cardinal de Sourdis rallied the citizens of Bordeaux to maintain the Irish in their midst. Later we shall describe the extraordinary happenings that led to the endowment of the college by Louis XIV and the queen-mother, Anne of Austria. Again, in 1683 Joseph de Montpézat, archbishop of Toulouse, made a pastoral appeal on behalf of the Irish students. In pithy phrases he commended the émigrés : 'it has pleased the divine goodness to inspire several of their [Irish] priests and seminarists to seek refuge in certain towns of France and amongst them, Toulouse. Having been cordially received here with Christian charity they have made such progress in theological studies as to become fit for ordination.' The archbishop made reference to the conditions under which newly-ordained priests returned to Ireland. The funds raised would be utilised to purchase the passage home and also to provide them with secular dress to avoid detection.[12]

After 1690 the Jacobite exodus and the later Irish infiltration to France helped consolidate the seminaries. The first and second

12. In 1636 a Flemish vessel was detained off Plymouth and a young man was removed. In a deposition before the justices of the peace at Plymouth Derby O'Callaghan admitted that he was a priest; that the box of rosaries and crucifixes were his possessions. He added that he was a native of Mallow, Co. Cork, and had been ordained at Bordeaux. After sundry journeys through France he had taken ship for Ireland at La Rochelle. *Cal. State Papers, 1633-47,* p. 120.

generation of Irish émigrés were mindful of the grave oppression of
Irish Catholicism by the Williamite penal code. Irish regiments in
the French military service and prominent Irish mercantile families
at Paris, Nantes, St Malo, Bordeaux, and elsewhere strengthened
the Franco-Irish nexus. The colleges were obvious channels of aid
to Ireland. Hence the series of burses and other educational foundations established by clerics and lay donors. The *pietas* of the
founder was usually expressed in the attached conditions : the
students nominated must be relatives of the founder or must come
from a specified Irish diocese or parish. We print a list of the
burses—to be read with certain qualifications.[13] The titles and
descriptions of the burses are taken from documents prepared in
1815 and later used to prosecute Irish claims for compensation
under the treaty between Britain and France.[14] Since 1802 all
burses and educational revenues had been vested in the Irish
college, Paris. Our list, therefore, affords little indication of the
distribution of the burses among the colleges under the *ancien
régime*. For other reasons the list is incomplete. Some of the legal
documents were lost in the revolutionary years; others were never
executed in strict accord with French law. As will be seen later lack
of legal proof of title militated against the presentation of Irish
claims in the law courts of Britain in 1825 and 1832.

In 1745 the last rally to the house of Stuart suffered final defeat
on the battlefield of Culloden. In Ireland, the penal legislators
breathed easily : the menace of Jacobitism was removed. Already
there was a run-down of the more vicious phases of the penal code;
now was the time for more cautious moves towards toleration. In
1750 every diocese in the country had its resident bishop. Spiritual
stocktaking showed several pastoral deficiencies. It became obvious
that the remedy lay in the implementation of the reforms imposed
by the council of Trent. One Tridentine decree required that
bishops must establish seminaries in their dioceses. Already Archbishop Butler of Cashel (1711-57) had led the way with the sem-
blance of a diocesan college. Other reforms, however, were more
urgent. During the acute penal era certain bishops in need of
pastoral clergy ordained young men of minimal education. There
was an accompanying injunction on the young priests to enrol at
some continental college when opportunity afforded for further

13. Appendix 1.
14. Some of the titles are intriguing : e.g. the burse entitled 'The Poor
of Macroom'.

training and education. Failure by many to obey led to abuses. There was a clash of views among the bishops. But there was agreement that any amelioration of pastoral conditions demanded that the bishops must accept their canonical responsibility to select and promote aspirants to the diocesan priesthood. A major obstacle was the privilege enjoyed since 1623 by the continental colleges of ordaining students without reference to diocesan bishops, a privilege utterly at variance with Tridentine discipline. Lille college was a case in point. Only students from Meath and the dioceses of Leinster were accepted. Yet the nomination and subsequent ordination of the students had no reference to the bishops of Leinster.[15] Hence in 1764 Patrick Fitzsimons, archbishop of Dublin, and his suffragan bishops, challenged the Capuchin rights at Lille. Although the supreme court of Flanders decided in favour of the Capuchins the omens were unambiguous : the continental colleges were gradually being outmoded. The original terms of their foundation were questioned.

Deep currents were also running in France threatening the foundations of the establishment from which the colleges drew life. Voltaire and Rousseau were the high priests of the new radicalism. In 1763 La Chalotais' *Essai d'éducation nationale* impugned and rejected the role of the Church as educator. A year later, the Jesuits and their 560 colleges were suppressed. In 1772 the encyclopaedists completed their synthesis of the new enlightenment in which supernatural belief and revelation were rationalised. The *ancien régime* was slowly undermined.

Outwardly, all such assaults on the established order bore little significance for the Irish seminaries. Nonetheless, there was a sharp reminder of growing animus at Bordeaux. Martin Glynn, superior of the college, writing in 1774 to Dr Charles O'Kelly, San Clemente, Rome, described how the students were reviled and insulted in the streets by the populace. In 1776 Patrick Geoghegan of Lille college in a letter to Father Norbert Shee at Bar-sur-Aube confessed that the seminary was plunged in misery without any possibility of relief. Francis Moylan, formerly of Toulouse, and now bishop of Cork, saw the gathering storm clouds and invited his friend, the Abbé Edgeworth, to join him in Ireland.[16] A few years later, the

15. On 26 September 1769 the provisors of the Irish college at Lille refused to accept students nominated by Patrick Fitzsimons, archbishop of Dublin. Burke MSS.

16. *Lettres de l'Abbé Edgeworth à ses Amis* (Paris, 1818), 26 ff.

ill-omened appointment of Loménie de Brienne, archbishop of Toulouse, as first minister of state in succession to Calonne, fanned the flames of anti-clericalism. When the cataclysm came in 1789 the National Assembly gave assurances of immunity to foreign institutions. There was a specific exemption of Irish establishments from the general confiscation of Church property. But the immunity was short-lived. In 1793 the Hébertist extremists of the Jacobins gained power. Then came the final reckoning with the Irish colleges.

Yet all was not lost. By a happy chance the seminary in rue du Cheval Vert (now rue des Irlandais), Paris, survived the general wrack. This institution now engaged the attention of Bonaparte. Franco-Irish *entente* had been weakened by the closure of the colleges; the First Consul devised a scheme of restoration. Centralising Irish funds and integrating the seminary with the Prytanée or university of France he endeavoured to create conditions that would induce a return of Irish students. There was no response from Ireland. When the concordat with the Holy See was negotiated in 1801 Bonaparte felt that his hand was strengthened. In the following year he established a federation of the former Irish foundations at Antwerp, Louvain, Lille, Douai, Nantes, Bordeaux, Toulouse together with the former English and Scots colleges. The federated institute was in rue du Cheval Vert. In 1805 by imperial decree Napoleon gave the college a new constitution and threatened to disburse Irish revenues if the students did not return. A year later he made a drastic suggestion. In the belief that a strong Irish nucleus in rue du Cheval Vert would give a fillip to his plans he invited Dr Bartholomew Crotty of Clonakilty, Co. Cork, superior of the Irish college, Lisbon, to transfer to Paris. Crotty was not unwilling but the Irish bishops entered a flat negative. In fact, the bishops now rested their hopes on the infant establishment at Maynooth, founded in 1795.

Irish educational enterprise in France that had lasted for two centuries did not die easily. A legal battle was begun for the recovery and repatriation of Irish burses and in default, compensation was sought for losses sustained. In the final chapter we shall trace from contemporary documents the last phase of the college movement. When the entire story has been told one cannot escape an acute sense of deprivation. True, the college at Rome is a flourishing institution. Also we find a certain comfort in the knowledge that Polish students now occupy the historic building in rue des Irlandais, Paris. One feels that its original purpose is still served

3 10, 184 / $941 \cdot 56$

when young men denied Catholic education in their homeland are occupants of Irish property. The last vestige of Irish educational activity in Spain disappeared in 1951 with the sale of the college at Salamanca to the Spanish government. The ancient building, so full of Irish memories, is now incorporated with the medical school of the university.

In the foregoing pages we have traced the broad outlines of a complicated episode in Irish history. In the following chapters we shall present a more detailed examination of the college movement with special reference to the colleges at Bordeaux, Toulouse, and Lille. Some questions must remain unanswered; perhaps a discovery of more Franco-Irish materials will add to our knowledge. In particular, examination of Hispanic-Irish sources of history will reveal a much more complete picture of the colleges in the peninsula. It is gratifying to know that research in Spanish archives is in the competent hands of Professor P. MacBride, University college, Dublin, and his team of devoted workers.

Most Irish parishes retain a tradition of some old-time priest trained and educated in a continental college. In our own day William O'Brien recalled boyhood memories of Mallow, Co. Cork. He gives a delightful pen-portrait of the lovable Abbé Moriarty— 'the delicious old French-trained angel in a shabby hat who knew of no country except France and Heaven'.[17] One finds occasional reminders in the scattered remnants of clerical libraries : names writter on flyleaves that tell us that the volume was once in the hands of a student at Salamanca, Bordeaux or Paris.[18] There are other memorials to the old-time priests who sought education abroad. In the countless churchyards and cemeteries of the countryside one finds eighteenth-century monuments. Inscriptions, worn by time and weather, often make mention of Paris, Bordeaux, Salamanca or some other continental college. In the hearts of the Irish people the inscriptions are unfading.

17. *Irish Fireside Hours* (Dublin, 1927), p. 81. The Abbé Moriarty is Father Phil in *When We Were Boys*.
18. A volume in the writer's possession (*Doctrina S. Concilii Tridentini*, Lyons, 1664) bears the names of Nicholas Kirby and James O'Donoghue. Both were students of the diocese of Cloyne at the college of Bordeaux.

MANUSCRIPT SOURCES

THE COLLEGE AT BORDEAUX

A—*Archives départementales de la Gironde, 14 rue d'aviau, Bordeaux*
   Séries G 525 — G 920, D, L, Q, E supplément.

B—*Archives municipales de la ville de Bordeaux, 74 rue de Loup, Bordeaux*
   État civil, série L.

C—*San Clemente, Rome,* Codex 11, D 106.

D—*Lambeth Library,* Carew MSS.

E—*Trinity College, Dublin,* MS. E.3.15.

F—*St Patrick's College, Maynooth,* Long Papers—collection of official documents relating to former Irish foundations in France.

G—*Mount Melleray, Co. Waterford,* Burke MSS.—notes on Irish continental foundations compiled by the late Canon W. P. Burke.

H—*Cork Diocesan Archives,* Murphy Papers—correspondence and memoranda of John Murphy, bishop of Cork, 1815-47.

THE COLLEGE AT TOULOUSE

A—*Archives départementales de la Haute-Garonne, 11 Boulevard Griffoul-Dorval, Toulouse*
   Séries G 427 — G 428.

B—*Public Record Office, Belfast,* MS. D 1514/9/70.

C—*Domestic Annals, South Presentation Convent, Cork*

THE COLLEGE AT LILLE[1]

A—*Archives départementales de l'Aube, quai du Comte Henri, Troyes*
   Séries D and E (1606-85), H 1-12 (1685-1790).

B—*Bibliothèque municipale, rue Chrestien, Troyes*
   Nicholas Archbold, *Historie of the Irish Capuchins* (1642), cabinet des MSS. no. 1103; Robert O'Connell, *Historia Missionis Hibernicae Fratrum Minorum Capuccinorum (1655),* pp. 724, cabinet des MSS. no. 706.

C—*Archives départementales de la Haute-Marne, Chaumont*
   Séries G 971 — G 974 (1700-1790).

1. Authenticated transcripts of the documents here noted are in the provincial archives of the Irish Capuchins, Church St., Dublin. A complete conspectus of Irish Capuchin materials of history is printed by F. X. Martin, O.S.A., 'Sources for the History of the Irish Capuchins', *Collectanea Franciscana,* vol. 26, 1956.

D—*Archives départementales du Nord, 1 rue du Pont-Neuf, Lille*
    Séries B 1642; D 568 — D 580; D 624 — D 626.
E—*Archives of the Congregation de Prop. Fid., Rome*
    i Lettere antiche vols. 74-297.
    ii Scritture riferite Irlanda vols. 298-698.
    iii Scritture riferite nei Congressi Irelanda vols. 1-28.
    iv Acts S. Cong. 1622-74.
    v Tabularium S. Cong. congreg. particolari, 1622.

A fortunate circumstance ensured the survival of some Franco-Irish materials during the revolutionary period. Records in many episcopal chanceries and the domestic documents of some collegiate and religious institutions ultimately reached the safe keeping of civic and municipal authorities. Hence the preservation of documents formerly in the diocesan chancery of Bordeaux; they are now in the departmental archives of the Gironde, Bordeaux. Again, some, not all, of the domestic records of the former Irish college at Toulouse are to be found today in the departmental archives of Haute Garonne at Toulouse. Similarly, the considerable volume of materials relating to the former Irish Capuchin foundations at Bar-sur-Aube and Vassy are preserved in the departmental archives of Aube and the municipal archives at Troyes. From such sources an attempt will be made in these pages to reconstruct the history of three Irish colleges in France : the seminaries at Bordeaux, Toulouse, and Lille.

At Bordeaux one finds a vast quantity of documents of a most diversified character pertaining to the administration of successive archbishops from the early years of the sixteenth century to the period of the revolution. The collection includes pastoral letters, episcopal correspondence, communications with the Holy See, letters to and from religious superiors, secular and regular. One could not give a general classification other than the day-to-day records of administration of an extensive diocese. When Abbé Bertrand compiled his monograph on the Irish college at Bordeaux he always referred to the above archival sources as *Archives de l'Archevêché*; doubtless, he repudiated the continued retention by the civil authorities of materials that were once ecclesiastical property.[2]

References to the Irish arrival at Bordeaux in 1603 are found in the liasse or series *Actes de l'Archevêché de Bordeaux sous le cardinal de Sourdis*. Very informative for our purposes are the

2. *Histoire des séminaires de Bordeaux et de Bazas* (Bordeaux, 1894).

letters patent of Anne of Austria, the queen regent, dated February 1654, taking the college into the royal protection. More valuable are the letters patent of Louis XIV, dated April 1654, conferring French citizenship on the priests and students of the college.

Diocesan historians naturally seek the names of students and dioceses of origin. A petition to Archbishop de Béthune, dated April 1665, to retain Dr Cornelius Scanlon in office as superior is a roll-call of the Irish community at that time. A recital of the names of those present at the election of a superior in 1672 adds to our knowledge of the student body.

A more obvious source of such information is the records of ordinations by various archbishops of Bordeaux. Recognition of Irish names under a French or Latin guise is not always immediate.[3] It seems that ordinations of Irish students took place in the chapel attached to the hospital of St André. Although the records are incomplete many Irish students are discovered.[4] The earliest record is the ordination of John O'Connor of Cork on 6 September 1622; the latest is that of Thomas Molloy of Ossory on 17 May 1782. One is grateful to the archbishop's secretary : in most cases he added the parentage and parish of origin in Ireland of the ordinand. Two Irish bishops officiated in the eighteenth century. In 1738 Robert Lacy, a former superior of the college and recently consecrated bishop of Limerick, ordained students from Cork, Emly, Limerick, and Kildare. In December 1756 and March 1757 John O'Brien, the exiled bishop of Cloyne, conferred Holy Orders on students from Cork, Cloyne, and Kerry.[5]

Here and there in the collection are found detached notes of Irish interest. For example, a brief letter, undated, addressed presumably to Archbishop Honoré-François de Maniban, contains an assurance that a named French nobleman had complied with the paschal precept. The note is signed by Robert Lacy, superior of the Irish college. This is the only known signature of a well-known bishop of Limerick in penal times. In a series containing copies of official correspondence entitled *Registre des expéditions du secretariat de l'archevêché* a single folio gives the names of fifteen Irish priests to whom *celebrets* were issued in 1759.[6]

3. Thus 'Heanoesoeus' for Hennessy and 'Squiddoeus' for Skiddy.
4. Printed in *Arch. Hib.*, xv (1950).
5. Lacy was bishop of Limerick, 1737-59; John O'Brien, author of the *Irish Dictionary* (Paris, 1769), was bishop of Cloyne 1748-68.
6. A *celebret* is the official approval by a bishop authorising a priest to celebrate Mass.

A question to be more fully discussed in a later context is—why did so many Irish priests, presumably alumni of the college, elect to remain on the French mission? Examination of registers of the communes in the area now included in the Gironde reveals the names of some scores of Irish priests and the parishes in which they served. This collection of MSS volumes which begins with the year 1595 is known as *E Supplément*. The series does not carry records beyond the years of the revolution. More Irish names are found in the series *volumes des nominations ecclésiastiques*—a summary of appointments to parishes made by archbishops of Bordeaux during the eighteenth century. References to Irish curés are found for the same period in *volumes des visites des paroisses par l'archevêque*.

In the *État Civil* in the municipal archives of Bordeaux are recorded the deaths of Irish priests and students of the college.[7] The system of registration is based upon the fourteen parishes of the city. Thus the *État Civil* of the parish of St Projet provides the names, dates of death, and often place of interment of Irish priests for the reason that the hospital of St André and the college were situated in the parish of St Projet. Also in the municipal archives is a four-paged folio which yields the names of six Irish priests to whom passports were issued during 1792-93.

The Abbé Bertrand's work on the Irish seminary at Bordeaux is largely based upon the above sources. Although he does not cite any particular file or liasse there is little difficulty in finding his materials. A valuable guide to the departmental archives is M. Allain's *Inventaire sommaire des archives de l'archevêché de Bordeaux* (Bordeaux, 1893).

At Toulouse the materials relating to the former Irish college (1659-1793) are far less extensive than the sources of Irish history at Bordeaux. The records now preserved in the departmental archives of the Haute-Garonne, Toulouse, are divided into two series : G 427 and G 428. The arrangement was made in a somewhat haphazard fashion with little thought for continuity or chronological sequence.

Amongst the first folios in G 428 we find the earliest dated document. It is an authenticated copy of the renewal in 1626 to Thomas Fleming, archbishop-elect of Dublin, of the privilege granted by Urban VIII in 1623 of ordaining students in the Irish continental colleges on the sole title of a mission in Ireland. The copy at Toulouse was authenticated at Paris on 15 September 1645.

7. Printed in *Arch. Hib.,* xv.

Included in G 428 are the lettres patentes of Louis XIV in 1659, *registre de réception des séminaristes* during 1660-69 and for the period 1684-94, *formula admissionis et juramenti quod in ipso ingressu praestabunt recipiendi in Congregatione Hibernorum apud Tolosates*—with autograph signatures. In addition there are original records of the *procès-verbaux* of meetings held during 1660-69 to pass college accounts and to elect a college superior. A fascicle entitled *pièces produits par l'archevêque de toulouse pour justifier son autorité dans le séminaire des irlandois* 1663-69 contains official statements concerning rivalries among the students at times of election. Here we find an autograph letter written in 1669 by Charles-François de Bourlemont, archbishop of Toulouse. A few *pièces détachées* have neither title nor date.

In G 427 is an undated copy, but written before 1683, of a remarkable document. It is a pastoral letter, addressed to the citizens of Toulouse, by Archbishop Joseph de Montpézat, urging support and sympathy for the young Irish students in their midst. We give the full text on a later page. In the series are also the statutes of the college drawn up by Archbishop Colbert in 1694, and an undated copy of an *ordonnance* by the archbishop reserving to himself the right to nominate a college superior to the exclusion of agitation among the students. Events in the college during 1696-1700 are relatively well-documented. A report, filling nine folios, by M. Raby, vicar general of Toulouse, contains his observations and recommendations following a visitation of the seminary in 1696. Amongst the *pièces detachées* are depositions made at this time by Modeste MacSwiney and M. O'Shihan (*sic*) who were rival claimants to the office of superior.

Series 427 also holds materials of the eighteenth century. There are authenticated copies of court decisions; a decree of the *conseil d'état* in 1703 confirming the appointment of Timothy O'Brien as superior, lettres patentes of Louis XV in 1730 and 1754, a printed copy of the new statutes drawn up in 1731. Perhaps the most informative document in the series is the ledger or domestic account-book of Francis O'Hea, superior of the college during 1751-66. The daily record of income and expenditure gives a close-up picture of the college at work. Unfortunately for our purposes, O'Hea seldom wrote the Christian names and dioceses of the students whose names appear regularly in his ledger. The latest document relating to the college is the decree in 1761 of Arthur Richard Dillon, archbishop of Toulouse, giving the institution the status of a French seminary.

Lille college was something of an anomaly among the Irish continental foundations. It was an institution, founded and controlled by Irish Capuchins, to supply priests to the dioceses of the pale. The diverse original sources of the history of the seminary require some explanation.

Irish Capuchin history begins in 1608 with the formal establishment of the mission to Ireland. Francis Nugent, pioneer Irish Capuchin, at once embarked upon a project that had two immediate objectives. Firstly, a recruiting ground for Irish Capuchin novices was imperative; secondly, Nugent felt impelled to include in his purview the pastoral needs of the dioceses of the pale. To the achievement of these purposes he founded the college at Lille in 1610. His plans for Ireland were carried a stage further in 1615 with the establishment of an Irish Capuchin novitiate at Charleville, a town on the river Meuse on the borders of the Low Countries.

Thenceforward to his death in 1635 Nugent was involved in controversy. His inflexible determination and forthright methods aroused antagonism on the continent and in Ireland. The college at Lille was a special target for criticism by Catholics in Ulster and Connacht on the grounds of its restricted entry in favour of young men from the pale. But Nugent withstood his critics. Hence, at Charleville, the headquarters of the Irish Capuchin effort, a considerable quantity of *Nugentiana* was accumulated.

Two Capuchin historians add to our knowledge of the early years of Lille college. In 1643 Nicholas Archbold, a colleague and associate of Nugent, wrote his MS *Historie of the Irish Capucins,* pp. 157.[8] Later, in 1655, Robert O'Connell completed his MS *Historia Missionis Hibernicae Fratrum Minorum Capuccinorum,* pp. 724.[9] Both writers used materials to hand at Charleville.

In 1685, by decision of Louis XIV, the Irish Capuchins at Charleville were transferred to friaries at Bar-sur-Aube and Vassy in Champagne. At the suppressions in 1793 most of the materials in the friary at Bar-sur-Aube were placed in the departmental archives of Aube, the remainder in the municipal library at Troyes.[10] The documents at Vassy were deposited in the depart-

8. Archbold was born at Mountainfoot, Dalkey, Co. Dublin. He was guardian at Charleville 1622-25. He died at Wexford in 1650.

9. O'Connell was born at Ballycarbery, near Cahirciveen, Co. Kerry. He joined the Capuchins at Charleville in 1645. He is best known as the author-in-chief of the *Commentarius Rinuccinianus,* Irish MSS. Comm.

10. The Irish materials at Troyes are now on microfilm in the National Library of Ireland.

mental archives of Haute-Marne at Chaumont.

Some records in the college at the time of its suppression are now in the departmental archives of Nord, Lille.

The present writer spent some time at Troyes and Chaumont in 1952. Beyond obtaining some materials in photostat and microfilm he did not make any extensive extracts for the following reason. At various times during the early years of the present century the late Father Stanislaus Kavanagh, O.F.M.Cap., D.Litt., archivist of the Irish Capuchin province, received authentic copies of the historical records set forth in the preceding list of sources.[11] The copies have been bound and are now in the provincial archives, Church Street, Dublin, where the present writer consulted them. In compiling the history of Lille college he relied on the copies.

Transcripts from the archives de l'Aube and de la Haute-Marne have been arranged in six folio volumes :

(a) Papers dealing with the missionary and domestic affairs of the Irish Capuchins from 1608 to the French revolution. Included are correspondence of superiors, firstly at Charleville and later at Bar-sur-Aube and Vassy, documents dealing with religious and missionary affairs, reports to the Holy See, memoranda of individual missionaries in Ireland from the time of Nugent to 1789. All such materials have been bound in three volumes lettered *Troyes Transcripts,* i, ii, iii.

(b) Historical materials relating specifically to Lille college have been segregated : the correspondence of Nugent, copies of deeds of title, affirmations and letters of Don Jean de Robles, Christopher Cusack, and Sedgrave, figures associated with the early history of the college. Also there are numerous documents relating to the many legal proceedings of the Capuchins in defence of their rights at Lille, letters from the bishop of Tournai, some decrees of the Congregation de Prop. Fid., memoranda dealing with administration in the eighteenth century. All such materials have been bound in three volumes lettered *Troyes Transcripts, Lille College,* i, ii, iii. The small collection from the archives du Nord, Lille, is a quarto sized typescript of twenty pages.

---

11. The copyists were M. Massiet du Biest, archivist of the Ardennes department, and M. Roger Geny, archivist of the department of Haute-Harne. Cf. Du Biest, *Notes sur les archives des Capucins Irlandais ayant en leur siège en France à Charleville, Sedan, Bar-sur-Aube et Vassy* (Nonce et Cie, 6 rue Houzean-Muiron, Reims, 1924), and Gigot, *Inventaire sommaire des archives communales antérieures à 1815* (Chaumont, 1948).

Chapter One

THE CONTINENTAL COLLEGE MOVEMENT

1

'ECCLESIA SEMPER REFORMANDA'

Our generation has witnessed the inception of the mighty reforms launched by the second Vatican ecumenical council. The *aggiornamento* of John XXIII, however nebulous the term when it first fell on our ears, has now achieved a real and personal meaning at all levels of religious life. There is unqualified acceptance of the overall purposes of the council : 'to fight scepticism and defeatism and to combine a necessary realism with hope and encouragement.'[1] For a world held in thrall by clashing ideologies the Church has a message of hope and encouragement. In missionary terms, the Church must always be ready in succeeding generations to meet the challenges and needs of redeemed mankind.

Were the terms of reference of the council of Trent in the sixteenth century different? At the first session in 1545 Cardinal del Monte, legate of Paul III, declared the conciliar purposes : 'for the increase of Christian clergy and people.' The council Fathers meeting at Trent had no illusions as to the nature and extent of the counter reform required to meet the religious malaise of the sixteenth century. Hence the Tridentine reforms were given their most precise and contemporary statement in the twenty-third session.[2] The theme was the priesthood. Without faithful shepherds there was no feeding the flock of Christ. The experience of four centuries is an endorsement of the shining ideals set forth at Trent in 1563. From the historical perspective it is legitimate to conclude that the reforming decrees of the twenty-third session were the touchstone, if not the measure, of the counter reform in England and Ireland.

Response in England and in Ireland to the Catholic revival was the establishment of clerical seminaries on the European mainland. Beyond that mere statement there was little parallelism between the movements in both countries.

1. Küng, *The Council in Action* (New York, 1963), p. 8.
2. Forma erigendi seminarium clericorum praesertim tenuiorum: in cujus erectione plurima observanda: de educatione promovendorum in cathedralibus et in majoribus ecclesiis, *Canones et Decreta Concilii Tridentini,* sessio xxiii. Cf. Alzog, *Manual of Universal Church History,* iii, 430 ff.

William Allen (1532-94) of Oriel college, Oxford, gave the first impetus to the English college movement in 1568 when he founded the seminary at Douai, the 'mother and nurse' of all the other seminaries. A second foundation was added in 1579, the *Venerabile* or English college, Rome. Soon Allen was joined by the Jesuit Robert Persons (1546-1610) formerly of Balliol college, Oxford, who established two colleges in Spain : at Valladolid in 1589 and at Seville in 1592. Under the guidance of Allen and Persons the Catholic revival in England was crystallised in the college movement. Hence the history of English Catholic recusancy is largely the story of the continental seminaries.

An important point is the distinctive origin and first expansion of the English foundations on the continent. The colleges at Douai, Rome, Valladolid, and Seville had their provenance in the universities of Oxford and Cambridge. Rejecting the acts of supremacy and uniformity the non-jurors of the universities turned to Europe. When Allen opened his college at Douai in 1568 the trickle of émigrés soon became a torrent. Nicholas Sanders of Winchester and New College, Oxford, was happy when he saw 'the very flower of the two universities carried away as it were by storm and scattered to foreign lands.'[3] In the words of Professor Beales a tide of scholarship and teaching power followed Allen across the channel denuding the universities and the schools.[4] In such circumstances during 1570-80 took place the first mobilisation of the forces of the English counter reform.

Elizabeth and secretary Cecil read the portents. Pius V's bull *Regnans in Excelsis* in 1570 and its excommunication of Elizabeth coincided with the first appearance of the seminary priests in the queen's realm. Little time was lost in deploying the power of the law; a penal enactment in 1571 (13 Eliz. cap. 1) made it treason to bring a copy of a papal bull into England. Seminary priests, said Cecil, presumed to have authority to absolve the queen's subjects from their allegiance. These were the terms of the indictment of Cuthbert Mayne in 1577, the proto-martyr of Douai college and the first of 123 Elizabethan priests to pay the supreme penalty.[5]

Nonetheless, the seminary priests continued to bring their message of hope and encouragement. Campion's *Brag* in 1580 was the missionary dialectic of the counter reform : 'My charge is free of

3. *Douai Diaries,* ed. Knox (London, 1878), pp. 3-4.
4. *Education under Penalty* (London, 1963), p. 3; cf. Bede Camm, *William Cardinal Allen* (London, 1908), chap. iii.
5. Anstruther, *The Seminary Priests* (Durham, 1969), i, p. 225.

cost to preach the gospel, to minister the sacraments, to instruct the simple, to reform sinners, to confute errors.'[6] The linkage between the council of Trent and Vatican II is more obvious in the words of another Elizabethan seminary priest who endured the *peine forte et dure* in the tower of London in 1597. For John Gerard the college apostolate was 'an outpouring of the Spirit for the health of souls in the last era of a declining and gasping world.'[7] John XXIII declared the reforming ideals of Vatican II in similar terms : 'The most pressing topics will be those which concern the spread of the Catholic faith, the revival of Christian standards of morality, the bringing of ecclesiastical discipline into closer accord with the needs and conditions of our time.'[8]

Reform, therefore, is an ageless and timeless process in the Church but in the setting of history during the sixteenth, seventeenth, and eighteenth centuries the counter reform launched by the Fathers of Trent found clear definition in England and Ireland in the continental college movement.

To the extent that the English college movement drew its strength from fidelity to the Old Faith among the recusant families throughout the land one could say that the foundations of Allen and Persons were calculated efforts to meet a national need for priests.[9] On the evidence of the *Douai Diaries* there was a ready organisation to receive the abundant recruitment. Thus the counter reform was launched in England. Persons were exultant; he avowed that the continental colleges were 'more fearful to the heretics than any armament of Catholic princes.' The savage legal riposte of 1585 (27 Eliz. cap. 2) allowed no ambiguity or uncertainty as to the attitude of Elizabeth and Cecil : henceforth the very presence on English soil of a priest from Douai, Rome, Valladolid, or Seville was treason. Shakespeare felt the temper of his generation. He caught the ears of the groundlings when the earl of Kent declaimed in *King Lear* :[10]

> True it is, from France there comes a power
> Into this scattered kingdom; who already,
> Wise in our negligence, have secret feet
> In some of our best ports.

6. Simpson, *Edmund Campion* (London, 1896), p. 226.
7. Gerard, *The Autobiography of an Elizabethan* (ed. Caravan, London, 1956), author's preface.
8. *Ad Petri Sedem,* 29 June 1959.
9. Cf. Aveling, 'The Catholic Recusants of the West Riding of Yorkshire', *Proceedings of the Leeds Philosophical and Literary Society,* 1963.
10. Act III, scene 1.

Elizabeth indulged in her own polemics in 1591 : the seminary priests were 'a multitude of dissolute young men who have, partly for lack of living, partly for crimes committed, become fugitives, rebels and traitors.'[11] The price was heavy. Between 1577 and 1603 one hundred and twenty priests were done to death.[12] In the English continental colleges martyrdom was placed on a new level of reality.

In Ireland, on the other hand, there were ambiguities and uncertainties. The Tudor reformers could not find recalcitrant clergy; flaming nationalism was hardly understood; outside the pale there was a disregard of English law. Henry VIII's statement of political theory concerning Ireland was axiomatic—sober ways, politic drifts and amiable persuasions. The Irish scene was complex.

Henry and Lord Grey, the lord deputy, went warily; their first approach to the Irish problem was by way of law. The Dublin parliament, representative only of the fractional English colony, passed the act of supremacy in 1537. Within the pale the measure carried a political rather than a religious meaning, without the pale in the vast area of Gaelic Ireland it remained a dead letter.[13] A firm step forward towards the establishment of the new order was made in the same year with the suppression of thirteen major religious houses in Leinster. Whatever qualms the official pro-English colony and some of the Anglo-Irish nobility might have felt were calmed by grants of rich abbey lands.[14] So far the English precedent was working well. A necessary corollary, however, was clarification of the king's legal position in Ireland. The Irish people regarded the pope as their temporal sovereign, acknowledging the king as merely lord of Ireland. Now was the time to offset such papal claims. The compliant Dublin parliament passed a measure, introduced by St Leger, the new lord deputy, which gave recognition to Henry Tudor as 'King of England, France, and Ireland, Defender of the Faith, and of the Church of England and also of Ireland.' If the English precedent could be enforced the way to royal absolutism in Church and State could not be impeded.

A major obstacle remained : what of the princely rulers of Gaelic Ireland? In the view of St Leger the introduction of the English

11. Quoted by Hughes, *The Reformation in England* (London, 1954), iii, 382.

12. *Ibid.,* p. 338.

13. Wilson, *The Beginnings of Modern Ireland* (London, 1914), p. 169.

14. Curtis, *A History of Ireland* (London, 1945), p. 167.

system of land tenure would win over the Irish chieftains. Between 1537 and 1541 MacGillapatrick of Ossory, O'Connor of Offaly, and O'Brien of Thomond had renounced the jurisdiction of the pope and consented to hold their lands from the king.[15] Here was an effective, if an oblique, method of extending the statutory religion in Gaelic Ireland. St Leger resolved to make the experiment.

Surrender and re-grant, as the new system of land tenure was termed, has but a limited relevance to our present purposes. Five-eighths of the land of Gaelic Ireland was held by the princely rulers and their attendant clansmen.[16] Under surrender and re-grant the chiefs surrendered their sept lands and received them back under royal patent with a new title of ownership, often with an added title of nobility. Few of the Irish chiefs resisted the attraction of enhanced personal prestige and power. In all parts of the country between 1541-43 there was a series of treaties between the Crown and the sept rulers. The chiefs did not demur at the religious overtones; they acknowledged Henry as their lawful sovereign and head of the Church in Ireland, renouncing the pope 'with a fervour which might have satisfied a modern Orangeman.'[17]

Despite the example of ten conforming bishops, despite the extensive suppression of religious houses and the enforced return of some three thousand religious to secular life, and notwithstanding the lavish disbursal of monastic property to enthusiastic acceptors, religious and lay, of the statutory religion, there was little erosion of traditional loyalties amongst the mass of the Old Irish and Anglo-Irish.[18] The impact of Henry's sober ways and amiable persuasions on the Irish people was slight. Nevertheless, Paul III, already contemplating the council of Trent, decided on remedial measures for Ireland. Two Jesuits, Paschasius Brouet and Alphonsus Salmeron, early associates of St Ignatius, were despatched to Ireland. They were accredited with special faculties to meet Irish conditions. In 1542 they began their work of preaching, administering the sacraments, and reconciling the lapsed. The mission was a failure. Depressed and disillusioned, Brouet and Salmeron returned to Rome. Their report was an alarming commentary on

15. Cf. MacCaffrey, *History of the Catholic Church from the Renaissance to the French Revolution*, ii, 273.
16. Butler, *Gleanings from Irish History* (London, 1925), p. 206.
17. Wilson, *op. cit.*, p. 259. Ronan, *The Reformation in Dublin*, p. 293.
18. Mooney, *The First Impact of the Reformation* (Dublin, 1967), 29 ff. Cf. Rothe, *Analecta*, p. 265.

religious and pastoral conditions of priests and people.[19] St Ignatius declared that the Jesuit visitors' account of religion in Ireland was more frightening than reports from Germany![20]

Little evidence has survived to give us a clear insight into pastoral conditions in Ireland during the first part of the sixteenth century.[21] That poverty, squalor, and ignorance abounded is accepted.[22] Pluralism, non-residence, the reservation of parishes to religious houses were grievous impediments to the shepherding of souls. At the highest level there was defection : in 1539 George Cromer, archbishop of Armagh, fell into heresy and was suspended from office by the Holy See.[23] Nevertheless, Ireland did not have a Wycliffe or a Tyndale.

In 1560 Elizabeth and Cecil, secretary of state, determined to extend the statutory religion by every means short of active persecution. The Dublin parliament received its mandate from Sussex, the lord deputy. New acts of supremacy and uniformity were passed. An oath acknowledging the queen as supreme head of the Church in Ireland was demanded of officers of state, mayors, and civic officials. Attendance at services of the Established Church was enforced, use of the book of common prayer was compulsory. In other words, in law Protestantism now supplanted Catholicism.

Meanwhile, Pius IV gave thought to Irish pastoral needs. Before the council of Trent had entered on its final sessions, David Wolfe, a Jesuit, was sent to Ireland as commissary. In general terms, Wolfe's mission was to initiate the Tridentine reforms.[24] He landed in Cork in 1561 and forthwith began his visitation of the country. It was the first instalment of far-reaching changes. The position in Ireland during 1560-61 may be summarised :

19. Hogan, *Ibernia Ignatiana*, 6 ff.; Broderick, *The Origin of the Jesuits* (London, 1940), p. 110.
20. Quoted by Mooney, *op. cit.*, p. 30.
21. Perhaps the best evidence of pastoral defects is found in the reforming legislation of later synods. Cf. synod of Clogher in 1582, synod of Kilkenny in 1614, Moran, *History of the Archbishops of Dublin* (Dublin, 1864), p. 89, p. 441.
22. Wilson, *op. cit.*, 142 ff.; Mooney, *op. cit.*, p. 6.
23. Brady, *Episcopal Succession*, 1, 216.
24. One of his first acts was to recommend the appointment of Thomas O'Herlihy to Ross, Eugene O'Hart to Achonry, Donald MacCongall to Raphoe; all three had attended the council of Trent. The first promulgation of the decrees of Trent was made by MacCongall, *De Praesulibus Hiberniae* (ed. O'Doherty, Ir. MSS. Comm.), ii, 170, p. 339; MacCarthy, *Collections on Irish Church History*, i, app. 116 ff.; *Hib. Dominicana*, p. 486.

'While the Holy See was preparing to begin the work of the counter reformation in Ireland, the reformation itself had not begun there.'[25]

There was a crispness in Wolfe's assessment of the Irish religious and pastoral scene.[26] He was gratified by the slight impact of heresy not only on the wide areas of Gaelic Ireland but in the walled towns of Leinster and Munster. He was emphatic, however, on the need to reform the spiritual and educational standards of the clergy. He was captured in 1567 and held prisoner in Dublin castle, eventually escaping to Spain. Fortunately for Ireland, his recommendations for the implementation of the counter reform were readily accepted by the Holy See. An official directive was given by Pius IV in the bull *Dum Exquisita,* issued on 31 May 1564.[27] In effect, the document was a blueprint for the Irish continental colleges.

In *Dum Exquisita* one can sense the sharp thorns of experience. Having stressed the exalted standards set up by the Fathers of Trent the pope indicated in the frankest terms the manifest inadequicies of priestly training and education in Ireland. In the whole country not more than one or two had doctorates in theology; none held a degree in canon law; not more than six or eight had gained the baccalaureatus. To meet the onslaught of heresy priests had little more than the slender instruction they had received in their schooldays. The most urgent need was a *studium generale* similar to the universities of Paris and Louvain. Accordingly, faculties were vested in David Wolfe and Richard Creagh, archbishop of Armagh, to make good the defect. The revenues of religious houses and ecclesiastical benefices were to be diverted to provide the necessary university endowments.

There was not a shred of possibility in such fantastic plans. Pius IV was a realist and he anticipated the objections. He recognised that 'the greater number of monasteries and ecclesiastical benefices, secular and regular, were partly suppressed or partly devoted to profane uses.' The pope's intentions were obvious in the repeated exemplification of the universities of Louvain and Paris. Any perspective of Irish clerical education must reach to farther horizons. Already the drift of students to the Low Countries had

25. Dudley Edwards, *Church and State in Tudor Ireland* (Dublin, 1935), p. 190.
26. Letter to Cardinal Moronius, protector of Ireland, *Ibernia Ignatiana,* p. 13.
27. *Ibid.,* p. 15; *Spicilegium Ossoriense,* i, 32 ff.

begun : the first Irish student was enrolled in the university of Louvain in 1548.[28] A more compelling factor was the failure, when conditions were more favourable, to found a *studium generale* in Ireland.

A constant theme in the history of Irish educational endeavour in late medieval times is the repeated attempts to establish a university. In 1312 Clement V approved a foundation, the *Academia Dublinensis,* proposed by John de Lech, archbishop of Dublin.[29] Troubles beset the path of de Lech; he died in the following year. Alexander de Bicknor, his successor, revived the scheme, and John XXII in a brief of approval outlined the framework of an Irish university in conjunction with St Patrick's cathedral. The project failed through lack of endowments.

In Scotland the problem was solved. The university of St Andrew, founded by Nicholas V in 1451, united academic training with priestly formation.[30] Ireland would do well to copy the Scottish model. In such terms Sixtus IV traced the plan of a university in a brief dated 1475.[31] He urged an Irish *studium generale* with the statutes and customs of the colleges at Lincoln and Oxford. Direction of the Irish university was vested in the Dominicans, Franciscans, and Augustinians. Careful provision was made for the necessary endowments.[32] Once more after a brief existence the foundation failed.

Of necessity, therefore, the Irish cleric who sought higher education was obliged to travel overseas. During the fifteenth century there were large numbers of Irish clerics at Oxford and Cambridge. Indeed the strength of the Irish enrolment warranted the reservation of four hostels at Oxford.[33] On the continent young Irishmen attended the universities of Paris, Cologne, and Bologna.[34]

It is not gratuitous to assume that the major religious houses of the pale, such as the Augustinian abbey of St Thomas the Martyr, Dublin, and Athassel, Co. Kilkenny, the Cistercian abbeys of St Mary, Dublin, Baltinglass, and Dunbrody provided for the training

28. Jennings, 'Irish Students at the University of Louvain', *Measgra Mhichíl Uí Cléirigh,* 1944.
29. *Hib. Dominicana,* p. 66; Gwynn, *Studies,* xxv-xxvii, 1936-38.
30. Theiner, *Vetera Monumenta Hibernorum et Scotorum,* p. 384.
31. *Hib. Dominicana,* p. 193.
32. *Calendar of Archbishop Alen's Register* (Dublin, 1950), p. 260.
33. Gwynn, *Studies,* lvii, 226, 1968.
34. Fitzmaurice and Little, *Materials for the History of the Franciscan Province of Ireland* (Manchester, 1920), pp. 156, 192.

and education of their own aspirants. Scattered references indicate that lay schools were also maintained by the communities. In Scotland endowments were attached to chantries for the maintenance of clerical students. The custom was not widespread in Ireland but there was one such chantry in Cork—attached to Christ Church in the South Main street.[35] There is evidence also that collegiate schools at cathedral centres survived to a late date.[36]

Pius IV's strictures in *Dum Exquisita* seemed to emphasise the deficiencies of priestly training and education in the wider areas of Gaelic Ireland. In Connacht clerical training and education depended to a large extent on the old monastic foundations that survived to late medieval times. Thus we are certain that aspirants to the secular or diocesan priesthood were received at the monasteries of Boyle, Assaroe, and Cong.[37] Little is known of the character or quality of the education. Reports on pastoral conditions in Tuam and Anaghduagh in 1555 are not encouraging.[38]

There may be comfort in Campion's picture of an Irish school in 1570—lusty fellows of twenty-five years, grovelling in straw, books at their noses.[39] But to recast and remould clerical education and priestly formation in the bracing air of the Tridentine counter reform was not possible on Irish soil. Irish Catholicism, perforce, turned to the continent.

2

THE DRIFT TO THE CONTINENT

Dum Exquisita and its drastic terms did not provoke questioning dissent. A major obstacle was the absence of Irish clerical leaders with the prestige of William Allen and Robert Persons to sponsor an academic move to the universities of the continent. Hence for want of a more apt word the early phase of the Irish college movement must be seen as a disjunctive process : individuals or small groups made their way to some European centre. The extent to which the initiative came from bishops or students cannot be determined. We see the process at work in the records of the university

35. Archdall, *Monasticon Hibernicum* (ed. 1873), p. 125.
36. Messingham, *Florilegium Sanctorum Insulae Hiberniae* (Paris, 1624), praefatio.
37. *Annals of the Four Masters*, ed. O'Donovan, s.a. 1230, 1322, 1328.
38. Moran, *History of the Archbishops of Dublin*, app. II and III.
39. *Historie of Ireland* (Hibernia Press, Dublin, 1809), p. 26.

of Salamanca. Records in the *Libros de Claustros* or Acts of the Senate for the years 1574-91 tell of assistance given to Irish students who had come to Salamanca without means of subsistence.[1] Oliver Eustace, an Irishman, applied to the university on 14 January 1574 for alms to continue his studies. He was granted a room in the college hospital and a daily allowance. A similar application was made in July 1574 by John Philipps, an Irish student-priest. He was appointed university chaplain with a salary. In the following years the university gave support to Thomas Prendergast of Tuam, Robert Lawless of Limerick, Nicholas Hickey of Waterford, Daniel Heffernan of Tuam, and Daniel O'Drehan. But there is no evidence that their presence in Salamanca was part of an organised movement.

Too little is known of Irish diocesan history to discover the extent of the movement to the continent of students of the secular priesthood during the immediate post-Tridentine period. The exodus to Louvain was not altogether a Franciscan story.[2] Richard Creagh was appointed archbishop of Armagh in 1564; he died in the tower of London in 1585. Dermot O'Hurley was named archbishop of Cashel in 1581; he was done to death in 1584. Both were alumni of Louvain.[3] There was a sudden acceleration in 1578 when John Lee, priest of the diocese of Meath, led six students to Paris. There is no evidence of intention to make an outright foundation; Lee was content to establish his little group at the collège Montaigu, then one of the ten colleges of *pleine exercice* that comprised the university of Paris.[4] From such small beginnings grew the best known of the Irish continental seminaries, the Irish college, Paris. In 1580 a joint Scots-Irish college was founded in Paris. Mary, queen of Scots, granted an annual subsidy of 400 crowns.[5] A year later the institution was moved to Pont-à-Mousson in Lorraine with an added papal subsidy of 1200 crowns. Provision was made for six Irish students. The seminary was affiliated to the Jesuit college to form part of the university of Pont-à-Mousson. Richard Fleming, an Irish Jesuit, was professor of divinity and ultimately

1. Amalio Huarte, 'Petitions of Irish Students in the University of Salamanca, 1574-91', *Arch. Hib., iv.*
2. Jennings, 'Irish Students in the University of Louvain, 1584-1794', *Measgra Mhichíl Uí Cléirigh*; 'Irish Names in the Malines Ordination Registers', *Ir. Ecc. Rec.,* 5th series, lxxvi-vii, 1951-52.
3. Rothe, *Analecta,* p. 398, intro. xiii.
4. Boyle, *The Irish College in Paris* (Dublin, 1901), p. 3.
5. Martin, *Friar Nugent* (London, 1963), 13 ff.

chancellor—a fact that drew Irish students.[6] How many is not known. It is certain that Lavalin or Francis Nugent, later founder of the Irish college at Lille, was a student at Pont-à-Mousson. The college lost part of its endowments with the execution in 1587 of Mary, queen of Scots. A year later the college ceased to exist. At its closure there was an enrolment of nine Irish students.

Although we anticipate somewhat mention must be made of Christopher Roche who in his own way was an outrider of the later Irish incursion to Bordeaux.[7] Roche sailed from Wexford in 1593 in a single-handed effort to gain entry to a French college. He reached Bordeaux and found employment as a porter in the college at Guyenne in Aquitane. Later he was admitted as a student. After ordination he was appointed to the staff of a college at Libourne, a little town on the banks of the Dordogne, some miles north of Bordeaux. By a curious coincidence the college at Libourne later fell to the charge of Irish priests.

Many years passed without an organised effort to implement the plan of education outlined in *Dum Exquisita*. The decade 1570-80 saw the Desmond or Geraldine rising in Munster during which many priests and religious were murdered.[8] On the continent the English recusant foundations at Rome and Douai and their alumni were already making history. The scroll of martyrs grew longer. An unfailing stimulus to heroic fortitude was the increasing penal proscription of the colleges and the seminary priests.[9] In Ireland, there was as yet no comparable outlawry of priests. Moreover, a new political factor may well have hindered constructive moves in Ireland. A logical consequence of the excommunication of Elizabeth in 1570 by Pius V was a plan for her dethronement. Pius V was prepared to consider military means to expel a heretical queen. He died in 1572 and was succeeded by Gregory XIII, a pope consumed with zeal for the counter reform.[10] He had a new perspective : the might of Spain must be allied to the decrees of Trent. In the alignment of Catholic powers there was a place for Ireland. For Gerald FitzGerald, fourteenth earl of Desmond, and for the Geraldines of Munster, defenders of the Church, this meant war, a religious crusade that lasted from 1569 to 1583.

6. Hogan, *Distinguished Irishmen of the Sixteenth Century* (London, 1894), p. 27.
7. *C.S.P.*, 1588-92, p. 455.
8. Cf. Dudley Edwards, *Church and State in Tudor Ireland*, app. 309 ff.
9. Bede Camm, *William Cardinal Allen*, pp. 64-67.
10. Jones, *The Counter Reformation* (Dublin, 1967), 17 ff.; Mourett, *The Papacy* (London, 1931), p. 56.

A growing nucleus of Irish abroad, mostly in the Spanish service, helped inject the new militancy into the Tridentine counter reform. Acting with the leaders at home they determined to recover Ireland for Catholicism by force of arms. James FitzMaurice FitzGerald of Desmond read the omens correctly. The attainder of Shane O'Neill and his defeat in 1567 meant disaster for Ulster. Three counties were confiscated and the name of O'Neill was legally extinguished.[11] The plan of Elizabeth and Cecil was a wholesale reduction of Ireland by the imposition of English law and religion. Only a military defeat of England could save Ireland for the counter reform.

FitzMaurice might well be reckoned the first of a long line of modern Irish statesmen. He visualised Ireland taking her place in the Catholic consortium of Europe, included in a Catholic armed confederation. In 1569 Maurice MacGibbon, archbishop of Cashel and kinsman of FitzMaurice, was despatched as emissary to the courts of the continent. MacGibbon addressed a memorial to Philip II of Spain. The appeal allegedly bore the signatures of four Irish archbishops, eight bishops and leading members of the nobility. The document was most probably the work of FitzMaurice himself.[12] The Catholic king of Spain was besought to save Ireland from the infection and ruin of the accursed and infectious heresy now raging in England. Philip was invited to accept Ireland as a fief of the Spanish Crown. At home FitzMaurice did not mince words. In the same year he called on the mayor and corporation of Cork 'to abolish out of their city the heresy newly raised and invented.'[13] It was the Geraldine's brusque affirmation of the anathemas of Trent.

MacGibbon's embassy at large accomplished nothing. Philip was reluctant to wage large-scale war on behalf of the Irish Catholics. Meanwhile Pope Gregory XIII in March 1575 approved a plan for the deposition of Elizabeth by military action.[14] An invasion of Ireland was part of the design. Philip II was a party to the negotiations and undertook to supply 2,000 Spanish troops on condition that the pope would bear responsibility for the enterprise. At Douai, William Allen and his associates in the college, Nicholas Sanders and Owen Lewis, were ardent supporters of the project.

11. Curtis, *History*, p. 192.
12. *Spic. Oss.*, 59 ff *.C.S.P.*, 1509-73, p. 401.
13. *C.S.P.*, 1509-73, p. 413.
14. Cleary, 'Dr Morys Clynnog's Invasion Projects of 1575-76', *Recusant History*, vol. 8, no. 6, 1966.

In Ireland, the first phase of the Desmond wars ended disastrously for the Geraldine leaders. Sir John Perrot, president of Munster, and Sir Humphrey Gilbert suppressed the rising with indiscriminate slaughter of garrisons and religious communities. FitzMaurice must have been apprised that Gregory XIII and Philip of Spain were contemplating joint action. In 1575 he sailed for Europe with a declared intention of gaining continental aid for the counter reform in Ireland.[15] His itinerary brought him to Paris, Lisbon, Madrid, and Rome. Only the Holy See offered constructive help. At length, a pitifully small force of seventy men, including FitzMaurice and Nicholas Sanders, landed at Dingle, Co. Kerry, in July 1579. A few weeks later FitzMaurice was killed on the banks of the Shannon in a miserable skirmish with the Burkes. Yet all was not over. The Geraldine defence of Catholicism was continued by Gerald FitzGerald, fourteenth earl of Desmond, now recognised by the Holy See as the 'Leader of the Catholic armies in Ireland.'[16] Another force comprising Spaniards, Italians and Irish, landed at Smerwick, near Dingle, in September 1580. The expected help from the Irish chieftains did not materialise; the entire force of six hundred was massacred. So ended the Geraldine crusade for the counter reform. The sequel was confiscation of the vast areas of the Desmond lands in Munster.

Contemporary documentation of the counter reform in Ireland follows closely the pattern of post-Tridentine history in other countries. The tasks of healing the ills of the religious and social order were formidable but not insuperable to a zealous and well-equipped priesthood. Gregory XIII with all his crusading ardour sought to restore the determining factor of faith amongst the Irish Catholics who had faltered. By apostolic brief in 1575 the pope empowered Richard Creagh, archbishop of Armagh, with special faculties to repair the religious and social ravages of heresy in the dioceses of Armagh and Dublin. Similar faculties were granted to Edmund Tanner, bishop of Cork and Cloyne.[17] In 1577 Tanner informed Everardo, Father General of the Jesuits, that in Cork there were few heretics and the people assisted at Mass and received the sacraments.[18] A wider problem transcended diocesan limits. In 1578 John White, an Irish priest, was sent to Ireland by the

15. *Ibernia Ignatiana*, p. 21.
16. *Spic. Oss.*, i, 81, Letter of earl of Desmond to Gregory XIII.
17. *Spic. Oss.*, i, 43.
18. *Ibernia Ignatiana*, p. 23.

Holy See with plenary faculties to dispense from matrimonial impediments and to sanate irregular marriages.[19]

Perhaps the best evidence of the extent to which the counter reform had penetrated religious life not only in Gaelic Ireland but in the chartered towns is found in hostile testimony. Most likely the old faith claimed the secret fidelity of many who made a bold front of their loyalty to the new. But the cross currents of political and religious allegiance occasionally brought strange motives to light. Richard Whyte on 8 May 1590 made choleric protest to Cecil that Sir Warham St Leger and Andrew Skydamore had assaulted him on the north bridge of Cork.[20] Whyte declared that his assailants were 'arrogantly barking and condemned the religion established and compared her Majesty's godly proceedings to the vile sect of the anabaptists.' Complainant put his finger on the root cause of disloyalty among the citizens of Cork : 'the sting of rebellion which in times past remained among the Irishry is transferred and removed into the hearts of civil gentlemen.' Lyon, the Elizabethan bishop of Cork, reported in 1595 that four prominent citizens had refused the mayoralty because they would not attend the services of the state religion.[21] He was more specific in his letter to Cecil : the dioceses of Cork, Cloyne, and Ross were far from being the Fortunate Isles.[22] The zealous persuasions of the new priests had driven the Protestant cause backwards. In 1596 the poet Spenser made a deeper diagnosis. Small good could be done for the people until one enormity was eliminated, namely, 'that both they be restrained from sending their young men abroad to other universities, beyond the sea, as Rennes, Douai, Louvain, and the like, and others be restrained from coming into them.'[23] Carew, lord president of Munster, warned Elizabeth in 1600 that grapes could not be gathered from thistles because incoming priests came from colleges 'where your Majesty is rather hated than honoured in.'[24] He stated his fears to the privy council in December 1602—the overmuch liberty enjoyed by Irish merchants sailing in and out of Spanish ports provided undesirable intercourse and intelligence.[25] Priests from colleges in Spain were contraband cargo.

In other words, the tenuous flow of priests from the colleges overseas was hastening the Catholic revival.

19. Moran, *Archbishops,* p. 82.
20. *C.S.P.,* 1588-92, 340 ff.
21. *C.S.P.,* 1592-96, p. 433.
22. Webster, *The Diocese of Cork* (Cork, 1920), p. 228.
23. *View of the State of Ireland,* p .254.
24. *Cal. Carew Papers,* 1589-1600, p. 480.
25. *Ibid.,* 1601-03.

3

GETTING UNDER WAY

A general conspectus of the college movement in its first phase shows that by 1612 there were eleven colleges at work, mostly in university towns and cities. In Spain there were four : Salamanca (1592), Lisbon (1593),[1] Santiago (1605), Seville (1612); in France three : Paris (1578), Bordeaux (1603), Rouen (1612); in the Low Countries four : Douai (1594), Antwerp (1600), Louvain (1607), Lille (1610). The rapid diffusion of so many institutions of diverse Irish origins imparts an almost accidental character to the initial stages of the movement. There were no formal acts of foundations, hence we cannot be sure that in some instance the dates of origin are more than approximations.

Apart from the overriding impetus of the Tridentine reform two factors in the last decades of the sixteenth century gave a strong stimulus to the continental movement. In Ulster following the death and attainder of Shane O'Neill in 1567 the grip of English law was tightened. In Munster during and after the Desmond wars religious houses which had hitherto escaped were suppressed. Again, there were vast confiscations of religious property and thus the already attenuated channels of education were closed. Inevitably, the very continuity of the pastoral priesthood was in peril. In 1600 Dermot Creagh, bishop of Cork and Cloyne, reported to the Holy See the grave shortage of priests : 'the harvest and the flock are increasing, workers and pastors are needed.'[2] Elsewhere the picture was the same.[3]

In addition, the changing political complexion of the counter reform helped give finality to designs for the future. The recognition of Philip II of Spain as the political overlord in Europe and military protagonist of the Tridentine reform was tempered not only by the defeat of the Armada in 1588 but also by a reversal of policy by the Holy See.[4] For Ippolito Aldobrandini, elected pope as Clement VIII in 1592, there would be less dependence on Spain and a discount of military alliances as an instrument of the counter reform. There would be no more military popes.

1. Portugal was under Spanish rule 1582-1640.
2. Letter to Clement VIII, *Arch. Hib.*, ii, 287.
3. Report of John Howling c. 1593, *Spic. Oss.*, i, 82 ff.
4. *Cambridge Modern History*, vol. iii, 509; Dickens, *The Counter Reformation* (London, 1968), p. 149.

Yet O'Neill and O'Donnell were the acknowledged leaders of Catholic Ireland in arms. Although O'Neill's secret overtures to Philip II of Spain won assurances of military help the burden of the Irish leaders' pleas to the Holy See was their dedication to the cause of the counter reform. In 1596 in a joint letter to Clement VIII O'Neill and O'Donnell declared their aims : 'Just now we would notify to your Holiness what is most needed by our Church, to wit, good prelates of unimpeachable morals and highly educated, not such as those inferior men who would exercise jurisdiction badly, to the detriment of religion and of whom we have daily experience.'[5] Despite the promised Spanish aid O'Neill knew that the hope of the counter reform lay in the infant foundations at Salamanca, Lisbon, and Douai. In 1599 he urged Philip III and Archduke Albert, viceroy of the Spanish Netherlands, to lend support to the college at Douai. In 1602 when Spanish and Irish hopes had been frustrated at Kinsale O'Donnell on his arrival in Spain presented a memorial to the king on behalf of the college at Salamanca.[6] In other words, whatever military co-operation might achieve through the Nine Years' War more enduring fruits were to be gathered in a different sphere—the continental colleges. Henceforth Spanish-Irish co-operation would be in the field of education. To the promotion of Irish colleges in Spain and France Clement VIII and Paul V extended a strong hand.

To bracket the Irish foundations in Spain and France under the common heading of the continental college movement without further distinction is to ignore obvious features. Philip II and Philip III breathed life into the colleges in Spain at a time when Spanish-Irish *rapport* took the form of a military alliance. The Irish foundations at Salamanca and Lisbon were period pieces. In contrast with the upsurge of Spanish sympathy for Ireland during 1592-1601 French readiness to receive Irish students had less spontaneity and gave evidence of more deliberate planning. While little is known of the earliest phase of Father John Lee's Irish nucleus in Paris in 1578 it was in 1621 that the Irish seminary had its first discernible proportions.[7] As we shall see Diarmuid MacCarthy of Cork was far-seeing in his design for a college at Bordeaux in 1603. In 1601 he went to Rome to seek counsel of Clement VIII. On his return journey MacCarthy consulted the Abbé Alexandre de la

5. Text in Meehan, *The Fate and Fortunes of the Earls of Tyrone and Tyrconnel*, app. p. 374.
6. *Ibid.*, p. 372.
7. Boyle, *The Irish College in Paris,* p. 5.

Rochefoucauld at Saint-Martin-en-Vallée, near Chartres. We may assume that the abbé, brother of Cardinal de la Rochefoucauld, made the initial approach to Cardinal de Sourdis, archbishop of Bordeaux. Thus when the first group of students arrived from Waterford all was ready. Similarly, at Toulouse there was an Irish student nucleus as early as 1645 but formal recognition of a seminary was not forthcoming until 1659.

Proposals for more Irish foundations in France and the Spanish Netherlands were carefully studied. In 1610 Cardinal Borghese, secretary of state, held discussions with the nuncios to France and the Spanish Netherlands with reference to proposed Cistercian and Capuchin-controlled colleges.[8] The projects were not realised. Nevertheless, the point is clear : any extension of the college movement in the seventeenth century must be the fruit of careful planning.

To minimise in the slightest degree the depth of French cordiality to Irish students would be less than just. Documents to be quoted in the following pages will show that Louis XIV, Anne of Austria, the queen regent, Louis XV, and successive archbishops of Bordeaux and Toulouse, were at all times ready to reinforce Irish Catholicism then under siege. Anne of Austria, mother of Louis XIV, was realistic in her appraisal of the Irish pastoral scene in 1654 : 'que chacun sait estre dans une des plus utiles et plus laborieuses missions qui se fassent dans l'Église.'[9] In many of the colleges at various times there were crises that tried the patience of church and civic authorities. The suggestion of withdrawal was never made.

An outline, however, must be given of a special difficulty which beset most of the Irish foundations in the first part of the seventeenth century : regionalism. If the frets and dissensions which divided the Irish people for several centuries were carried overseas there is small ground for surprise. The concept of Irish nationalism was still remote; local or provincial interests were paramount. For the seminaries abroad there were unhappy sequels. At Salamanca the charge was that Munster dominance was aimed at the exclusion of students from western and northern dioceses. Florence Conry, later the Franciscan archbishop of Tuam, pilloried the administration of Father Thomas White. In 1602 with the authority of the northern chieftains, O'Neill and O'Donnell, Conry sought the

8. Fondo Borghese, Arch. Hib., ii, 264; Arch. Hib., xxii, 84.
9. Bertrand, op. cit., p. 356.

intervention of Philip III of Spain.[10] Conry recalled the heroism of the men of Connacht and Ulster at Kinsale in 1601 : Spain must not forget their sacrifice. He felt the enrolment at Salamanca must be reserved to students from western and northern dioceses. Controversy raged amongst the exiles in Spain.

In the Spanish Netherlands the position was different. Christopher Cusack, president of the Irish colleges in the Low Countries, faced a tumult at St Patrick's, Douai, in 1614—Old Irish versus Anglo-Irish. The bishop of Arras must have been driven to desperation when he agreed to an apartheid—a segregation of the dissident students in the same building. Fortunately, Guido Bentivoglio, the nuncio at Brussels, and the viceroy, Archduke Albert, saw that wiser counsels prevailed.

As we shall see, by far the most uncompromising advocate of regional exclusiveness was Francis Nugent, Capuchin, scion of one of the most prominent Anglo-Irish families in the pale. His college at Lille, founded in 1610, was forbidden territory to all but students of Meath and the dioceses of Leinster. Heavy pressure was brought to bear on him to widen the terms of entry but Nugent remained adamant. His successors, the Irish Capuchins at Lille, maintained the reservation to the final suppression of the seminary in 1793.

At Bordeaux the issue of regionalism was raised much later. The college, from its beginnings in 1603, was an enclave of Cork, Cloyne, Kerry, and Waterford. For more than a century the exclusiveness was unchallenged. In 1717 seven Irish bishops framed a severe indictment of the administration; they urged that Munster dominance in the seminary militated against the faith in Ireland.[11]

Some circumstances other than mere provincialism provoked the extraordinary happenings at Toulouse at intervals between 1669 and 1700. The documentary evidence to be submitted is taken from French official sources. Nevertheless, we have failed to discover the precise reason why two students, allegedly for insubordination, were committed to prison in 1669. Reviewing the evidence one is forced to ask—could twelve students cause such stresses and strains that finally compelled Louis XIV to intervene? One wonders whether the jarring episodes in the early history of Toulouse college must be seen against a background of Jansenism. If such is the

10. Text in Meehan, *op. cit.,* app. p. 352.
11. '... supra dictum seminarium ab unica hujus regni provincia, Momonia scilicet, in magnum damnum et dispendium rei Catholicae in hac patria usurpari', Bertrand, *op. cit.,* p. 369.

case, one's sympathies move towards a group of ebullient young Irishmen who chafed under Jansenistic control. Of the prestige and stature of the seminary in later years there can be no question. The names of Francis O'Hea of Ross, Francis Moylan, bishop of Cork, and the Abbé Henry Edgeworth, confessor of Louis XVI, remove all shadow of mediocrity.

By the middle years of the seventeenth century there was a score of Irish foundations on the continent. The question arises—whence their maintenance and sources of revenue? Detailed consideration of the revenues of the colleges at Bordeaux, Toulouse, Lille, and educational endowments in general will be discussed later. Summarily, the institutes in France fared best by reason of the considerable Irish settlement in French towns, especially after 1690. But the seminaries in Spain and the Low Countries waged a constant struggle against poverty. At various times it seemed that some colleges had lost the fight: closure and sale of buildings were imminent; for example, at Seville in 1619, at Douai in 1625, and at Lille in 1682. Under God's providence they survived.

In 1592 when Philip II directed the rector and chancellor of the university of Salamanca to receive Irish students he undertook to pay 'a good annual stipend' to the new Irish foundation.[12] The exact amount of the stipend is not stated, but the equivalent of £100 paid to the seminary at Santiago in 1605 was a figure common to all Irish establishments in the peninsula. Other subventions were minor in character. Nonetheless, the college at Salamanca was hardly a year old when James Archer, the Jesuit, was obliged to seek financial aid in Ireland.[13] On his own testimony his journey was not fruitless. In 1599 Hugh O'Neill appealed to Philip III to sustain the seminary at Douai, then only five years old. In general, the economic status of the foundations in the Spanish dominions was gravely affected by the slow decline of Spanish power and wealth. Without decrease of good will towards Ireland the statutory grants were chronically in arrears. Doubtless, awareness of the fact prompted three Irish bishops in 1627 to address a memorial to Cardinal Ludovisi, protector of Ireland, to use his influence with the king of Spain and Archduchess Isabella, joint viceroy of the Spanish Netherlands, to expedite the state subsidies payable to the

---

12. M'Donald, 'The Irish Colleges since the Reformation', *Ir. Ecc. Rec.*, 1874, 361.
13. Hogan, *Distinguished Irishmen*, p. 323.

Irish foundations.[14] When chaos threatened to engulf the establishments in Spain the Jesuits were invited by the king to accept responsibility for the conduct and administration of the seminaries. A recent writer has given a realistic picture of the period 1620-40 —an Irish Jesuit, intent on securing payment of the state subventions, eating his heart out awaiting a royal audience at the court in Madrid![15]

When the armies of Louis XIV overran the Spanish-Netherlands in 1667 the colleges at Antwerp, Louvain, Douai, and Lille were faced with utter collapse. The Holy See came to the rescue. The series of disbursements by Sebastiano Tanari, internuncio at Brussels, warded off the pending catastrophe.[16] But brighter days were ahead for the foundations on French soil.

A turning point in the history of the college movement in France was the arrival of the Jacobite exodus after 1690. In its first onset the Irish *diaspora* bore the character of a military caste but in later years the Irish attainded commercial and civic eminence in many cities and towns of France.[17] At the present day one does not have to probe deeply in Paris, Rouen, St Malo, Angers, Nantes, and Bordeaux to find traces of Irish ancestry. The unfaltering support of the first and second generation of Irish émigrés is seen in the lengthy but incomplete sequence of burses and educational foundations.[18] This close association with the colleges was understood in terms of proprietory rights. The establishments in France reached the end of the road in 1793—to be replaced in Ireland by the college at Maynooth. We shall see with what tenacity and zeal Irish military and political interests in France resisted any repatriation to Ireland of educational endowments. In 1814 famed veterans of the Irish brigades protested : 'Maynooth is a stranger to us!'

Distinct from subsidies, endowments, the favour of kings and governments, a unique canonical privilege was enjoyed by all the Irish continental colleges. This was the faculty vested by the Holy See in every college superior of promoting students to holy orders on the sole title of a mission in Ireland. In simple terms, a major

14. Fleming of Dublin, Rothe of Ossory, Tirry of Cork, *Collectanea Hibernica,* no. 10, 1967, p. 49.

15. Finegan, 'Irish Rectors at Seville, 1619-87', *Ir. Ecc. Rec.,* cvi, no. 1183, 1966, 48.

16. *Coll. Hib.,* no. 3, 1960, 80-81.

17. Cf. Hayes, *Old Irish Links with France* (Dublin, 1940), *passim.*

18. See appendix, Irish Educational Foundations.

Tridentine reform was that every cleric must be attached to a diocesan bishop or religious superior so that in no circumstances will there be an unattached cleric.[19] The promotion of a student to holy orders for a stated diocese may be done only on the express authorisation of the bishop in whose diocese the cleric will serve. This authorisation of the ordaining prelate must be expressed in dimissorial letters. Such legislation envisages that normal conditions prevail when bishops are free to communicate with superiors of colleges. In the abnormal conditions of the seventeenth and early eighteenth centuries in Ireland there were few bishops and they were *in loco refugii* whence communication with continental seminaries was impossible. Dimissorial letters could neither be sought nor issued.

At an early stage the difficulty arose at Salamanca : students could not be ordained in the absence of dimissorial letters. In 1600 Hugh O'Neill sent a postulation to Clement VIII urging that the faculty to promote students to the priesthood, as laid down by the council of Trent, should be amended to meet Irish conditions.[20] Very soon the same difficulty presented itself in the colleges in Spain, France, and the Low Countries.[21] The first step towards a removal of the obstacle was taken in 1614 by Paul V when he issued a brief to the Irish foundations in Spain, Portugal, France, and the Low Countries permitting the ordination of their students on the sole title of missionary or pastoral work awaiting them in Ireland. The final recommendation rested with the college superior.[22] The privilege was valid for five years. The procedure bristled with difficulties, with the result that some restrictions were imposed upon its use in the seminaries in Spain. Elsewhere more difficulties were encountered. As a final solution, Urban VIII by apostolic indult, dated 23 December 1623, allowed the ordination of students in all the Irish colleges on the sole title of a mission in Ireland, without recourse to the Irish bishops.[23] Lest any abuse should arise from the absence of a direct nexus between the cleric and his bishop the indult demanded that every student should promise on

19. *Codex Iuris Canonici,* canon 111.
20. Fondo Borghese, *Arch. Hib.,* ii, 296.
21. In 1600 twenty dioceses in Ireland were without bishops. Of the other nine sees five bishops were in exile, 'Archiepiscopatus et Episcopatus totius regni Hiberniae', *Arch. Hib.,* ii, 300-301.
22. Moran, *Archbishops,* p. 282.
23. *Hibernia Dominicana,* supp. 874 ff.

oath, duly signed and witnessed, that after ordination he would return to his mission in Ireland.[24]

It would be difficult to exaggerate the relevance and importance of the privilege in the evolution of the Irish continental colleges. It made them viable institutions, capable of the function for which they were founded. Nevertheless, the departure from Tridentine discipline had inherent dangers. To ordain students without the express authorisation of diocesan bishops could have disastrous consequences. Not only was there an invasion of episcopal responsibility but in the circumstances the spiritual and moral fitness of the candidates was not assured.

Whenever the rigour of persecution was relaxed bishops in Ireland were ready to resume the direction of their dioceses. On such occasions they voiced their anxiety concerning the procedure that governed the ordination of students in the seminaries overseas. As early as 1635 a number of Irish bishops addressed a petition to Urban VIII protesting that undesirable candidates were ordained in the continental colleges. They urged the enforcement of the Tridentine rule which required that students must provide testimonial letters from their bishops.[25] Apparently, the petition went unheeded.

Throughout the two centuries of the college movement Irish priests were ordained abroad *in titulo missionis in Hibernia* and without patrimony. Whatever the theoretical advantages in the departure from the law of Trent the practical consequences were oftentimes disadvantageous, even disastrous. In 1687 John Brenan, archbishop of Cashel, in a report to the Holy See, ascribed his pastoral difficulties to the privilege enjoyed by the continental colleges.[26] In the following century when persecution was eased the practice was called into question. Sharp controversy broke out among the Irish bishops.[27] In 1764 the anomalous conditions arising from the exercise of the privilege in the Capuchin college at Lille precipitated legal action in the courts of Flanders by Patrick Fitzsimons, archbishop of Dublin, and his suffragans, against the Capuchins. The matter will be more fully discussed in a later context.

No picture of the Irish college movement would be complete

24. For specimens of the oath see *Arch. Hib.*, i, 126; *Arch. Hib.*, ii, 5.
25. *Coll. Hib.*, no. 10, 1967, 24 ff.
26. Power, *A Bishop of the Penal Times* (Cork University Press, 1932), p. 86.
27. *Coll. Hib.*, no. 10, 1967, 87; Renehan-MacCarthy, *Collections on Irish Church History* (Dublin, 1861), p. 191.

without emphasis on the vital part played by the Jesuits. That the animation, encounters, and risks of the new education should summon up the zeal and fortitude of the Jesuits was altogether in accordance with the ideals of St Ignatius Loyola. Too little acknowledgment has been made of our indebtedness to such men as John Howling, Thomas White, Henry Fitzsimon, James Archer, and William Bathe. Without them, there would have been no Irish foundations at Salamanca, Santiago, Seville, and Lisbon.

Implementation of the educational reforms launched by the council of Trent was for the greater part imposed upon the Jesuits. The society was the only group with adequate organisation and skill to undertake the task. Before long the typical Jesuit *schola* took shape—a combination of residential university for clerics and a secondary boarding and day school for lay pupils. The formula was widely accepted.[28] Between 1551 and 1650 more than 155 Jesuit colleges were at work in the countries of western Europe. A summary of Jesuit educational theory and practice points to the necessary involvement of the society in the Irish college movement : 'Local bodies, when asking for the help of the Jesuits, knew that they were bringing into their schools the spirit of the Catholic reformation : order, hierarchy, and methodical organisation, as well as a severe type of moral discipline, resting on ardent piety.'[29]

Scots Jesuits founded a college at Tournai (1576), while English Jesuits made foundations in the peninsula : Valladolid (1589), Seville (1592), a school at St Omer (1593), and a novitiate at Louvain (1607).

Irish Jesuits made a beginning at Salamanca in 1592. Perhaps they were aware of a precedent : Ignatius Loyola once tried his fortunes at Salamanca and constituted himself a sort of student-relief agent.[30] Several years previously, in 1582, Thomas White, a native of Clonmel, gathered a number of Irish youths at Valladolid. When he heard of Howling's move at Salamanca White and his young men hastened to form the first nucleus at the university. In the following year Howling and White made another Irish foundation at Lisbon.

Opposition to the Jesuits was soon forthcoming—from Irishmen. In 1602, as we have already told, the Franciscan Florence Conry protested to Philip III that White, the rector of the Salamanca college, maintained a rigid Munster monopoly. Conry avowed that

28. Janelle, *The Catholic Reformation* (Milwaukee, 1951), p. 147.
29. Janelle, *op. cit.,* p. 149.
30. Broderick, *The Origin of the Jesuits* (London, 1940), p. 36.

the Catholic landed families and the mercantile groups of the Munster towns cared little for Irish continental schools : if it were possible they would send their sons to Oxford! Irish exiles at Valladolid made counter charges, stating that the Munster chieftains, O'Sullivan Beara and O'Driscoll, had made possible the landing of Spanish troops in Ireland during the late wars. The differences among the Irish were referred to the superior of the Jesuits, who found the Irish bickering incomprehensible. Nevertheless, Father White was removed from office at Salamanca; a Spanish rector was appointed. The innovation had not happy results; three Spanish Jesuits succeeded each other within four years. In 1608 the Irish Jesuits were restored when Richard Conway was named rector of the college. Florence Conry, now archbishop of Tuam, continued his opposition. Twenty years later he was still objecting to Jesuit control of the seminary at Salamanca.[31]

Growing dissatisfaction with the working conditions of the foundation at Santiago was the occasion of another royal directive. From its beginnings in 1605 the seminary was under the control of Father Kilian MacCarthy, formerly of Fermoy, Co. Cork. From the slender evidence available it seems that MacCarthy had the practice of admitting children of tender years, sons of Irish exiles in Spain.[32] Thus the college assumed a semi-lay character. Moreover, MacCarthy had neglected the obligation of requiring clerics to take the customary oath of service to the Irish mission. In 1611 representations were made to Philip III that remedial measures were necessary at Santiago. In the following year, David Kearney, archbishop of Cashel, through the Spanish ambassador in London, urged the king to commit the college to the Jesuits as had been done at Lisbon and Salamanca with satisfactory results.[33] Philip, in a letter dated 9 March 1611, issued instructions to Louis Henriquez, governor of Galicia, to make arrangements for the transfer of the seminary to the Jesuits.

MacCarthy registered his protest. In the names of the students he appealed to the provincial superior of the Jesuits of Castile. He accused the Jesuits of ambition and self-interest, of arrogating to themselves control of Irish foundations in Spain and France.

31. Cf. Thomas Walsh, archbishop of Cashel, to John Roche, bishop of Ferns, 14 March 1627, *Wadding Papers,* p. 244.

32. M'Donald, 'Irish Colleges since the Reformation', *Ir. Ecc. Rec.,* x, 1874, 170 ff.

33. Mooney and Healy, MS. Report on Documents relating to Ireland at Simancas, p. 71, N.L.I.

He alleged that they had made attempts to wrest the college at
Bordeaux from its founder, Diarmuid MacCarthy of Cork. Protests
notwithstanding, a peremptory order by the king to the duke of
Lerma on 1 April 1613 contained a directive to the Jesuit provincial to accept responsibility for the college at Santiago. But the
episode was not over. Daniel O'Sullivan, count of Bearehaven, son
of the famed Donal O'Sullivan of Dunboy, addressed a petition to
the king giving reasons why the sons of Irish exiles should be
educated at the seminary, thus retaining its semi-lay character.
There were arguments and counter-arguments but the royal decision remained unaltered. Thomas White, Richard Conway, and
William White, Irish Jesuits, took charge at Santiago. There was
a dramatic sequel when the students refused to take the oath of
Irish missionary service. They argued that the oath was a Jesuit
innovation. Dissenters were dismissed from the college.

At Seville college, founded in 1612, student restiveness and
maladministration combined to provoke crisis in 1619. Approaches
were made to Vitelleschi, Father General of the Jesuits, to remedy
the troubles. Once again came a decision from Philip III. On 25
July 1619 from Lisbon the king sent a firmly-worded instruction to
Augustin de Quirros, provincial superior of the society in Andalusia, to place Jesuits in the Irish seminary at Seville. A month later,
Richard Conway was installed as rector—to make order out of
chaos.[34] Apparently, student restiveness was not easily calmed.[35]

Jesuit prestige as educators within the framework of the counter
reform was the basic reason which prompted the general demand
that the Irish foundations in Spain be placed in the charge of the
society. Already the *Ratio Studiorum* of 1599 was a tried and
proved medium of pedagogy in the schools and colleges of the Low
Countries. Its psychological insight, wide experience, and an intelligence in advance of contemporary educational science were the
needed supports of Irish institutions on the verge of collapse.[36]

Jesuit responsibility at Seville has been described as a *damnosa
hereditas;* the inheritance included the seminaries at Salamanca
and Santiago.[37] Student unrest, pressing for payment of delayed

34. M'Donald, quoting records of Seville preserved at Salamanca, stated
that when Father Conway arrived at Seville he found that most of the
furniture and domestic chattels had disappeared. The remaining appointments were valued at £12, *loc. cit.,* vol. ix, 1873, 209.
35. On 9 April 1630 the students sent a memorial to Cardinal Ludovisi,
protector of Ireland, seeking a change of rectors, *Wadding Papers,* p. 352.
36. Cf. Janelle, *op. cit.,* p. 150.
37. Finegan, 'Irish Rectors at Seville, 1619-87', *loc. cit.*

THE CONTINENTAL COLLEGES

state subventions, and sectional opposition were minor difficulties compared to the shortage of Irish Jesuit personnel. As yet an Irish Jesuit province had not been established. In 1609 there were sixty-two Irishmen in the society; eighteen served as missionaries in Ireland.[38] According to a summary in 1617 the Jesuit provinces of Castile and Toledo included eighteen Irishmen but not more than ten were priests.[39] During the years 1619-87 scarcely half a dozen Irishmen joined the Andalusian province in which the Seville college was located. Nevertheless, in that period Irish Jesuits were appointed rectors on nine occasions. In some instances the provincial superior was constrained to seek men seconded from the neighbouring provinces of Castile and Toledo. After 1687 Spanish Jesuits were chosen for the post. The procedure was similar at Salamanca and Santiago. Failing a Jesuit nominee, a Spanish secular priest acted as rector—the experiment did not make for harmony among the students. Within such limitations the colleges remained under Jesuit control to the suppression of the order in Spain in 1767.

4

FOUNDATIONS

SPAIN

Nearly a century ago Mgr William M'Donald, rector of the Irish college, Salamanca, compiled his *Irish Colleges since the Reformation*.[1] He limited his study to the seminaries in Spain; his sources were materials in the college archives. M'Donald admitted that he had not examined the documents exhaustively and that more light might be hidden under the dust of years. Early in the present century Mgr D. J. O'Doherty, his successor at Salamanca, added some valuable extracts from the same sources.[2] Biographical studies of pioneer Irish Jesuits in Spain fill in the story of Irish educational enterprise in Salamanca, Lisbon, Santiago, and Seville.[3]

38. *Ibernia Ignatiana*, p. 228.
39. M'Donald, *loc. cit.*, 527 ff. He also notes a move by the Jesuits at this period to convert one of the Irish colleges to an institution for the training of Irish members of the society.

1. *Ir. Ecc. Rec.*, vols. vii, viii, ix, x, 1871-74.
2. *Arch. Hib.*, ii-iv, 1913-1915.
3. Hogan, *Distinguished Irishmen*, 'Father Henry FitzSimon, S.J.' and 'Father James Archer, S.J.', *Ir. Ecc. Rec.*, ut supra; Ware's *Works* (ed. Harris, 1745).

In 1592-93 John Howling, a native of Wexford, was attached to the Lusitanian (Portuguese) province of the Jesuits. Quoting records of the society M'Donald gives details of pastoral problems that Howling encountered among Irish arrivals at Spanish ports. Here was the bitter aftermath of the expropriations and plantations of the Desmond wars. Howling described the scene :[4]

> Many, especially priests and youths of thirteen and fourteen years, not even bidding farewell to their friends, have gone overseas, choosing with little hope of subsistence to live a needy life among Catholics but with their faith untarnished.

Theirs was the tragedy of a displaced people. A formidable figure, Don Francisco Arias Davila y Bobadilla, el Conde de Puñoenrostro, member of the Spanish supreme council of war, and Protector of the Irish in Spain, was the official reception agent.[5] Young men of physical fitness were recruited for the *tercios* in Spanish Flanders; the unfit and aged were often shipped back to Ireland. Castaways and wanderers remained—a harassing pastoral problem to two Irish Jesuits, Thomas White and John Howling. White was already committed to the work. In 1582 he established a school at Valladolid for Irish youths who lived in misery 'having no means to continue their studies, nor language to beg.' His long cherished project was to provide a regular foundation with adequate educational facilities and sufficient revenue. In 1592 the opportunity came. White presented his students when Philip II visited Valladolid. The king spoke words of encouragement and gave a generous subvention. White pressed home his petition : a regular college was necessary to accommodate the growing numbers of Irish youths. Philip undertook to give full effect to White's request—at Salamanca. A royal directive, dated 15 August 1592, to the rector and chancellor of the university of Salamanca guaranteed the right of admission to Irish students.[6] So under White and Howling was organised the first Irish educational institution in Spain—*El Real Colegio de Nobles Yrlandeses*. White was named rector, assisted by Richard Conway and James Archer.

4. *Spic. Oss.,* i, 109.
5. El Conde de Puñoenrostro was also official registrar, cf. Walsh, *Spanish Knights of Irish Origin,* p. 1.
6. Text in Hogan, *op. cit.,* pp. 53-54. M'Donald adds that in 1592 there were 6,631 matriculated students in the university of Salamanca.

The omens were favourable for further educational effort; John Howling hastened to Lisbon. The *Portuguese Annual Letters* of 1593, as cited in the *Life* of Father Henry FitzSimon, S.J., give details of Howling's pastoral anxieties at Lisbon.[7] Some of the Irish arrivals were exiles for the faith, others were released prisoners of pirates. Ships from Ireland brought still more youths, destitute and homeless.

A generous sympathy was extended to the work of Howling. With funds raised by an Irish merchant named Leigh and a group of Portuguese noblemen Howling purchased a disused convent of the Discalced Carmelites. Thus on 1 February 1593 with an initial enrolment of thirty youths the Irish college at Lisbon was established—*Collegio de Estudiantes sob a invoçacaon de S. Patricio.* At this point the sequence of events is confused. It is clear, however, that Howling had not sufficient maintenance for his college and students. Another sympathiser, Don Antonio Fernandez Ximenes, offered help.[8] From his own purse he repaired the dilapidated buildings and set up a permanent endowment for fourteen students. Ximenes spent the last years of his life in the college and at death bequeathed his estate for the maintenance of Irish students.

Meanwhile Howling and White continued their quest for students at the Spanish seaports. One of the early admissions to the seminary was Stephen White, scholar of the recently founded Trinity college, Dublin.[9] In 1595 at Coruña Thomas White met Dominic Collins of Youghal, a commander of a cavalry corps.[10] He joined the Jesuits as a professed brother. Later with James Archer he sailed for Ireland with the expedition commanded by Don Juan de Aguila. In 1602 Collins was captured at Dunboy and hanged in his native Youghal.

Another benefactor gave assured permanence to the seminary. In 1613 Edward da Costa, a Portuguese nobleman of considerable wealth, entered the society of Jesus. Not only did he expend his wealth on the Irish college but he shared in the educational work and arranged for the instruction of the students at the Jesuit school at Lisbon.

7. *Ir. Ecc. Rec.,* viii, March 1872, 281.
8. Ware states that Ximenes was the founder of the college, *Works* (ed. 1704), ii, 257.
9. Murphy, *History of Trinity College* (Dublin, 1951), p. 13.
10. Hogan, *op. cit.*, p. 55.

Salamanca and Lisbon now assumed a new significance for Irish Catholicism. On the other hand, Santiago Compostella in Galicia, the scene of the next educational venture, already bore a religious meaning for Ireland. The pageant of medieval history found a spiritual focal point in the tomb of Santiago. Well-defined pilgrim paths across Europe led to the miraculous resting-place of the elder of the sons of Zebedee. Memories of Charlemagne and echoes of the *Chanson de Roland* may have counted for less in Ireland than on the mainland of Europe but Irish devotees found a place in the pilgrimage. Thus in 1472 Finghin Mór O'Driscoll and his son Tadhg sailed from Dunasead castle in Baltimore, Co. Cork, to pray at the tomb of St James.[11] Perhaps the tradition was still strong enough to give a point of assembly to the Irish who sought exile in Spain after the defeat at Kinsale in 1602. We do not know. But it is certain that Eugene or Kilian MacCarthy, parish priest of Fermoy, Co. Cork, sought refuge at Santiago in 1604 after the edict of expulsion of the clergy from Ireland. We know also on the testimony of Diarmuid MacCarthy, founder in 1603 of the college at Bordeaux, that Kilian or Eugene MacCarthy organised the exiles at Santiago and established a centre of education.[12] 1605 is the approximate date of foundation. Philip III allowed an annual subsidy of £100 to which was added alms from the townsfolk.

Whatever the reasons the seminary was a scene of contention from the outset. Donal O'Sullivan Beara of Dunboy, hero to the Irish exiles, insisted that lay pupils, children of Irish parents, should find accommodation in the college. MacCarthy, the superior, was in agreement. Powerful interests thought otherwise. In 1611 the king desired to place the seminary under the control of the Jesuits but the society was reluctant to shoulder the college debts. Finally, in 1613, as we have already told, there was a royal directive. Three Irish Jesuits, Thomas White, William White, and Richard Conway, took charge at Santiago.

One finds it difficult to see a planned educational economy in the Irish infiltration to Spain during the first years of the seven-

11. *Annals of the Four Masters* (ed. O'Donovan).

12. In a pamphlet published at Bordeaux in 1619 Diarmuid MacCarthy named the priests, secular and regular, who found refuge at Bordeaux after the edicts of expulsion in 1604 and 1611. The first name on the list is: *Pere Eugenius Cartaeus du diocese de Cluanen. abbe de Fermoy, qui a este superieur du College Hibernois dix ou douze ans a St Jacques de Gallice,* cf. *C.S.P.,* 1615-25, 316 ff.

teenth century. From Santiago in Galicia in 1605 to Seville in Andalusia in 1612 was the next step forward in the Irish college movement. Real, although remote, historical associations could have explained the Irish appearance in Santiago; one is at a loss to discover the attraction to Seville. True, the old Moorish city was the scene of St Teresa's Carmelite reform; one can still see in the *Calle de Zaragoza* the white building, with its patio and Moorish arches, bearing the inscription *Casa de Santa Teresa, 1576*. But St Teresa and the Carmelite reform must have meant little to the young Irishmen who foregathered in Seville some thirty years later. Perhaps they hoped to gain admission to the English college, founded by Persons, in 1592. Indeed it seems probable that the English recusant establishment held a few Irishmen.

Once again we cannot be sure when the Irish students reached Seville. M'Donald, quoting documentary materials in Salamanca college, cites a licence, dated 8 June 1612, granted by Don Antonio Caetano, archbishop of Capua and nuncio in Spain, to collect alms for the *junta* of Irish students in Seville.[13] Clearly, in 1612 the Irish were an identifiable group. A contemporary Spanish source yields more graphic details. Father Richard Pichardo, twice rector at Seville, quoted Don Diego Ortiz de Zuñiga who noted in the *Annales de Sevilla* under the year 1618 :[14]

> About this time some pious people of Seville, and particularly a devout and zealous priest, who afterwards entered the Society of Jesus, seeing the advantage which resulted to the secret Christianity of England from the College that nation had in Seville, desired to establish one in favour of the Irish, no less in need, and for many reasons more deserving of it from Spain, which took place, as I find in some records in the year 1612. They had a house with some form of College which was fostered and assisted by the Christianity and piety of Don Felix de Guzman, a Sevillian noble, archdeacon and canon, who thought it would be useful and advantageous if the Society of Jesus would charge itself with its government, as it did with that of the English.

A fragment, dated 1620, of Irish authorship is much more informative. The document, entitled *Origin, Progress and State of the Irish Seminary of Seville, of the Pure Conception of the Mother of God,* bears erasures and emendations by Father Richard

13. M'Donald, *op. cit.*, viii, 1872, 467.
14. *Ibid.*

Conway who was appointed rector of the college in 1619.[15]
According to the fragment many Irish youths destined for the
divine ministry sought education in Spain; some found a home at
Salamanca and others at Lisbon. 'Many noble youths, virtuous and
deserving' came to the royal and noble city of Seville. The first body
of Irish students all perished of plague. Then a young man, Theobald Stapleton, a native of Tipperary and a student at the college
at Lisbon, approached the duke of Braganza with a petition to
bring relief to the young Irishmen at Seville.[16] In this way we
learn the circumstances that led to the foundation of the college :

> A zealous youth, called Theobald Stapleton, otherwise Gal-
> duf [Gall Dubh], with the desire of increasing the number of
> Catholics in his country, left Lisbon, where he was a student,
> without telling anyone of his intention. Recommending himself
> to God and the Blessed Virgin, he reached the residence of
> the noble and pious Duke of Braganza, and told him he
> wanted to found a seminary of his nation at Seville. The Duke
> gave him letters of recommendation to the archbishop and
> governor and other persons in Seville, with a good viaticum,
> a part of which he spent in purchasing a blue habit and the
> cross which the students of Lisbon wore on their breast. And
> thus he arrived in Seville, animated more by the confidence he
> had in the Holy Virgin than by the human favours he received.
> A good number of his fellow-country students united with him
> in a short time. He took a house and sought food for them for
> which he neglected his own studies, that they might prosecute
> theirs with more freedom, and be able to give a good account
> of themselves.

Stapleton was joined by two more Tipperarymen, Charles Ryan
and James Kearney, a young priest from Salamanca. At this stage
the little college gained a new benefactor, Don Geronimo de
Medina Farragut, who gave the students accommodation in his
own house. In 1619 when the Jesuits assumed direction of the
seminary Don Geronimo made over his house, valued at 4,000
crowns, as an absolute grant for use as an Irish college.[17] M'Donald adds a piquant detail. In his day (1872) the street in which the

15. M'Donald, op. cit., 468.
16. Not to be confused with the Theobald Stapleton who published a
Catechism in Brussels in 1639. Theobald of Lisbon and Seville was martyred
in Ireland in 1647. Cf. Murphy, Our Martyrs, p. 307.
17. A crown at this period was worth about 5s. 8d.

seminary once stood was still known as *Calle de los Chiquitos* or the street of the little ones. The term was said to have been used by Philip III in reference to the Irish foundation—*El Colegio de los Chiquitos.*

James Kearney and Maurice Regan, both secular priests, were the first superiors. They were succeeded by four Spanish secular priests. Under their *régime,* as we have already described, there was recurring student restiveness and the institution was threatened with closure. In 1619 the Jesuits took charge; the student enrolment was then fifteen. In the following years the seminary became a subsidiary to the college at Salamanca. The students studied humanities and philosophy at the Jesuit College of St Hermenigild, Seville, after which they were transferred to Salamanca to read theology.

Although Madrid was not a university town an Irish foundation was made in the city in 1629.[18] Don Dermisio O'Brien, chaplain to Philip IV, received a number of Irish students in his own house in the *Calle de Humilladero,* Madrid. The municipality allotted sufficient revenues to maintain ten to twenty students. In 1692 the revenues failed but Don Baltasar Moscoso, cardinal archbishop of Toledo, converted the establishment to a hostel for priests from the other colleges who came to Madrid seeking the viaticum for their return to Ireland. The custom was continued to 1759. The history of the foundation is obscure.[19]

If the colleges at Salamanca, Santiago, and Seville maintained a policy of regionalism in favour of the province of Munster the last Irish seminary in Spain was professedly reserved for students from the dioceses of Ulster.[20] In 1657 at Alcalà de Henares Baron George de Paz y Silveira whose mother was a MacDonnell of Antrim gave a capital endowment of £5,000 towards the foundation of a seminary to serve the northern dioceses of Ireland.[21]

18. The university of Madrid was founded in 1836.

19. One finds occasional references in Spanish sources: e.g. when Domingo O Mouroghu [Murphy] was made knight of Calatrava in Madrid in 1663 among his sponsors was Dr Guillermo Nugencio, rector of the Irish college of San Patricio, Madrid. Walsh, 'Further Notes Towards a History of the Womenfolk of the Wild Geese', *Irish Sword,* no. 20, 1963.

20. In later years the reservation cannot have been too strictly enforced; in 1740 Michael O'Gara, former rector of the college, was nominated archbishop of Tuam, cf. *Coll. Hib.,* no. 10, 1967, 87; Brady, *Episcopal Succession,* ii, 147.

21. Walsh, 'The MacDonnells of Antrim on the Continent', *O'Donnell Memorial Lecture,* University College, Dublin, May 1960.

The college was incorporated with the university of Alcalà. Under the terms of the foundation the office of rector was filled by a student, elected by his fellow students. This extraordinary procedure, adopted in most continental seminaries, frequently precipitated rivalries and student unrest. In 1729 the Irish bishops intervened with a request that the institute be placed under Jesuit administration but their plea was not accepted.[22] In 1778 Charles III, king of Spain, forbade the admission of students with the result that the college was closed in 1785 and its endowments were vested in the seminary at Salamanca.

Such in broad outline was the first phase of the Irish college movement in Spain. Only when Spanish archival sources have been fully examined will it be possible to discover the later developments of foundations from which for more than two centuries hope and comfort flowed to Irish Catholics.

St Patrick's college, Salamanca, was the major institution; the Colegio de Nobles Irlandeses figured largely in Irish history. Happily, a wealth of its historical materials has been published by O'Doherty.[23] The materials may be classified : *Juramentos* or oaths of obedience and missionary service, with some small lacunae, for the periods 1595-1700, 1715-1778, 1789 and 1796, giving us the names of students from hundreds of parishes in Ireland; reports of college examinations for the years 1617 and 1626-1766; the *Diario* of John O'Brien, Waterford, rector of the college 1743-78.

What was the relationship between the colleges and the extensive Irish settlement in Spain after 1602?[24] During the seventeenth and eighteenth centuries bearers of historic Irish names sought admission to the knightly orders of Santiago, Calatrava, and Alcántara. Irish sponsors or witnesses testified to the noble ancestry of the candidates. The list of witnesses is a remarkable cross-section of the Irish *diaspora* in Spain : officers in the military and naval

22. M'Donald, *op. cit.*, ix, 1873, 546.

23. *Arch. Hib.*, ii (1913), iii (1914), iv (1915).

24. In more recent times the financial resources of the colleges were concentrated in the college at Salamanca. In 1951 the Irish bishops entered into negotiations with the Spanish government with a view to transference of the college at Salamanca. Eventually the college was transferred to the university of Salamanca. The villa, investments and other property were sold for two million pesetas (£20,000), conveyed to the Irish college, Rome. Under the auspices of the National University of Ireland two 'Salamanca' scholarships were founded, one for a clerical and one for a lay student, tenable at any Spanish university. Cf. Browne, 'Irish College at Salamanca —Last Days', *The Furrow*, no. 11, November 1971.

service, clerics, secular and regular, landowners, merchants, bankers.[25] Although no list of educational foundations, comparable to that of the colleges in France, is yet forthcoming there is evidence that the Irish colony in Spain had a deep solicitude for the foundations in the peninsula. For example, when the foundation was made at Seville in 1612 Irish officers in the Spanish service offered a percentage of their pay to support the students.[26] A Captain French continued his alms even when he had been transferred to the West Indies. Irish merchants in Seville and Cadiz likewise paid a levy on every pipe of wine exported to England, Scotland, and Ireland as augmentation of Irish revenues.

THE LOW COUNTRIES

Irish tradition in the Low Countries drew its first strength from missionaries such as Foillan and Rumold in the eighth and ninth centuries. Whatever the vitality of medieval tradition, there was a new and powerful magnetism in Louvain when the call of the counter reform reached Ireland. Thither came the earliest response: the first Irish student was admitted to matriculation in 1548. Understandably, to generations of Irishmen Louvain is more than a university town; it is a period of time when the trusteeship of Irish culture and scholarship rested with Hugh Ward, John Colgan, Michael O'Clery, and Hugh MacCaghwell. During the years 1590-1616 the Irish college movement made its greatest penetration—with five foundations. Significantly, there was an element of reciprocity : newly-formed Irish regiments were distinguished units in the armies of the Spanish Netherlands then engaged in war against the seceding seven provinces of Holland.

Oddly enough, the first major Irish involvement in the war culminated in an act of secession. After the Desmond wars, William Stanley, a former sheriff of Co. Cork, recruited 1,000 Irishmen to serve the cause of the revolting provinces. In the summer of 1586 the Irish fought at Dixmude and Zutphen. Then they went into winter quarters in the town of Deventer. Only then, apparently, did the Irish troops realise that they had espoused the cause of Calvinism against the Catholic Philip II of Spain. In January 1587 they seceded—holding Deventer for Spain. Later, Stanley's regi-

25. Walsh, *Spanish Knights of Irish Origin,* passim.
26. M'Donald, *op. cit.,* ix, 1973, 211.

ment, augmented to 2,000 officers and men, was recognised as a separate command in the armies of the Spanish Netherlands.[1] After the defeat at Kinsale in 1601 Irish recruitment grew steadily. Henry O'Neill, second son of Hugh O'Neill, earl of Tyrone, was given command of an Irish regiment in 1605. On his death in 1610 the command passed to his half-brother, John O'Neill. Official records show that during 1610-28 thirty-three Irish priests acted as chaplains to the regiment of O'Neill.[2] The formidable Irish mustering in the Low Countries was viewed by Chichester, the Irish lord deputy, and his privy council, as a prelude to another Spanish landing in Ireland.[3] In 1607 the flight of the earls, Hugh O'Neill and Rory O'Donnell, to the Spanish Netherlands seemed to confirm the suspicions. The Irish military and clerical mustering was ominous. Chichester warned the lords of the council in London of what might befall, directing them to employ many eyes and ears to understand the considerations that brought O'Neill and O'Donnell to the Low Countries.[4]

Chichester need not have been alarmed. If one were to assess the effect of the earls' arrival in the Spanish Netherlands one must look to the college movement. The passing of the Irish cavalcade through the towns of southern Flanders and on to Antwerp, Malines, and Louvain has been described by O Cianáin. The chronicler of the earls' itinerary briefly recorded the visit of O'Neill to the first of the Irish foundations in the Low Countries—St Patrick's college, Douai.[5] Seven years previously, in 1599, O'Neill had made a strong plea to Philip III of Spain to grant a subsidy to the college at Douai which then held 100 students. Now in October 1607 O'Neill was received in the seminary where he met the founders and directors of the colleges : Christopher Cusack, founder and president of Douai college, Florence Conry, founder of St Anthony's, Louvain, and later archbishop of Tuam, Eugene Mac-Mahon, founder of the Pastoral college, Louvain, and later archbishop of Dublin, and Dr Robert Chamberlain, later professor at St Anthony's, Louvain. O Cianáin noted the odes and orations in Latin, Greek, and English by students and professors in honour of

1. *Wild Geese in Spanish Flanders, 1582-1700*, pp. 3-4.
2. *Ibid.*, p. 7.
3. 'List of Irish Officers in the service of the king of Spain in the Low Countries in 1606', *C.S.P.*, 1603-6, 396 ff.
4. Chichester to the Lords of the Council, quoted by Meehan, *op. cit.*, p. 93.
5. 'Flight of the Earls', ed. Walsh, *Arch. Hib.*, ii, app., 37.

the visitors. One must wish that he had treated the historic occasion in greater detail. But he dwelt at some length on the meeting between the earls and the joint viceroys of the Spanish Netherlands, Archduke Albert and the Infanta Isabella Clara Eugenia. Their names figure largely in the documentation of the Irish colleges in the Low Countries.[6] The Archduke Albert came five leagues from his residence at Binche to greet the earls. At the palace they were received with 'honour and respect, with welcome and kindliness.' It is not gratuitous to assume that the Archduke's cordial sympathy for the Irish college movement in the Low Countries was awakened at his meeting with O'Neill and O'Donnell. Three years later, in 1610, the viceroys made possible the achievement of Francis Nugent at Lille.

To the extent that the first organisation and launching of the college movement in the Low Countries are attributable to one man, the father figure of the Irish foundations was Christopher Cusack. Notwithstanding the considerable documentation of his educational activities he remains a somewhat elusive or mysterious personage. His parentage and date of birth are uncertain; most probably he was the son of Sir Robert Cusack, second baron of the Irish exchequer.[7] Little is known of his advent to the Low Countires, but most likely his interest was aroused by an appeal in March 1587 by the Holy See to the chancellor of the university of Douai on behalf of homeless Irish students. In 1594 Cusack established the seminary of St Patrick, Douai. Although the foundation had an enrolment of 100 students in 1599 more young Irishmen continued to arrive. In 1600 in collaboration with his cousin, Laurence Sedgrave, Cusack founded a second college at Antwerp, There is fleeting mention of two other Irish colleges at Douai : an institution of the Irish Cistercians and a seminary begun by Gelasius Lorcan, an Irish diocesan priest, but both foundations were short-lived. Little is known of them.[8] Nor is it known if Cusack was

6. 'Documents of the Irish Colleges at Douai', ed. Jennings, *Arch. Hib.*, x. Albert was the son of the Emperor Maximilian II. He married the Infanta Isabella Clara Eugenia, daughter of Philip II and Elizabeth of Valois. In 1598 Philip appointed them joint viceroys of the Spanish Netherlands. They are always referred to as the Archdukes.

7. Brady, 'Father Christopher Cusack and the Irish College at Douai', *Measgra Mhichíl Uí Cléirigh,* 1944.

8. Father Jennings thinks that the Cistercian foundation at Douai may have been responsible for the Irish Cistercian revival in the seventeenth century, *Documents &c.,* p. 163.

associated with the foundations. In 1616, however, he added another Irish seminary—at Tournai. Relatively little is known of its history. In 1636 it was given a charter by Maximilian Vilain, bishop of Arras, who also founded a burse for the education of Irish students.[9]

Inevitably, the greatest concentration of Irish effort in the Low Countries was at Louvain. The university, founded in 1425, was, after Paris, the most celebrated centre of learning in Europe. To the fifty colleges affiliated to the university flocked students from many lands. The rector magnificus of Louvain ruled with almost the rank and power of a local sovereign.[10] Amongst the early Irish alumni were Richard Creagh, archbishop of Armagh (1564-65), who died in the tower of London, Dermot O'Hurley, archbishop of Cashel (1581-84)), who was done to death in Dublin, and Peter Lombard, archbishop of Armagh (1601-25).

The Franciscan Florence Conry (1560-1629) was the pioneer founder at Louvain.[11] For many years he was a central figure and participant in Spanish efforts to bring help to Ireland. In 1601 he sailed to Kinsale with Don Juan del Aguila. Later he returned to Spain with Hugh O'Donnell to elicit further military aid. Subsequently, Conry was in the van of the college movement. In 1607 he was among the group of Irishmen that greeted Hugh O'Neill at Douai college. In the same year he founded the Franciscan college of St Anthony, affiliated with the university of Louvain. Thenceforward St Anthony's was welded into the tradition of Irish culture and scholarly achievement. Without Louvain, the Irish literary scene in the seventeenth century would have been a barren landscape.[12]

Some years after the foundation of the Franciscan college of St Anthony, Dr Eugene MacMahon or Matthews, archbishop of Dublin, moved to make provision for the secular or diocesan clergy. He surrendered part of his own slender revenues to the project. His petition to the Holy See in January 1623 was a frank evocation of the Tridentine educational decrees :[13]

9. App. Irish Educational Endowments: Brady, 'Irish Colleges in the Low Countries', *Arch. Hib.*, xiv.
10. Cf. Healy, *Centenary History of Maynooth College* (Dublin, 1895), 69 ff.
11. Ceyessens in *Father Luke Wadding* (ed. Mooney, Dublin, 1957), p. 303.
12. Cf. Flower, *The Irish Tradition,* p. 169.
13. Moran, *Archbishops,* p. 280.

Eugene Matthews, archbishop of Dublin, knowing by experience the fewness of the spiritual labourers in Ireland, and reflecting on the Tridentine decree, which commands the erection of diocesan seminaries, although he himself is deprived of the revenues of his see, and therefore being guided more by his zeal than his resources—resolved to devote a portion of what was offered by the faithful for his own subsistence, to make some beginning, at least, of so desirable a work.

Matthews was able 'to put together a mite sufficient for the scanty maintenance of two students.' To this the Holy See added an annual grant of 300 escudos, an endowment of six burses.[14] So in 1624 in a house in the rue des Orphelines, the Irish Pastoral college was established. The first president was Nicholas Aylmer, former tutor to Brian, youngest son of Hugh O'Neill, murdered in Brussels in 1617.[15]

Alumni of the Pastoral college won prominence in later years : Edmund O'Reilly, archbishop of Armagh, 1657-82, Nicholas French, bishop of Ferns, 1646-78, Thomas Stapleton who ten times was elected rector magnificus of the university, and Florence O'Sullivan of Kerry who was elected rector magnificus in 1715.[16] The college continued its work down to October 1797 when French armies entered Louvain and the university was suppressed.

On Mont-Caesar, Louvain, stood the third Irish foundation— the Dominican college of Holy Cross. In 1624 Richard Bermingham of the Dominican priory at Athenry leased a house from James de Mattinet, a military knight of St John of Jerusalem.[17] The first superior was Oliver Burke of the Galway priory. A memorial by Ross MacGeoghegan, provincial of the Irish Dominicans, dated 18 December 1626, was readily received by the viceroy, the Infanta Isabella Clara. With the commendation of Cardinals Ludovisi and Bandini the court of Madrid and the Archduke Albert gave proof of good will; an annual grant of 1,200 florins was allowed and the community at Mont-Caesar was admitted to the university.[18] In 1648 the Holy See added 320 crowns annually on condition that

14. Acta Cong. Prop. Fid., ed. Jennings, *Arch. Hib.*, xxii, 36.
15. O Fiaich, 'Edmund O'Reilly', in *Luke Wadding*, p. 177.
16. Jennings, 'Irish Students in the University of Louvain', *Measgra Mhichíl Uí Cléirigh.*
17. O'Heyne, *Epilogus Chronologicus* (Louvain, 1706), ed. Coleman, 1902, p. 275.
18. O'Heyne, *op. cit.*, p. 113; *Coll. Hib.*, no. 11, 1968, 9.

four students, fully trained and equipped, were sent to Ireland every six years.

Seen in retrospect each of the Irish colleges we have named—at Douai, Antwerp, Lille, Tournai and the three foundations at Louvain—is a theme of history. Life in the seminaries was a rough adventure for the young men who arrived from Ireland seeking admission. Want and penury were hard taskmasters.

One may assume that official grants, both from the court at Madrid and from the archdukes, were less than adequate. It is certain, however, that the grants were either delayed or withheld as Spanish finances fluctuated. In the first decades of the seventeenth century Spanish funds were in a precarious state. In 1623 bankers in the Low Countries refused to accept the credit of the state treasury.[19] Soon the Irish foundations were in debt. There was a cancellation of the subsidy to the college at Douai. In 1610 Cusack made known his needs to Philip III at Madrid.[20] On 12 September 1613 Feliciani, papal secretary, sent a sharp note of remonstrance to Antonio Caetano, nuncio at Madrid, to remind the king of Spain of the unpaid subsidies to Irish institutions.[21] Obviously, there was no lack of willingness on Philip's part. On 24 October 1613 he instructed the Archduke Albert that 'the reduction of payments should not extend to the alms and grants which are given to the convents, seminaries, and persons mentioned by the nuncio.'[22] But performance fell short of promise.

As was the pattern of development in the colleges in Spain so was the evolution of the foundations in the Low Countries. Extant documents present a general picture of impoverished institutions.

Cusack died probably in 1622. His successors, Nicholas Aylmer and Laurence Sedgrave, shouldered the burden of maintaining the colleges. John Roche, bishop of Ferns (1624-36) and agent at Rome of the Irish bishops, made a report to Cardinal Ludovisi, protector of Ireland, giving stark details of many Irish foundations on the continent.[23] The report refers to the years 1625-26. Roche stressed the precarious state of the Douai college from which in times past so many worthy priests had gone forth to labour in the vineyard of

19. Jennings, *Wild Geese etc.*, p. 628.
20. 'Documents of the Irish Colleges at Douai', ed. Jennings, *Arch. Hib.*, 1902, p. 277.
21. Fondo Borghese I, *Arch. Hib.*, xxiii, 143.
22. Jennings, *Wild Geese etc.*, pp. 141-42.
23. 'Two Reports on the Catholic Church in the Early Seventeenth Century', *Arch. Hib.*, xxii.

the Lord. The other foundations, Roche added, were similarly placed : unless adequate provision was forthcoming the loss to Ireland would be very grave.

Indeed in 1625 at Douai all seemed lost : the college buildings were about to be sold to meet the creditors. Nicholas Aylmer, as president, appealed for help to the bishops of Flanders and abbots of Benedictine monasteries.[24] In April 1627 there was alarm in Ireland and three bishops moved to save the seminary. Thomas Fleming of Dublin, David Rothe of Ossory, and William Tirry of Cork addressed a memorial to Cardinal Ludovisi to urge the king of Spain and the Infanta Clara Isabella to sustain the college.[25] The plea of the bishops was reinforced by strong representations by the Holy See through the nuncio at Madrid. Aylmer added his plaint in two letters written in 1628 : subsidies promised by the court of Spain and by the Holy See were unpaid.[26] The appeals were heard. On 11 June 1628 the bishop of Segovia, president of the council of Flanders, gave an assurance that everything would be done to maintain the Irish foundations.[27] Evidently, the subsidies were paid; how and when is not clear. But the college of St Patrick, Douai, survived.

Douai college and its recurring crises were typical of all the Irish foundations in the Low Countries. Extant documentation has little variation of the theme of impoverishment. The college at Antwerp was small—it held six priests and ten students in 1613—but it was always facing dissolution. Only the efforts of Nicholas Eustace, appointed president in 1650, gave the college some measure of security. Nonetheless, there is a hint of exasperation in the comment in 1680 of Paul van Halmale, archpriest of Antwerp—the college needed a Maecenas of superlative munificence![28] The passing years did not bring an economic improvement. As late as 1703 the revenues of the benefice of St Martin of Duffel, Antwerp, were attached to the seminary to defray current expenses.[29]

In 1635 the Holy See decided to investigate the affairs of the Irish colleges but there was no practical result.[30] Nevertheless, there was some kind of investigation; in 1641 the Holy See

24. Acta S. Cong. Prop. de Fid., *Arch. Hib.*, xxii, 38.
25. *Coll. Hib.*, no. 10, 1967, 49.
26. *Ibid.*, pp. 48-49.
27. *Ibid.*, p. 51.
28. Brady, 'Irish Colleges in Douai and Antwerp', *Arch. Hib.*, xiii.
29. *Coll. Hib.*, no. 10, 1967, p. 105.
30. Acta S. Cong., *Arch. Hib.*, xxii, p. 90.

commended the diligence of Matthew Teige, president of the Pastoral college, in extricating the institute from its embarrassments.[31]

Rarely is there mention of support from Ireland. This is surprising in view of the generous contributions given to Francis Nugent at the foundation of Lille college in 1610.[32] One significant contribution was made to the Pastoral college in 1639—900 florins from some Irish bishops.[33]

Nor did the Irish in the Spanish Netherlands give material support. A possible explanation is that despite the heavy Irish military influx there was little Irish penetration into the commercial life of the country. The Irish remained an exclusively military caste. Another factor was the cessation of Irish military recruitment in 1641.[34] Whatever the reason, the extent of Irish almsgiving was limited.

Records of educational foundations or burses are few. One of the earliest was established by Pope Urban VIII in 1624. In the same year the first burse of purely Irish origin was founded by Eugene Matthews, bishop of Clogher (1609-11), and later archbishop of Dublin (1611-23). He made two foundations : one reserved to the diocese of Clogher and the other to the diocese of Dublin.[35] Such reservations were a feature common to most educational foundations in the Irish colleges. Thus a burse established by James Normel, president of the Pastoral college in 1653, was limited to students who were natives of Clonmel and Lismore. Similarly, an endowment made in 1666 by John Sinnich, also of the Pastoral college and rector magnificus of the university, was cconfined to students of Munster. A narrower restriction was attached by Florence O'Sullivan of the diocese of Kerry; in 1699 he established fifteen foundations for his own collateral descendants and in default to O'Sullivans and MacCarthys of Co. Kerry.[36] Although burses in the colleges of the Low Countries were relatively few in comparison with the seminaries in France there is

31. *Ibid.*, p. 117. Cf. statements of accounts of Pastoral college 1627 and 1631, 'Miscellaneous Documents', *Arch. Hib.*, xii, 134, 161.

32. Archbold, *Historie of the Irish Capuchins,* p. 109, Martin, *Friar Nugent,* p. 167.

33. Acta S. Cong., *Arch. Hib.*, xxii, 109.

34. Jennings, *Wild Geese,* p. 500.

35. App. Educational Foundations in the Belgian Netherlands.

36. Jennings, 'Irish Students in the University of Louvain',. *Measgra Mhichíl Uí Cléirigh.*

evidence that there were other educational foundations of which nothing is now known.[37]

In the documented anxieties of the Holy See, Irish bishops, and local superiors to assure maintenance of the colleges one discovers very little relating to the ordinary day-to-day routine of the students, their names and dioceses, dates of ordination and departure for the Irish mission. Doubtless, the ordination registers of Belgian dioceses may hold some evidence.[38]

Agitations of another and extravagant nature distrubed the calm tenor of student life. Fissures and divisions between Old Irish and Anglo-Irish spilled over into the continental colleges. While it is easy to exaggerate and decry the serious disciplinary implications of such rivalries one must bear in mind that racial cleavages of various kinds had halted for many generations attempts to forge national unity. A contributory influence towards regional bias was the provincial or local origin of many foundations. They were not the result of hierarchical initiative; indeed the absence of Irish episcopal control was eventually to their detriment. As we have already seen, in 1602 there were protests at high level against the Munster dominance in the college at Salamanca. Florence Conry, in the names of O'Neill and O'Donnell, addressed a memorial to Philip III requesting an allocation of half the places in the seminary to students from Connacht and Ulster.[39]

In the foundations in the Low Countries the emphasis was on the dioceses of Leinster. Although Christopher Cusack was a palesman he did not submit to such regional exclusiveness. As president of all the Irish colleges, he was party to an agreement in 1607 under which there was a reduction of admissions from the Leinster dioceses to increase the intake from non-pale areas.[40] By strange irony, in 1614 his own college at Douai became the focal point of protests : the Old Irish accused Cusack of partiality towards the dioceses of the pale. The bishop of Arras was willing to adopt a solution which apparently was suggested by Old Irish elements : a segregation of the students.[41] Bentivolgio, the internuncio at Brussels, refused to sanction such a drastic action on the

37. As appears from the letter of Vincenzo Montalto to Cardinal Banchieri, 29 June 1731, *Coll. Hib.*, no. 9, 1966, 23.

38. Cf. Jennings, 'Irish Names in the Malines Ordination Registers, 1602-1794, *Ir. Ecc. Rec.*, fifth series, vols. lxxvi-vii, 1951-52.

39. Cf. Meehan, *Fate and Fortunes* etc., App. p. 352.

40. Martin, *Friar Nugent*, p. 164.

41. Miscellanea Vaticano-Hibernica, *Arch. Hib.*, iv, 284 ff.

grounds that the expenses of the foundation, already in financial straits, would be increased and racial prejudices would be perpetuated. The archdukes, Albert and Isabella, declared their uncompromising objections.[42] The viceroys discounted regional bias by a directive to the president and provisors to admit students from the four provinces of Ireland without discrimination.[43]

Regional rivalry was not so easily terminated. Undaunted, Francis Nugent in his college at Lille refused admission to students from non-pale dioceses. His reservation in favour of the dioceses of Meath and Leinster was recognised by Urban VIII in an apostolic brief, dated 28 July 1636.[44] The regional controversy also aroused feelings at Antwerp. In 1631 Bonaventure Magennis, the Franciscan bishop of Down and Connor, approached the Holy See with a request to investigate the conditions of entry at Antwerp, where due equality was not observed in admitting students from the different parts of Ireland.[45] But provincial rivalry continued to agitate the college. In 1680 new rules and statutes were approved for the Antwerp foundation. Rule 20 asserted the need for peace and harmony among the students; any student who despite repeated admonitions continued to foment provincial discord would be expelled from the college.[46]

History has its victories. In the seminaries of the Low Countries all obstacles were overcome. The order of closure came only with the outbreak of the French revolution.

FRANCE

In early medieval times Irish scholar exiles were major influences in the creation of French religious culture.[1] St Columbanus, Sedulius, John Scotus Erigena, and Dungal were in the van of the Irish *peregrini*. Erick of Auxerre avowed that 'almost all Ireland with a vast train of philosophers removed to France in the ninth

---

42. Jennings, 'Documents of the Irish Colleges at Douai', *Arch. Hib.*, x.
43. In 1579 in the English college, Rome, the student body, numbering thirty-three Englishmen, broke out in open revolt against the admission of seven Welsh students, *Douai Diaries*, p. lxxi.
44. *Bullarium Ordinis FF. Minorum Capucinorum* (Rome, 1748), V, f 281.
45. *Coll. Hib.*, no. 10, 1967, p. 37.
46. Brady, 'The Irish colleges at Douai and Antwerp', *Arch. Hib.*, xiii.

1. Cf. Flower, *The Irish Tradition*, chap. ii.

century.'[2] Hence a modern French commentator on Franco-Irish relations sees the establishment of Irish colleges in France during the seventeenth and eighteenth centuries as an acknowledgment of French indebtedness.[3]

As we have noted, the first Irish post-Tridentine foundation on the continent was made in 1578 when Father John Lee of Meath and his group of six students settled in Paris. Little is known of the Irish nucleus during the following decades save that it had a tenuous continuity. Further educational expansion in France was slow in contrast to the rapid diffusion of colleges in Spain and the Low Countries during 1594-1610. Internal conditions in France postponed the Irish educational advance. Incessant religious wars during the last quarter of the sixteenth century effectively delayed the Catholic counter reform. In 1594 Henry of Navarre was acknowledged king of France and pledged himself to accept the Tridentine reforms.[4] More importantly, in 1598 he put an end to religious strife with the publication of the edict of Nantes. Soon the work of national reconstruction was begun. When Henry died at the hand of an assassin in 1610 much had been accomplished. France, once distracted, impoverished, desolated, impotent, was now 'united, prosperous, peaceful, flourishing, powerful.'[5] Hitherto on the margins of the counter reforms, France suddenly became its main focus.[6]

There was a timeliness, therefore, in the second Irish educational advance into France : in November 1603 Diarmuid MacCarthy, priest of the diocese of Cork, accompanied by a dozen students, arrived at Bordeaux. Other Irishmen also felt the French contagion. In 1610 dispersed Irish Cistercians made proposals to the Holy See to erect seminaries in France.[7] In the same year, Cardinal Borghese papal secretary of state, considered a Capuchin plan to establish colleges on French soil to meet 'the needs of the languishing faith in Ireland.'[8] Neither design was successful.

Perhaps the most enigmatic figure at this period was Gelasius Lurcan, an Irish priest. In 1608 he was associated with Christopher

2. Ware's *Writers* (ed. 1704), I, 57.
3. Pauly, *Les Voyageurs Français en Irelande au Temps du Romantisme* (Paris, 1939), p. 2.
4. MacCaffrey, *History*, 165.
5. *Cambridge Modern History*, III, chap. xx, 691.
6. Dickens, *The Counter Reformation*, 172 ff.
7. Miscellanea Vaticano-Hibernica, *Arch. Hib.*, iv, 264.
8. Fondo Borghese 1, *Arch. Hib.*, xxiii, 85.

Cusack at Douai but relations between them were strained. Nonetheless, Lurcan won official favour and was licensed to quest for alms to maintain Irish students.[9] Somewhat inexplicably, in 1612 he succeeded in establishing an Irish college at Rouen in Normandy. In the following year Cardinal Borghese appealed to Cardinal Joyeuse, archbishop of Rouen, and Ubaldini, the nuncio in France, to aid Lurcan's foundation.[10] It seems that the little seminary was submerged in debt; in 1614 Lurcan was back in Douai. Whether we regard it as a survival or a revival there was an Irish college at Rouen in the latter part of the century.[11]

Naturally, the Irish resurgence in France largely expanded from the first settlement at Paris in 1578. The earliest students resided at first at the collège Montaigu and then at the collège de Navarre, institutions that were affiliated to the university of Paris. Boyle, in his short history, traces the gradual emergence of the Irish college.[12] In 1605 a munificent benefactor, John de l'Escalopier, Baron St-Just, president of the parlement de Paris, provided a house of residence and maintenance. He shared the common life of the students.[13] When he died in 1620 his widow continued his benefaction to the Irish exiles. The proportions of the college were

9. 'Documents of the Irish Colleges at Douai', *Arch. Hib.*, x; *ibid.*, xviii, 202.

10. *Ibid.*, xxiii, 44, 70.

11. In 1704 the following declared under the act of registration that they had been ordained at Rouen: James Kearney, Fethard, Co. Tipperary, 1666; Teige Daly, Doneraile, Co. Cork, 1666; Loughlin Meagher, Ballyoyne, Co. Carlow, 1667; Edward Comerford, Thurles, 1669; William Tobin, Tallow, Co. Waterford, 1671; Dermod Driscoll, Creagh, Co. Cork, 1674; Maurice Gallagher, Kilfergus, Co. Limerick, 1675; William Ronan, Dromin, Co. Limerick, 1676, *Ir. Ecc. Rec.*, xii, 1876. Today one finds at Rouen many reminders of the former Irish settlement. In the church of St Patrice is a stained glass window commemorating an incident in the life of St Patrick. In the rue St Patrice there was a community of Irish priests in 1641, Hayes, *Old Irish Links with France*, p. 217; Licquet, *Rouen, its History and Monuments* (trans. Barguet, Rouen, 1858), pp. 56-57.

12. *The Irish College in Paris, 1578-1901* (London, 1901).

13. The Abbé MacGeoghegan, a provisor of the college in 1734, thus describes the piety of de l'Escalopier: 'They [the Irish] were brought by this illustrious Frenchman from an obscure dwelling, and settled in a more commodious place, while he was providing a regular seminary and funds necessary for their support. He was frequently with them in the refectory, where his humility was such that, forgetful of rank as first magistrate of France, and as a proof of his respect for the exiled clergymen, he always chose the last place at table.' *History of Ireland* (trans. O'Kelly, Dublin, 1844), p. 480.

clearly defined in 1621. Boyle cites an anonymous writer who stated in 1621 that there was an Irish seminary in Paris with at least twenty-four priests and students. By then the institution must have been in exitsence for several years. In his brief of appointment to the see of Meath, dated 5 May 1621, Thomas Dease is described as former rector of the Irish college, Paris.[14] The status of the seminary was clarified by letters patent issued by Louis XIII at St Germain-en-Laye on 16 September 1623.[15] Thus the foundation was recognised as a corporation under French law.

Despite the favourable auspices the seminary was in financial straits within a short period. In 1624 five Irish bishops addressed a moving appeal to the city and university of Paris and to the Sorbonne to sustain an institution which had already rendered priceless service to the church in Ireland : closure would be calamitous to the Irish people.[16] We must conclude that French generosity eased the burden. In 1626 the archbishop of Paris approved the rules and statutes of the college.[17]

Distinct from the purely pastoral value of the seminary the foundation, through its superiors and many alumni, had a large relevance to the wider picture of seventeenth-century Irish history. Thomas Messingham, superior, was the author of a standard work on Irish hagiology : *Florilegium Sanctorum,* published in Paris in 1624.[18] Malachy O'Queally, graduate of the collège de Navarre and the Sorbonne, was consecrated archbishop of Tuam in 1630. As one of the first members of the supreme council of the Confederation of Kilkenny O'Queally was an active figure in the wars of the period. He was killed near Sligo in 1645.[19] Edward Tyrell of the diocese of Meath also graduated at the collège de Naverre. In 1633 he was appointed proctor of the constituent of the university of Paris known as the Nation d'Allemagne which oddly included Ireland. Later during the confederate wars he acted as French agent of Rinuccini, papal nuncio to Ireland. Under his will, dated 1671, Tyrell made a bequest of £200 to the college with the expressed hope that the superior would always be a priest from

14. Brady, *Episcopal Succession,* I, 238.
15. Boyle, *op. cit.,* app. doc. 5.
16. *Spic. Oss.,* i, 133 ff.
17. Boyle, *op. cit.,* app. doc. 3.
18. Brenan, *Ecclesiastical History of Ireland,* p. 539. Messingham was also the author of *Officii SS. Patritii, Columbae et aliorum Hiberniae Sanctorum* (Paris, 1620.
19. Brady, *Epis. Succession,* i, 139; Murphy, *Our Martyrs,* p. 302; Meehan, *The Confederation of Kilkenny,* p. 46; *Comm. Rin.,* ii, 256.

Meath or some other diocese of Leinster.[20] Today in the Irish college, rue des Irlandais, one sees a memorial tablet to John O'Molony 'of ancient lineage, ardent champion of faith and fatherland whose death was often sought by heretics.' O'Molony was admitted as a student in 1642 and later graduated at the university of Paris. He was a close friend of Colbert, minister of state under Louis XIV. During 1662-66 O'Molony was deeply involved in French plans to bring military aid to Ireland. He was consecrated bishop of Killaloe in 1671 and later was transferred to Limerick. Owing to persecution he was obliged to return to the college in Paris where he died in 1702. Under his will he founded six burses for the benefit of kinsmen in Clare and Limerick.[21]

A stirring episode was the intervention of the Irish priests and students during the bitter controversies of the first phase of Jansenism. Was there an Irish dalliance with Jansenism? Did John Sinnich of the diocese of Cloyne, regent of the faculty of theology in the Pedagogium Lilii and rector magnificus of the university of Louvain, compile the index to the *Augustinus* of Jansen published posthumously in 1640? In the spate of controversial pamphlets printed at Paris during 1651-53 Irish names appear as trenchant proponents of the heresy : Dr Clonsinnil, Philip O'Lonergan, and the stormy figure of John O'Callaghan, of Carbery, Co. Cork, doctor of the Sorbonne, and Edward Rothe. From the Irish college came a strong disclaimer. In a brief statement and with telling emphasis twenty-seven priests of the college asserted that for more than a century Ireland had borne the insults and harassments of heretics.[22] A new heresy must not be allowed to contaminate either Irish students in Paris or the faithful people at home. The signatories repudiated the five Jansenistic propositions submitted to the Holy See by Nicolas Cornet, syndic of the university. The Irish counter move was unexpected and drew the censure of M. Courtin, rector of the university. O'Lonergan in a pamphlet berated his countrymen who, he alleged, had committed themselves to a doctrinal declaration beyond their comprehension. The aftermath was a pamphlet war involving the Jansenistic archbishop of Paris, the Jesuit Père Brisacier, and the doughty John O'Callaghan. But

20. Hayes, *Biographical Dictionary of Irishmen in France* (Dublin, 1949), p. 300.

21. Brady, *op. cit.*, 120, 49; Hayes, *op. cit.*, p. 245.

22. Text in Boyle, *op. cit.*, p. 22; Wall, 'Irish Enterprise in the University of Paris', *Ir. Ecc. Rec.* (fifth series), no. 921, Sept. 1944. *Comm. Rin.*, vi, 520 ff.

the faculty of theology of the university upheld the action and the orthodoxy of the Irish college. The condemnation of the Jansenistic propositions by Alexander VII in 1653 was a clear vindication of the Irish protest. For some years anti-Irish feeling ran high in Paris. Rulhière, a satirist of a somewhat later period, described the Irish as scruffy monks arriving in Paris to seek theological encounters. Having fled their own country, they were a scourge to learned teachers.[23]

The passing of the Cromwellian régime and the restoration of Charles II to the throne of England in 1660 gave the church in Ireland a breathing space. One of the most urgent tasks of reorganisation was the filling of the depleted ranks of the pastoral clergy. Moreover, most dioceses were bereft of bishops. At one period Patrick Plunket of Ardagh was the only resident bishop in the kingdom.

Edmund O'Reilly, archbishop of Armagh (1657-69), returned from exile in July 1660. He forthwith supplied the Holy See with statistics revealing the extreme gravity of the position throughout Ireland.[24] The colleges abroad were unable to supply the pastoral needs and there was no time for delay. O'Reilly ordained twenty-nine priests within eighteen months; in a shorter time Anthony MacGeoghegan, bishop of Meath (1657-64) ordained eight; during the years 1664-69 Plunket of Ardagh ordained 200 priests from various parts of the country.[25] In 1669 Oliver Plunket was appointed to the see of Armagh and William Burgat to Cashel. They also promoted many to the priesthood in the following decade. What of the educational standards of such men? Perforce, the standards of priestly formation and theological training were far from the norms of the council of Trent.[26] The bishops were conscious of the departure from Tridentine principles and demanded under oath that all priests so ordained must supplement their education in a continental college when opportunity served.

23. Venez-y, venez voir, comme sur un théâtre
   Une dispute en règle, un choc opiniâtre,
   Des moines echauffés vrai fléau des docteurs,
   Des pauvres Hibernois, complaisants disputeurs,
   Qui fuyant leur pays pour les saintes promisses,
   Viennent vivre à Paris d'arguments et de Messes.
          Quoted by Boyle, *op. cit.*, preface.
24. O Fiaich, 'Edmund O'Reilly, Archbishop of Armagh', in *Father Luke Wadding*, pp. 192-93.
25. Millet, *Survival and Reorganisation* (Dublin, 1968), pp. 14-15.
26. Millet, *The Irish Franciscans, 1651-65* (Rome, 1964), pp. 346-47.

Most of the priests obeyed; in later years many betook themselves to the college in Paris. Thus we find that in 1672 there were as many as eighty priests studying at the college Montaigu.[27] The influx of priest-students posed problems of accommodation and supervision for the superiors of the college at Paris.

Influential Franco-Irish figures were ready to help : William Bailly, abbot of St Thierry, near Rheims, Patrick Maginn, abbot of Theulay, near Langres, first almoner of Catherine of Braganza, wife of Charles II of England, and Malachy Kelly, prior of St Nicholas de Chapouin, Paris, almoner at the court of Louis XIV. The disused and semi-ruinous Italian collège des Lombards in rue des Carmes was acquired. By letters patent issued by Louis XIV in August 1677 the transfer of the Italian foundation to the Irish was ratified.[28] The buildings were repaired and normal accommodation was found for most of the Irish ecclesiastics studying in Paris. Under letters patent given in 1681 the chancellor of Notre Dame and the abbot of St Victor's, Paris, were appointed major superiors. Priest provisors were also named—one from each of the four provinces of Ireland. Somewhat incongruously, the old Italian designation—des Lombards—was retained in what was now an Irish institution. The new college in rue des Carmes became a centre of Irish life and activity in Paris. It was here that James II held a levée on his return after his defeat in 1690 at the battle of the Boyne.[29] How great was the Jacobite exodus to Paris in those years can be estimated from the pages of Lart.[30] The many émigrés, clerical and lay, fell on evil days, making heavy demands on charity. Generous subsidies were forthcoming from the Holy See; collections were made in the churches of Paris.[31] We may guess at the strain borne by the college. Its necessities were the theme of a sermon preached in 1696 before *la haute noblesse* of Paris by Bourdaloue, the renowned Jesuit preacher of the *ancien régime*.[32] But changes were pending in Irish pastoral life that Bourdaloue

27. O'Boyle, *op. cit.,* p. 25.
28. MacGeoghegan, *History,* p. 480; Boyle, *op. cit.,* app. doc. 9. Maginn died in 1683. In his will he bequeathed 10,000 livres to the college and 2,500 livres for burses to be held at the university of Paris by students from the dioceses of Ulster, Hayes, *op. cit.,* p. 198.
29. Boyle, *op. cit.,* p. 28.
30. *Jacobite Extracts from the Parish Registers of St Germain-en-Laye* (London, 1910).
31. *Spic. Oss.,* ii, p. 347; Burke, *Irish Priests in the Penal Times* (Waterford, 1914), p. 133.
32. Text in Boyle, *op. cit.,* app. doc. 1.

could not have foreseen. In the early decades of the new century the outlawing of the Church in Ireland had repercussions in the continental colleges, especially in the Lombard or Irish college, Paris.

By 1720 it was obvious that the more severe edicts of the penal code were no longer enforceable. Dioceses without bishops since the act of banishment of 1698 were gradually filled. By the middle years of the century every diocese had its resident bishop. An aftermath of the penal *régime* was an acute shortage of secular priests. Again, the supply from the colleges abroad was inadequate. With the first easement of persecution some bishops resolved to avail themselves of the privilege contained in the bull of Urban VIII in 1623—namely, to ordain young men without patrimony on the sole title of a mission in Ireland. The step was drastic but the position was critical. Evidence of the pastoral position is seen in the returns under the act of 1703 requiring registration of the clergy.[33] In all, 1089 diocesan priests registered; of that number only 249 declared that they had received holy orders overseas. In other words, the vast majority of the secular clergy in Ireland had been ordained under the conditions we have outlined above. The history of Irish Catholicism has only one verdict on the men who registered in 1704 : they were the *milites Christi*.

But continued derogation from the principles of the council of Trent led to unfortunate happenings. Many priests failed to comply with the injunction imposed at ordination—to seek further education in a continental college. Cornelius O'Keeffe, appointed to the see of Limerick in 1720, took immediate steps to call the defaulters to order. In 1721 he forbade such priests under penalty of suspension to say Mass : he ordered them to present themselves at a continental college within three months to obtain priestly training and education.[34] Other critical voices were heard. In 1729 Hugh MacMahon, archbishop of Armagh, forwarded to the Holy See some pungent criticisms of his colleague, Thomas Flynn, bishop of Ardagh. MacMahon complained that Flynn 'ordains as many as come before him, no matter what condition they are in, so long as they know a few words of Latin.'[35]

In Paris, John Burke, one of the clerical provisors of the Irish college, took alarm at the deplorable trends in Irish pastoral affairs.

33. *Ir. Ecc. Rec.*, xii, April-Sept., 1876.
34. Wall, *The Penal Laws, 1691-1760* (Dublin, 1961), p. 39.
35. *Coll. Hib.*, no. 9, 14.

In a letter written on 6 December 1733 to an unnamed correspondent Burke gave details of a report that 'would make a good Catholic's hair stand on end.'[36] There were daily scandals caused 'by an exorbitant number of priests roving about without any function but to say Mass, to marry young couples.'[37] He pilloried the Dominican bishop of Achonry, Dominick O'Daly, who 'if not stopped will ordain enough for the whole kingdom.' Burke added that in the college at Paris there were five of O'Daly's priests awaiting the removal by the nuncio of censures and other irregularities. In Burke's opinion it was time that some approach was made to Cardinal Imperiali, the cardinal protector of Ireland, to obtain a papal brief to the four Irish archbishops prohibiting such ordinations.

Hugh MacMahon, archbishop of Armagh, made an oblique effort to call a halt to the ordinations.[38] He objected that priests going to Paris for further education were invading and appropriating burses that were intended for younger students. He believed that if college burses were not available there would be less ordinations of unsuitable subjects in Ireland.

Other bishops thought differently. Without the priests ordained in Ireland pastoral needs could not be met. A protest against the proposals of MacMahon was drawn up and signed by three archbishops and six bishops.[39] The signatories gave power of attorney to James O'Daly, bishop of Kilfenora and then resident at Tournai, to present their views to the Holy See. Thaddeus MacCarthy Rabagh, bishop of Cork, and Eugene O'Sullivan, bishop of Kerry, did not mince words.[40] Twice, in September 1740 and in January 1741, they stated their case to Luca Melchiore Tempi, the nuncio at Brussels. The bishops sought faculties to ordain young men at home *sub titulo missionis* on the grounds that 'the few poor little Irish seminaries in France and elsewhere whose subjects enjoy the papal indult of being promoted to orders *sub titulo missionis* are not in a position to meet the needs of the afflicted Irish Church.' When forwarding the bishops' request to Rome Tempi added his own misgivings : if such faculties were granted Ireland would be flooded with uneducated priests !

36. *Coll. Hib.*, no. 8, 1965, 60 ff.
37. Newspapers in 1748 reported that six priests were excommunicated in Dublin 'for solemnising clandestine marriages'. Wall, *op. cit.*, p. 57.
38. *Coll. Hib.*, no. 9, 1966, 62.
39. *Ibid.*
40. *Coll. Hib.*, no. 10, 1967, 87 ff.

Early in 1742 John Kent, president of the Pastoral college, and canon of the chapter of St Peter, Louvain, was directed by the Holy See to investigate the missionary scene in Ireland.[41] Without waiting, apparently, for Kent's report a rescript of Benedict XIV to the Irish bishops was promulgated on 7 April 1742 : no Irish bishop was permitted to ordain more than twelve priests during his own lifetime; the oath imposing the obligation of seeking further education on the continent must be enforced.[42]

That priests seeking extended education should have sought admission to the Lombard college, Paris, was to be expected. They could hope for an Irish response in the university of Paris, where Michael Moore of Dublin was appointed rector in 1701. Some years later Irishmen occupied professorships in the constituent colleges of the university: James Wogan and John Plunket at the college of Navarre, and James MacDonagh at the college of Plessy.[43] Contacts with relatives and friends could be made among the Irish émigrés in Paris. There was also a continuous drift of Irishmen seeking to serve in Irish regiments. The popularity of the Lombard college did not lessen; in 1762 the enrolment of priests and students was 165.[44]

While Irish bishops argued heavy pressures were building up in the Lombard college, Paris. So many priests came from Ireland in pursuit of education that they slowly monopolised the institution to the exclusion of junior clerics or students. For the college authorities it was not only a question of accommodation but also of priorities. In the early 1700s the junior students had temporary lodging in a house in rue Traversine, with the result that a division arose between priests and students. A sharper division of opinion was concerned with the allocation of funds : should burses, the annual grant of 1,000 livres from the *clergé de France,* and other revenues, be expended on priests or students? Finally, at the instance of Andrew Donlevy, superior of the junior students (1728-46), the debate was referred to the archbishop of Paris.[45] In 1728 the constitutions of the Lombard college were remodelled.[46] The archbishop assumed much greater control. The provisors, hitherto

41. *Ibid.,* p. 94.
42. *Coll. Hib.,* no. 8, 1965, 63n.
43. Boyle, *op. cit.,* pp. 44-45.
44. Boyle, *op. cit.,* p. 40.
45. Donlevy was the author of *An Teagasg Críosduidhe do réir Ceasda agus Freagartha,* published at Paris in 1742.
46. Text in Boyle, *op. cit.,* app. doc. 7.

appointed by election, were now named by the archbishop. There was a similar reservation of the post of superior of the junior students. In addition, the college was made subject to the university. To the two major superiors, the chancellor of Notre Dame and the abbot of St Victor's, Paris, a third was added as the archbishop's personal representative—the Abbé de Vaubrun of the Sorbonne.

The Abbé de Baubrun took steps to deal with pastoral necessities in Ireland. He made provision for incoming priests by extending the Lombard college. As soon as the buildings were completed they were occupied by fifty or sixty priests. In 1735 priests and students were housed in the institution but with separate living quarters.

Under the new constitutions the university had the right of inspection. In 1735 Baltasar Gibert, rector of the university, made an official visitation of the college. His report applauded the unblemished lives of the entire Irish community, priests and students.[47]

The slow recovery of the Church in Ireland from the penal era coincided with the last phase of the college movement. There was a steady diminution in the numbers of priests from Ireland.[48] Much more urgent consideration was given to young students who came to the continent to begin their studies in humanities, philosophy, and theology. This necessitated a reorganisation of the Lombard college, Paris. In 1769 Laurence Kelly, superior of the clerics or junior students, acquired a plot of land in the rue du Cheval Vert at a cost of 47000 francs. A considerable part of the purchase money was contributed by Bartholomew Murray, former regent professor of medicine in the university of Paris.[49] Extensive new buildings were erected to serve the junior students. Henceforth, to the suppression of 1793, there were two Irish seminaries : the older establishment in the rue des Carmes and the new college in the rue du Cheval Vert, known today as rue des Irlandais.

Financial resources were adequate. In 1788 there were fifty-two educational educations—all made with Irish funds, an annual grant of 3000 francs from the *clergé de France*, together with an

47. *Ibid.*, p. 38.

48. Father Michael Murphy, one of the leaders of the '98 insurrection, was ordained in Ireland but went to the college at Bordeaux in 1785 to study theology. Father James O'Coigly, also ordained in Ireland, studied at the Lombard college in 1785. He was hanged at Maidstone in 1798.

49. Murray was born in Co. Clare. He also founded sixteen burses to be allocated to his own relatives, Hayes, *op. cit.*, p. 208.

allowance of 380 livres from Louis XVI. The latest figures of enrolment in the entire Irish establishment do not bear a specific date; they simply refer to the eve of the revolution. Enrolment in the Lombard college was 100, in the new college there were 80 students. Edmund Burke visited the Irish community at this period. He recalled the occasion in *A Letter to a Peer of Ireland* (1782) :[50]

> When I was in Paris about seven years ago . . . I saw there the Irish college of the Lombard, which seemed to me a very good place of education, under excellent orders and regulations, and under the government of a very prudent and learned man (the late Dr. Kelly). This college was possessed of an annual fixed revenue of more than a thousand pounds a year; the greatest part of which had arisen from the legacies and benefactions of persons educated in that college, and who had obtained promotions in France, from the emolument of which promotions they made this grateful return. One in particular I remember, to the amount of ten thousand livres, annually, as it is recorded on the donor's monument in their chapel.

In the first onset of revolution in 1789 there was little direct interference with the foreign colleges. A decree of the National Assembly on 7 November 1790 decided that the colleges should be maintained as under the *ancien régime*. With the increasing tempo of revolution the position of the institutions became less secure; on 30 August 1792 the buildings and property of the colleges were placed under sequester. A year later, on 10 October 1793, when Britain and the republic were at war, the National Convention ordered that all movable and immovable goods of the colleges were state property. The buildings passed into the hands of the administrators of the national domains. So the Lombard college passed into history. Under circumstances to be explained later the seminary in the rue du Cheval Vert was spared the final closure. In 1802 the institution was revived—to be the centrepiece of the protracted legal battle to recover Irish losses incurred during the revolutionary years.

Nantes college, last of the Irish foundations in France, must be fitted into a category different from that of the earlier institutions in Paris, Bordeaux, and Toulouse. The Tridentine counter reform,

---

50. *Edmund Burke on Irish Affairs* (ed. Arnold, London, 1881), p. 191.

in so far as it supplied the initiative in the first foundations, had passed its peak at the close of the seventeenth century. Whether we date the college at Nantes to 1689 or 1725 the origins of the enterprise must be sought in France rather than in Ireland.

In the aftermath of the Nine Years' War (1592-1601) Irish refugees made their home in the coastal towns of Brittany. By 1625 Irish merchants formed progressive trading communities at Nantes and St Malo. In 1645 Rinuccini, papal nuncio to the confederation of Kilkenny, made final preparations at Nantes for his voyage to Ireland.[51] Massari, secretary to the nuncio, commented in his diary on the great numbers of Irish Catholics in the municipality.[52] Later, during the Cromwellian period, there was a considerable accession to the Irish settlement. A contemporary report told of sixty exiled Irish priests at Nantes.[53] Two bishops who had borne prominent parts in the wars of the confederation remained to the end : Patrick Comerford of Waterford (d.1652) and Robert Barry of Cork (d.1662).[54]

At this period an Irish priest, Richard MacGibbon, established courses in philosophy for young Irish exiles but he was discredited by the university of Nantes. In 1659 by order of the French courts MacGibbon was obliged to desist.

The steady expansion of the Irish families may be traced in the *archives communales de la ville de Nantes* :[55] Whites of Waterford, Archers of Kilkenny, Wolfes of Limerick, O'Meaghers of Tipperary, Gallweys, MacCarthys, and O'Riordans of Cork, but by far the best known of the Irish merchants were the Walshes of Ballynacooly, Co. Kilkenny. Several members of the family won distinction in the Franco-Irish military service.[56] In 1754 Francis Walsh was ennobled by Louis XV as Count Walsh de Serrant.

51. *Comm. Rin.,* i, 732 ff.

52. 'My Irish Campaign', trans. Moran, *Catholic Bulletin,* vi, March 1916, 155.

53. 'Miscellaneous Documents', ed. Jennings, *Arch. Hib.,* xv, p. 26.

54. *Hibernia Dominicana,* p. 657; *Comm. Rin.,* iv, 325-327. A memorial to Comerford and Barry may be seen in the church of St Similien, Nantes. Cornelius O'Keeffe, bishop of Limerick (1720-47), also sought refuge at Nantes. In his will, dated 1734, he made provision for three burses for students bearing the name O'Keeffe, Windele MSS., University college, Cork.

55. Quoted by Hayes, *Old Irish Links with France,* 150 ff.

56. O'Callaghan, *History of the Irish Brigades,* pp. 92-94. In 1745 the Young Pretender was brought to Scotland by Antony Walsh of Nantes in his brig, the *Du Teillay,* Compton Mackenzie, *Prince Charlie* (London, 1932), pp. 39-40.

Among such Irish groups there was no withering of Irish memories or withdrawal from Irish needs. About 1680 the bishop of Nantes provided a place of residence for the exiled priests. At the outbreak of the Jacobite wars more clerical émigrés began to arrive. In 1689 Dr Ambrose Madden of Clonfert and Dr Edward Flannery of Waterford with local help established a hospice in the rue de Paume, Nantes. In 1694 the refugees were so numerous that a move to a more commodious building was necessary. The manoir de la Touche, former residence of the dukes of Brittany, was purchased. The Irish college now took shape.

Although Irish priests were ordained at Nantes[57] at an earlier period few notices have appeared concerning the history of the college.[58] About 1710 the institution was flourishing with an enrolment of thirty-five students. In 1765 by royal letters patent the seminary was given the status in law of a French corporation subject to the jurisdiction of the university of Nantes. There is no record of struggle against economic stress; the foundation was self-supporting.

It was short-lived. During the first phase of the revolution the college shared the immunity accorded to foreign institutions. When French priests who refused to subscribe to the civil constitution of the clergy sought refuge in the college the animosity of the revolutionaries was stirred up. In February 1793 the local committee of public safety decreed the arrest of the entire community; Patrick Byrne, the superior, made his escape but seventeen students were held in the Carmelite prison.[59] Finally, all the students were placed on board the Irish ship, *The Peggy,* and landed at Cork.

In 1813 the college buildings were partly destroyed by fire. On the authority of the minister for public instruction in 1857 the former Irish college was sold for 100,000 francs and the sum was added to the *Fondations Catholiques Irlandaises.* A remnant of the buildings is now part of the Museum Dobrée, Nantes.

---

57. In 1704 under the act for the registration of the clergy the following declared that they had been ordained at Nantes: Luke White, Clonmel (1656); Robert Esmond, Ballydungan, Co. Wexford (1685); Francis Esmond, St Peter's, Drinagh, Co. Wexford (1695), *Ir. Ecc. Rec., loc. cit.*

58. Walsh, 'Irish Exiles in Brittany', *Ir. Ecc. Rec.,* fourth series, i-iv, 1897-98; Boyle, *The Irish College in Paris,* p. 122; Hayes, *Old Irish Links etc.,* 68 ff.

59. On the eve of the revolution the total enrolment in the college was three masters and eighty students, Healy, *Centenary History of Maynooth College,* p. 696.

A Jesuit foundation at Poitiers is sometimes included among the Irish continental seminaries. Historical evidence indicates that Catherine of Braganza, wife of Charles II of England, was the actual foundress.[60] The institution was never a clerical seminary. From its foundation in 1674 to its suppression in 1762 it was a lay school for the education of Catholic youth. Amongst its endowments were two burses with a capital value of 16,000 francs established by Mrs John O'Meagher, Co. Tipperary, and three burses with a capital value of 30,000 livres invested in East India bonds, established by Jeremiah O'Crowley of Cork. At the closure of the school the burses were transferred to the Irish college, Paris.[61]

THE REGULAR ORDERS: LUKE WADDING

At the close of the sixteenth century the major monastic foundations, Cistercian, Benedictine, and Canons regular of St Augustine, were but a dim memory in Ireland—with little hope of revival. For the mendicant orders the threat to continuity was, despite prevailing perils, less ominous. The Franciscans, Dominicans, Augustinian eremites, and Carmelites were members of widely spread religious families in Europe, thus having a vital lifeline to the continent.

Although St Anthony's, Louvain, founded in 1607, was the first bulwark of the Irish Franciscans, Luke Wadding looked to wider horizons. In 1625 he established St Isidore's on the Pincian hill, Rome. Before his death in 1657 Wadding, directly and indirectly, extended Irish Franciscan friaries in several countries : Prague (Bohemia) 1629, Vielun (Poland) 1645, Paris (1653), Capranica (Italy) 1656.[1] Understandably, seventeenth-century Irish history could be largely written to a Franciscan theme.

In 1603 the Irish Dominican province faced extinction. Six aged priests living in the homes of friends were the sole survivors of a religious order which two generations previously comprised several hundreds.[2] Then Teige O'Duane, provincial, and his successor,

60. Finegan, 'The Irish College at Poitiers', *Ir. Ecc. Rec.*, fifth series, civ, July 1965.
61. See app. Irish Educational Foundations in France.

1. Millet, *The Irish Franciscans, 1651-65,* chaps. vi-vii; *Father Luke Wadding,* 154 ff. The friary at Vielun was closed in 1653, cf. 'The Irish Franciscans in Poland', ed. Jennings, *Arch. Hib.,* xx.
2. O'Heyne, *Epilogus Chronologicus,* p. xv.

Ross MacGeoghegan, turned to the task of conservation—and looked to their Dominican brethren in Spain. Irish aspirants were trained and educated at Victoria, Segovia, Salamanca, Bilbao, Burgos, and Pampeluna.[3] Consolidation of the Dominican province was ensured with the foundation of Holy Cross college, Louvain, in 1626 and Corpo Santo, Lisbon, in 1659. San Clemente, Rome, was added in 1677.

In 1656 the Irish Augustinian eremites established a college at San Matteo Merulana, Rome, but the foundation was shortlived. It was revived in 1739 and was the ancestor of the present St Patrick's college, Rome. Continuity among the Carmelites was assured by their continental brethren. In 1638 some fifty priests remained of the Irish Carmelites; the normal means of training and educating aspirants at home had long since ceased to exist. With the sanction of the Carmelite chapter of Aquitane the monastery at La Rochelle was surrendered to the Irish province to serve as a novitiate and college but actual possession was deferred to 1665. Another Irish Carmelite foundation was made at Aix-la-Chapelle in 1677.[4]

Gregory XIII (1572-85), the reforming pope, gave first priority to the establishment of Roman seminaries. From Rome the reforms of the council of Trent would radiate to the countries of Europe. In quick succession Gregory founded the *collegium Germanicum* and the *collegium Romanum*. In 1579 William Allen gave a sure base to the English counter-reform movement with the establishment of the *collegium Venerabile*. Ireland was also included in Gregory's plan of Roman colleges. Money for the project was raised in 1579 but the funds were diverted to aid the Catholic confederation of James FitzMaurice.[5] The beginnings of the Irish college at Rome were perforce long delayed.

When Cardinal Ludovisi was appointed protector of Ireland in 1623 Luke Wadding urged the necessity of a Roman seminary for the Irish diocesan clergy. As a first step Ludovisi agreed to maintain six Irish students to be accommodated in the English and Maronite colleges. The arrangement had not happy results; under pressure from Wadding the cardinal rented a house adjacent to the Franciscan friary of St Isidore where the students could live under

3. *Ibid.*, passim.
4. Rushe, *Carmel in Ireland* (Dublin, 1903), p. 57, supp. p. 54, p. 66.
5. Corish, 'The Beginnings of the Irish College, Rome', in *Father Luke Wadding*, 284 ff.

Irish supervision. Thus in 1627 the Irish college, Rome, had its origins.

Although Ludovisi and Wadding were of one mind as to the spirit and ideals which must prevail in the new foundation, internal frictions amongst the small body of students caused anxiety to the cardinal whose munificence maintained the college.[6] Differences between Old Irish and Anglo-Irish and regional rivalries, the recurring problems of the seminaries in the Low Countries, now cropped up in Rome. Rothe, bishop of Ossory, took alarm and warned Wadding : 'do not let the unruliness of a few ruin another foundation. You know well how near we were this time also to such a mishap had there not been people at hand to warn the Cardinal of what was afoot.'[7] There was no mistaking the reference to the crisis at Douai in 1625. When Eugene Callanan of the diocese of Killaloe and first superior died in 1629 direction of the college was vested in the Franciscans of St Isidore. In effect, the institution was now under the control of Wadding. Before long critics alleged that Wadding was partial to the Anglo-Irish and gave priority to students of Munster dioceses.

Cardinal Ludovisi died in 1632. In his will, dated 11 April 1629, he gave his own solution to the difficulties of the Irish college : he handed the seminary over to the Jesuits. Wadding and the Franciscans were non-plussed. Prince Ludovisi, brother of the deceased cardinal, declared his support of the Franciscans. Irish reactions came swiftly. A memorial, undated but probably prepared in 1633, signed by the students of the college, was addressed to Cardinal Barberini requesting that the Franciscans be retained in control.[8] A counter-memorial in the same year from the nobles and clergy of Ireland petitioned Barberini that the Jesuits should be placed in charge.[9] Then in August 1634 Thomas Messingham, superior of the Irish college, Paris, urged the Holy See to commit the seminary to the Irish secular clergy.[10] An authoritative settlement of the matter was sought in the Roman courts. The judgment of the Rota was promulgated in 1635 : the terms of Cardinal Ludovisi's will were upheld. So the foundation was transferred to the Jesuits and

6. A searching questionnaire containing fourteen questions was submitted to every student on admission, cf. *Wadding Papers,* ed. Jennings, p. 281.
7. Quoted by Corish, *op. cit.,* p. 290.
8. *Coll. Hib.,* no. 8, 1965, 35, text in *Arch. Hib.,* xii, p. 116.
9. *Coll. Hib.,* no. 8, p. 35.
10. 'Miscellaneous Documents', *Arch. Hib.,* xii, 192.

their supervision was continued down to the suppression of the society in Italy in 1773. When a French army under Napoleon occupied Rome in 1798 the seminary was closed. In 1826 Leo XII in the bull *Plura inter collegia* re-established the foundation under Irish superiors. The modern college on the Coelian hill, Rome, today is the only Irish continental seminary in which aspirants to diocesan or secular clergy are educated.

Chapter Two

THE IRISH COLLEGE AT BORDEAUX 1603-1793

1

FOUNDATION AND FIRST PHASE

When Paul V gave pontifical approval in 1618 to the Irish college at Bordeaux he named the founder as Diarmuid MacCarthy, priest of the diocese of Cork. It can be shown that the founder was the son of Sir Callaghan MacTeige MacCarthy, fifteenth lord of Muskerry, by his first wife, Ellen, daughter of James, Lord Barry.[1]

Few Irish families are of greater antiquity and none was more prominent in the history of Munster. There were three major branches : the MacCarthys Mór of Kerry, the MacCarthys Reagh of Carbery, and the MacCarthys of Muskerry in mid-Cork. The Muskerry line became in time the most powerful and affluent, living in semi-baronial state in more than a score of castles.

To trace the personal ambitions and jarring motives of successive lords of Muskerry is a baffling task. One of the most enigmatic was Sir Cormac MacTeige, fourteenth lord. Religious loyalty meant little to him. In 1578 he subscribed to the Elizabethan system of land tenure and conformed to the state religion.[2] At the same time, he sheltered and protected Thomas O'Herlihy, bishop of Ross, one of the three Irish prelates who attended the council of Trent.[3] When the bishop died in 1579 Sir Cormac MacTeige gave him burial in the Franciscan friary at Kilcrea, a MacCarthy foundation. In 1583 the unpredictable lord of Muskerry repudiated on his deathbed his newly-found religion and loyalty. In his last will and testament he reinstated the ancient usages and customs of his fathers. In defiance of English law he named his brother, Callaghan MacTeige, as his successor.[4]

1. In the Craobhscoileadh Cloinne Carrthaigh Diarmuid is not included among the sons of Sir Callaghan MacTeige, *Leabhar Muimhneach*, ed. Tórna (Irish MSS. Comm., 1940), p. 152. Lainé, the French genealogist of the MacCarthys, does not enlarge on the family of Callaghan MacTeige, *Généalogie de la Maison MacCarthy anciennement souveraine des deux Momonies ou de i'irlande méridionale* (Paris, 1839), p. 90. In the MacCarthy Muskerry pedigree as found in the Carew MSS., vol. 635, f. 154v (Lambeth library), Diarmuid MacCarthy, priest, is noted as the son of Callaghan MacTeige.
2. Butler, *Gleanings in Irish History,* 114 ff.
3. Lynch, *De Praesulibus Hiberniae,* p. 171; Rothe, *Analecta,* ii, p. 438.
4. Gillman, 'The Will of Sir Cormac MacTeige MacCarthy', *J.C.H.A.S.,* no. 10, 1892.

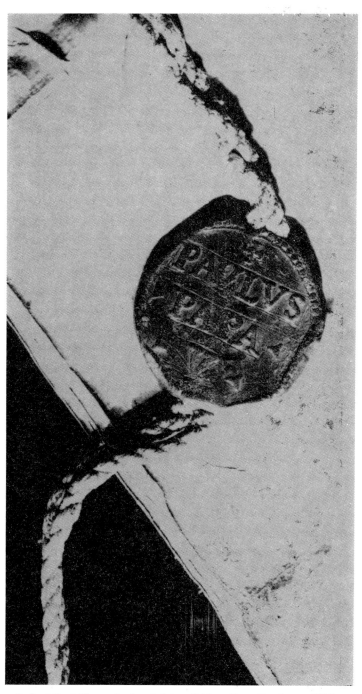

Seal of Paul V attached to brief to Irish college, Bordeaux, 1618.

Seal of Paul V attached to brief to Irish college, Bordeaux, 1618.

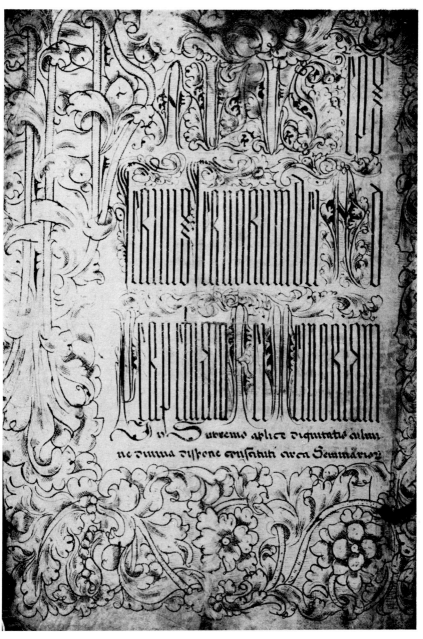

First folio of Brief of Paul V, granting pontifical recognition to Irish college, Bordeaux. Original in archives départementales de la Gironde, Bordeaux.

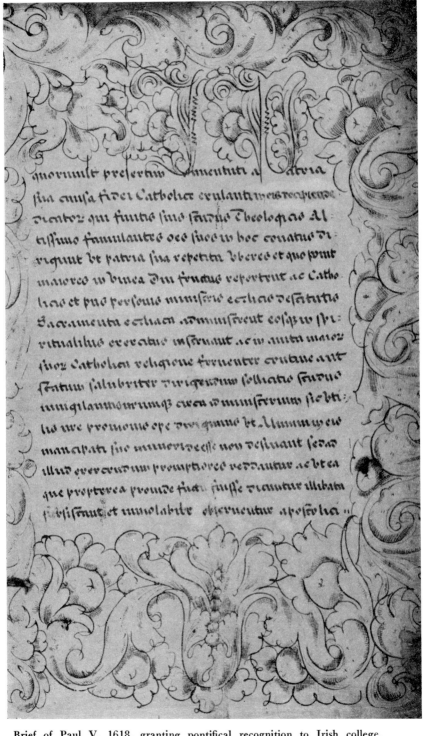

quorumlibet presertim ... incutiuntur a ... toria
sua causa fidei Catholica exulantur nostra recipiens
dicantur qui finitis suis studiis Theologicis Al-
tissimo famulantes deo suo in hoc conatu di-
riguunt ut patria sua repetita uberes et quo pont
maiores in vinea Domini fructus reportent ac Catho-
licis et pro personis ministerio ecclesie destitutis
Sacramenta ecclesiae administrent eosque in spi-
ritualibus exercitiis instruant ac in antea maior
suos Catholica religione feruenter erudiant aut
statuum salubriter dirigendum sollicitos studio
uuigilantiorumquz eos ad ministerium stabili-
tus ure promouis ope dei gratia ut Alumni eius
mancipati suo muneri deesse non desinant seorsd
illud exercendum promptiores reddantur ac ut ea
que propterea prouide facta fuisse dicuntur illibata
subsistant et inuiolabiliter obseruentur apostolica "

Brief of Paul V, 1618, granting pontifical recognition to Irish college,
Bordeaux. Original in archives départementales de la Gironde, Bordeaux.

The former Irish college, rue du Hâ, Bordeaux.

L

Compte de la recette et de la depense qui seront faites —
par moi François O'Hea prêtre Docteur en Theologie natif de l'Isle —
d'Island Diocese de Roscarbery Conté de Corck en Irlande pour le
Seminaire des Irlandois de Toulouse à commencer ce vint et —
deuxieme jour de Janvier mil sept cens cinquante et un au=
quel jour j'ai été chargé du gouvernement et de l'administra=
tion du dit Seminaire

Doivt au Seminaire quarante et trois livres onze sols que j'ai...

First entry by Francis O'Hea, superior, in the book of accounts, Irish college, Toulouse, 22 January 1751.
Original in archives départementales, Hte-Garonne, Toulouse.

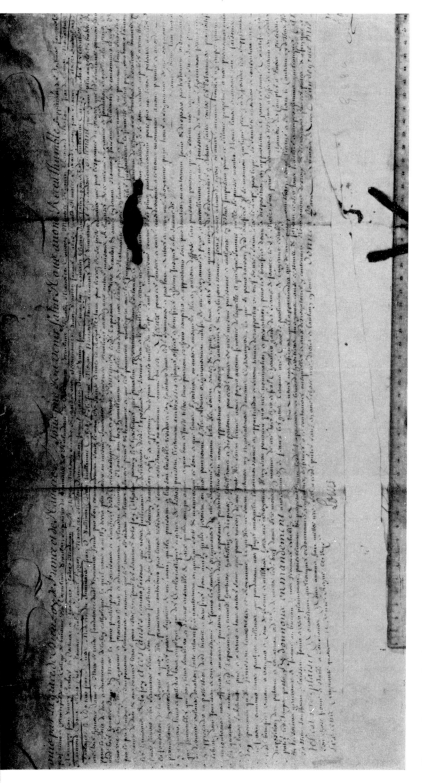

Lettres de naturalisation granted by Louis XIV to priests and students of the Irish college, Bordeaux, April 1654. Original in archives départementales de la Gironde.

Sir Callaghan MacTeige, father of the founder of Bordeaux college, held the lordship for less than a year. In 1584 he gave way to his ambitious and thrusting nephew, Cormac MacDiarmuid, who succeeded as sixteenth lord of Muskerry.[5] Secure in his massive castle at Blarney Sir Cormac MacDiarmuid gave and withheld religious and political allegiance as expediency prompted.[6] In 1601 he joined forces with Mountjoy in besieging the Spaniards at Kinsale.[7] After the defeat at Kinsale Cormac MacDiarmuid changed sides and was charged by Carew 'with treasons so foul as would fill a large book.'[8] He was imprisoned in Cork but escaped to join Donal O'Sullivan Beara.[9] Although the wily lord of Muskerry was completely discredited by Mountjoy, the lord deputy, and the English authorities, not an acre of the vast lands of Muskerry was confiscated—to the chagrin of the rapacious Raleigh. Such in brief was the family background of Diarmuid MacCallaghan MacCarthy.

Of the founder's early life little is known save that he studied at the college at Douai. A list of the alumni of St Patrick's college, Douai, published in 1622, would justify us in concluding that MacCarthy was ordained before 1600.[10] We must assume that in accordance with missionary procedure the young priest returned to Cork within a year. He found much in Cork that was disturbing. Dermot Creagh, the bishop, had been driven from his diocese.[11] Loyalty to the old faith was not a determining factor amongst the Catholic merchants and burgesses of the city. The ancient monastic foundations were suppressed, the parish churches of Holy Trinity and St Peter were confiscated. When the Gill abbey, the medieval cathedral of Cork, and its lands fell to the lot of the Elizabethan buccaneer, Sir Richard Grenville, in 1591 the Catholics of Cork made no protest.[12]

With the passing of the aged Elizabeth in March 1603 the citizens of Cork seized their opportunity to assert adherence to the old faith. In April Sir George Thornton, on receipt of a commission

5. Butler, op. cit., p. 115.
6. Fiants 5330 and 5333, 16th Report, D.K.R.
7. Pacata Hibernia (ed. 1810), ii, 362.
8. Cal. Carew Papers, 1601-03, p. 339.
9. Pacata Hib., ii, 632.
10. 'Exhibitio Consolatoria', ed. Brady, Arch. Hib., xiv.
11. Brady, Epis. Succession, ii, 89.
12. Smith, History of Cork, ed. 1892, i, 377.

from lord deputy Mountjoy, called on Thomas Sarsfield, mayor of Cork, to proclaim James Stuart of Scotland as king of Ireland.[13] The mayor demurred, declaring that the matter must be considered by the common council. Thornton chafed at the delay and rebuked William Mead, the recorder, for the corporation's dilatory tactics. There were heated words and Thornton counselled the recorder not to 'break out' in such an insolent fashion, only to be assured that several thousands in Cork were ready to break out. Then came days of excitement when the people gave full vent to long-suppressed feelings. Owen MacRedmond, a schoolmaster, was spokesman for the townsfolk. He told the deputy's commissioner that a few years previously James Stuart of Scotland was pilloried as a buffoon in English stage plays. How could the people of Cork proclaim as king one whose chief source of wealth was plundered abbeys and church lands? Led by two priests, Robert Mead and John FitzDavid Roche, the citizens took possession of Holy Trinity church and St Peter's church. The buildings were re-hallowed and Mass was celebrated publicly. To the people of Cork it seemed that the tyrannous usage of a generation was undone.[14]

Mountjoy was not prepared to see the hardwon fruits of the victory at Kinsale so easily lost. The Catholic *risorgimento* of 1603 was almost stillborn. The deputy moved in troops and put a halt to the pageantry. Some of the popular leaders, including Mac-Redmond, were hanged. Mayor Thomas Sarsfield was heavily fined. We may assume that Father Diarmuid MacCarthy saw it all and read the portents. There were grim years ahead for the diocese of Cork, but his own plans were already made.

Continuity of the pastoral clergy in the united dioceses of Cork and Cloyne was threatened.[15] In 1600 Dermot Creagh, bishop of the dioceses, reported the gravity of the position to Clement VIII.[16] Creagh died in 1603 after many years in exile;[17] Robert Mead

13. 'A Declaration of the Proceedings of the Commissioners and Council of this province with the Mayor and Corporation of Cork in the publishing of the proclamation of King James VI', *Lismore Papers* (2nd series, ed. Grossart, 1887), i, 43 ff.
14. Similar outbreaks took place at Waterford, Clonmel, Kilkenny, Wexford. Cf. Lynch, *Cambrensis Eversus*, iii, 523 ff. The Venetian secretary in London apprised the Doge and senate of Venice of the happenings at Cork, *Venetian State Papers*, 1603-07, p. 66.
15. The dioceses of Cork and Cloyne were united by Martin V in 1430 they were divided by Benedict XIV in 1748.
16. *Arch. Hib.*, ii, 287.
17. Lynch, *De Praes. Hib.*, ii, 146. *C.S.P.*, 1603-06, 380.

was appointed vicar apostolic but in 1604 he also was driven into exile—to Naples where he died. Hence we must see MacCarthy's plans as his own personal effort, the result of careful preparation. At this point we follow the Abbé Bertrand's narrative based on *actes de l'archevêché de Bordeaux*.[18] In 1602 MacCarthy sought the counsel of Alexandre de la Rochefoucauld, abbé of St Martin-en-vallée, near Chartres, brother of Cardinal de la Rochefoucauld.[19] The abbé assuredd MacCarthy that Bordeaux was an ideal choice as a theatre of Irish educational enterprise : Cardinal de Sourdis, archbishop of Bordeaux, would extend a helping hand to the Irish struggling to preserve their faith.

It was in Waterford, and not in Cork, as we would expect, that MacCarthy completed his arrangements for going to the continent. In November 1603 accompanied by ten or twelve youths he sailed for Bordeaux.[20] There seems little doubt that their arrival was expected. Cardinal de Sourdis received them with the utmost hospitality. A house in the rue du Hâ, the property of the cathedral chapter of St André, was given as a place of residence, and a small oratory or chapel, dedicated to St Eutrope, was allotted for spiritual exercises. No delay was made in providing educational facilities. De Sourdis arranged that the students would attend philosophy and theology courses at the Madeleine university under the direction of the Jesuits.

An immediate necessity was a steady source of income for the young foundation. Cardinal de Sourdis made an appeal through a diocesan synod for support. In 1611 an additional source of revenue was added when the Irish community was allowed to quest for alms. The warm-hearted approval of the Irish college by Cardinal de Sourdis is the first extant French reference to Diarmuid Mac-Carthy and his students :[21]

> We beg and we entreat all the Christian faithful to whom Father Dermitius shall address himself to give alms in proportion to their means and goodwill, having regard for the fact

18. *Histoire des séminaires de Bordeaux et de Bazas,* livre troisième, 324 ff.

19. *Ibid.,* p. 323.

20. Among the group was Patrick Comerford in whose house MacCarthy had stayed. Comerford later joined the Augustinian Eremites at Lisbon. He was bishop of Waterford 1629-52, *De Praes. Hib.,* ii, 115.

21. Bertrand, *op. cit.,* p. 326.

that it is not a question of helping our neighbour driven from his own land for the Faith but is a matter which proceeds from the worship of God.

Another, and to us an extraordinary, means of maintenance was attached to the college. The *Tretzenna,* whose community chapel of St Eutrope was now used by the Irish, was a pious sodality engaged in a corporal work of mercy—burying the dead. As successors to the *Tretzenna* the duty of acting as funeral bearers and gravediggers was transferred to the Irish students.[22] The task was faithfully discharged throughout the years down to the suppression of 1793. During the immediate pre-revolutionary period the custom was the source of much unhappiness to the Irish and drew the strong protests of the superior Martin Glynn.[23]

Very little has survived to tell us of the internal organisation of the seminary during its early years. It is clear, however, that the intake of students was entirely from the dioceses of Munster and in particular, from Cork, Cloyne, Kerry, and Waterford. Means of access to Bordeaux was easy. Shipping between Cork and Bordeaux was constant; 'the small barque of Gascon wines' was a familiar sight on the river Lee.[24]

Events in Ireland enlarged considerably the area of MacCarthy's responsibilities. Orders of exclusion and expulsion in 1604 and 1611 drove many priests, regular and secular, into exile. The good tidings of the Irish venture at Bordeaux induced some 215 refugees to seek a home with Diarmuid MacCarthy.[25] Although Cardinal de Sourdis received them with unfaltering kindness the entire number could not be accommodated at Bordeaux; the overflow was directed to Toulouse, Cahors, and Agen. When active persecution ceased in Ireland most of the refugees made their way home. There was, however, a significant sequel. Out of the Irish settlement at Toulouse arose in later years another college, a sister foundation to that at Bordeaux.

MacCarthy was a good strategist. In 1619 after the return to Ireland of the exiles he published a pamphlet or manifesto giving

22. Gaufreteau, *Chronique bordelaise,* t. ii, 27, quoted by Bertrand, *op. cit.,* p. 327.

23. Status Seminarii Burdigalensis Hibernorum exhibitus a D. Rectore Glynn anno 1774 et ab ipso ad P. Mgrum O Kelly transmissus. Archives San Clemente, Rome, Codex IID, 106.

24. *Council Book of the Corporation of Cork* (ed. Caulfield, Guildford, 1876), pp. 87, 88, 100, 109, 164-166.

25. *C.S.P.,* 1615-25, pp. 316-22.

the historical background of the recent Irish incursion.[26] He explained that the Irish priests who had sought refuge with him were exiles for the Catholic, Apostolic, and Roman Faith. For the same reasons, he, Diarmuid MacCarthy, priest of the diocese of Cork, was constrained to make an educational foundation at Bordeaux in 1603. He thanked the people for their sympathy but the college was now almost bereft of resources. Hence we must see in MacCarthy's pamphlet a frank appeal for continued French support.

In the state papers of the period there is evidence that the Irish colleges overseas were closely observed by the authorities in Dublin.[27] A spy, James Tobin, went to Bordeaux and won the confidence of MacCarthy. He sent Carew a copy of MacCarthy's pamphlet along with another document revealing a deep conspiracy between MacCarthy and Daniel O'Sullivan, count of Bearehaven, to effect a landing of French and Spanish troops in Ireland to restore the earl of Desmond.[28] Tobin assured Carew that he knew of no better way to serve his majesty the king than by revealing the nefarious plots hatched at Bordeaux. The spy's flights of fancy were worth the £50 he asked in payment.

As a close kinsman of the notorious Sir Cormac MacDiarmuid MacCarthy of Blarney castle MacCarthy and his foundation remained under a cloud of suspicion. An anonymous agent affirmed that the colleges were nurseries of treason, especially the seminary at Bordeaux.[29] Here were a son and nephew of Sir Cormac MacDiarmuid MacCarthy, a brother of David Roche, viscount Fermoy, of Ballyhooley castle, near Mallow, and two sons of Sir Christopher Plunket of Meath. The agent summed up his investigations : 'There are hundreds in the Colledges whose names I have the list sent (sic) from Waterford, Limerick, Clonmell, Corck, Gallway, Kilkenny and Drogheda and from the counteyes throughout

26. Catalogue de quelques clercs ecclesiastiques Hibernois, qui ont esté receus, nourris et eslevez aux lettres en le reguliere congregation, establie par Monseigneur l'illustrissime et reverendissime Cardinal de Sourdis, archevesque de Bordeaux, Primat d'Aquitane &c., en la ville et cité de Bordeaux depuis seize ans: le nombre desquels s'est tellement acreu, quils se sont despartis, les une a Tholose, Cahors, Aux, et Agen, exilez de leur pays pour le foy catholique, apostolique et Romaine, par Pierre de la Court, rue Sainct Jammes, Bordeaux, 1619; cf. Ir. Ecc. Rec., fourth series, no. 378, 1899, 507 ff.
27. C.S.P., 1606-08, 438 ff.; C.S.P., 1608-10, 350 ff.
28. C.S.P., 1615-25, pp. 316-17.
29. T.C.D., MS. E.3.15, undated.

the realme.' The anonymous spy may not have been too far from
the truth.

More comforting was the commendation of the little Irish college
in 1609 by Paul V to Henry of Navarre and Marie de Medici, the
king and queen of France. The pope spoke earnest words to Marie
de Medici :[30]

> The college at Bordeaux for the education of young men
> from Ireland has our warmest support. We commend it to
> your Majesty. We seek your help for further its interests in
> order that with your assistance these young men may the more
> efficiently devote themselves to the acquirement of sanctity and
> learning.

So far the only status enjoyed by the foundation was the limited
diocesan recognition granted by Cardinal de Sourdis. In 1617
Diarmuid MacCarthy journeyed to Rome to present the case for
full canonical status as a pontifical seminary. In the following year
Paul V issued the bull *In Suprema Apostolicae Dignitatis* which
conferred on the college all that the founder had sought. The
original bull, on vellum bearing the seals of Paul V, is now preserved in the departmental archives, Bordeaux.[31]

Paul V made a rigorous application of Tridentine ideals to Irish
pastoral conditions. There are eleven specific references to Ireland.
The young student living his daily routine of prayer and study in
college and university was constantly reminded that he must take
his place in the battleline of the Church. The stark realities of the
Irish mission field were not minimised. The rule stated that the
priest, at the time appointed by competent authority, must return
to Ireland to teach, to preach, to administer the sacraments. However great the persecution by heretics he must persevere 'because
the end and aim of all our labours is to fight valorously and daunt-
lessly under the standard of Christ.' To this heroic purpose every
student on admission to the college was required to make an oath
of promise, signed and witnessed. Thus the young men at Bordeaux
were prepared for the deadly encounters that awaited them at
home.

Little more is known of Father Diarmuid MacCarthy. In 1619
he was named vicar apostolic of Waterford and Lismore, but the

---

30. Fondo Borghese, 1, vol. 429, *Arch. Hib.*, iii, 271.
31. G 886. The complete text is printed in *Arch. Hib.*, xv.

appointment was not confirmed.[32] He died in 1620-21.[33] By then his college at Bordeaux had been added to the other Irish continental foundations at Paris, Douai, Salamanca, and Lisbon.

2

LE GRAND SIÈCLE

A more tolerant age has closed its eyes to the true character of Louis XIV; we pay him homage in the very title of his age—*le grand siècle.*

The splendour of the Sun King was part of the metamorphosis of despotic royal power. Richelieu prepared the way for royal absolutism by taming a turbulent nobility. And the boy-king was carefully tutored by his mother, Anne of Austria, the queen regent.[1] Rapid ascent to supreme political power is usually by way of revolution, and the young ruler of France encountered such a crisis in the rebellion of the Fronde in 1649-53.[2] The bitter struggle between Louis and the quasi-autonomous nobility allied to the parlement de Paris found a focal point in Bordeaux. An unexpected turn of events gave the Irish community an opportunity of aiding the hard-pressed royalists. The prominence thrust upon the Irish college had far-reaching consequences on its later history. In gratitude Louis XIV and the queen regent gave a royal accolade to the small foundation. Almost overnight it acquired a new and endowed status in the French economy.

In its origins the rebellion of the Fronde was the protest of the parlement de Paris and the nobility against reforms and land taxes imposed by Mazarin. The rebellion was reinforced by the accession of the powerful legal profession and great landowners. In 1648 the streets of Paris saw 'a revolutionary spirit comparable in many ways with that of 1789, though on this occasion the capacity for leadership was to be found in the Court, not on the barricades.'[3] An uneasy peace was signed at Rueil in March 1649 but with the

32. Fondo Borghese, 1, vol. 902, *Arch. Hib.*, xxiii, 82.
33. As appears from *Exhibitio Consolatoria* (1622), *Arch. Hib.*, xiv.

1. Anne, Louis XIV's mother, was the daughter of Philip III of Spain. She is known to history as Anne of Austria because the Spanish dynasty at that time was part of the Habsburg empire.
2. One of the mob leaders reproached the Parisians for their cowardice. He compared them to small boys who threw stones from their slings and then ran away (fronde, a sling).
3. Petrie, *Louis XIV* (London, 1938), p. 56.

defection to the rebels of Louis, prince de Condé, the civil war flared up anew. Nowhere was feeling against the king more intense than at Bordeaux. Condé fled to Spain to seek the help of Philip IV while his wife and her sister, the Duchesse de Longueville, rallied the city of Bordeaux to take up arms against the king. The city was too important to be allowed remain in revolt. After a hard-fought siege it fell to a royalist army under Marshal de la Meilleraye. With the capture of Orleans in 1652 it seemed that the rebellion of the Fronde was over. Then came intervention by Philip IV of Spain, brother of the queen regent. In 1653 a formidable army led by Condé crossed the Pyrenees. Among the Spanish forces were Irish regiments largely composed of veterans of the confederate wars in Ireland. Most likely, they included part of the 7,000 men who had been shipped to Spain in 1652 from Waterford, Kinsale, Bantry, Limerick, and Galway.[4] The Irish units were under the command of Colonels Dillon, O'Faral, and O'Scanlon, brother of Dr Cornelius O'Scanlon of Kerry, then superior of the Irish college. The Spanish interventionists were welcomed in Aquitane; they occupied Bordeaux. Leaving the Irish troops in garrison at Bordeaux and Perigueux Condé pushed northwards to Paris.

At Bordeaux the garrison had little reason to be happy with their lot in the Spanish service.[5] Since their arrival in Spain they had endured hunger, inadequate pay, and poor clothing. On the other side, former comrades in the Irish wars fared better in the French service; many were now in the armies of Louis XIV under the command of Cormac MacCarthy, son of Donough MacCarthy, Lord Muskerry. Moreover, the Franciscan George Dillon, brother to Colonel James Dillon on the Spanish side, was chaplain to an Irish regiment in the French army.

There was a strange turn of events after a meeting between Colonel O'Scanlon and his brother of the college. Colonel Dillon and his Irish garrison renounced their allegiance to Spain and entered the French service en bloc. The crushing defeat of Condé's rebel army by Turenne at the faubourg St Antoine outside Paris was the crowning disaster. The secession of the Irish at Bordeaux and Perigueux severed communications with Spain.[6] The rebellion of the Fronde was over.

4. Prendergast, *The Cromwellian Settlement in Ireland* (Dublin, 1922), p. 87.
5. *Comm. Rin.*, v, 100 ff.
6. Cromwell was an interested observer of the Irish action at Bordeaux, Rawl.A.20 (Thurloe Papers XX, November 1654), *Anal. Hib.*, i.

With little delay the king and the queen regent devised means of showing their appreciation of the part played by the Irish priests and students at Bordeaux. Representations by the duc de Vendôme concerning the penurious state of the college were sympathetically received. By letters patent issued at Châlons on 22 November 1654 French citizenship and civic status were conferred in perpetuity on the superiors, priests, and students of the college. In addition, the municipality of Bordeaux was ordered to pay an annual subsidy of 1200 livres, the tax to be levied on the *convoi de Bordeaux* of which the first moiety was to be paid on 1 January 1657.[7] Anne of Austria, the queen regent, also showed her personal regard for the Irish. Her letter, dated February 1654, recalled that the Irish came to Bordeaux in 1603 because they were exiles from their motherland through fidelity to the faith.[8] In times past God had given many proofs of His love for France but never more visibly than during the recent wars. As a token of her gratitude nothing could be more fitting and opportune than increased support for the college. Wherefore the foundation for the future would be under royal patronage with the right to use the royal titular—Sainte-Anne-la-Royale. The queen's crest was to be affixed to the doors of the seminary.[9]

Local feeling towards the Irish was not as enthusiastic as the cordiality of Louis and the queen regent. The obdurate parlement de Bordeaux from its place of exile at La Réole refused to accept the royal decisions. Hence the endowments of the Irish college were the subject of a constitutional struggle waged for some twenty years between the Grand Monarque and a local semi-autonomous body. To understand the jousting one must point out that France in the *ancien régime* was a mosaic of provincial and local barriers, tolls, exemptions, all acting in restraint of trade and dispersal of national effort. The aim of Louis in his striving towards absolutism was to render the Crown the one effective force in the country.[10] In the anti-royalist city of Bordeaux a determined effort was made to resist payment of Louis' subsidies to the Irish college. A number of contemporary documents dealing with the episode came to light

7. Bertrand, *op. cit.*, p. 349. The *convoi de Bordeaux* was an export duty on wines payable to the municipality.

8. A.Dep. (archives départementales Gironde), G 886.

9. The queen regent also established foundation Masses for the repose of the soul of her husband Louis XIII and for her own soul after death—to be celebrated in the Irish church of St Eutrope.

10. Petrie, *Louis XIV*, p. 106; cf. Behrens, *The Ancien Régime* (London, 1968).

98 THE IRISH CONTINENTAL COLLEGE MOVEMENT

several years ago in the manuscript department of the library in Maynooth college.[11]

M. Coupeau, president of the parlement de Bordeaux, sent a blunt reply to the king stating that the *chambre des comptes* was unable to sustain such heavy obligations.[12] He offered a compromise, namely, to pay 1,200 livres annually for a limited period of nine years. As regards conferring French citizenship on the Irish personnel M. Coupeau added that the parlement would consider each application on its merits but an unqualified acceptance of the directives in the letters patent of 1654 was impossible.[13] Louis mistakenly concluded that the subsidy would be paid but he was soon disillusioned. The first payment—due on 1 January 1657— was withheld. Dr O'Scanlon reminded the king of the omission. There was a peremptory communication, sent from Toulouse on 21 December 1659, in which Louis demanded ratification without limit or qualification of the letters patent of 1654.[14] The parlement submitted; the letters patent were ratified on 30 April 1660. Although payment was made, the matter was by no means settled.

Although Dr Cornelius O'Scanlon, his colleagues, and the students of the college were passive spectators of the constitutional collision they were not content to await the final outcome. In April 1654 the entire Irish community claimed the rights of French citizenship. A single folio holds the first roll-call of the college personnel. Judging by the family names Cork and Kerry were well to the fore :[15]

James Pierce, professor and principal of the college at Guyenne, Cornelius Scanlon, superior of the Irish seminary, Cornelius Whooley, Maurice Courcey, Maurice Honan, Bernard Mahony, John Burke, Moriart Parruquy (*sic*), John Sweeney, Thadie Madogan, Morgan Mahony, Richard Ronan, Edmund Scanlon, James Casey, Hugo Cash—all priests and doctors of theology.

Thomas Healy, Daniel Hogan, Maurice Maloney, Denis Craven, James Hannon, Daniel Sweeney, John Hanrahan, Germain Gleeson, Denis Falvey, John Rhody, William Canty —priests.

11. 'Documents relating to the Irish College at Bordeaux', *Ir. Ecc. Rec.*, fifth series, xlvii, January 1936.
12. 'Documents etc.', *loc. cit.*, p. 100.
13. *Ibid.*, p. 209.
14. Bertrand, *op. cit.*, p. 353.
15. A.Dep. (Gironde), G 886.

Gerald Morris, Richard Burke, John Harny, Patrick Foud-
agan, [Egan?], Raymond Burke, John Pierse, medical doctor
to the seminary, John O Sullivan Beara, the young Morgan
Mahony—students.

Whatever reluctance was felt by the municipal authorities, the
Irish application was accepted, granted, and registered.
Now that the college had an assured place in the French
economy O'Scanlon felt justified in embarking upon a plan of
expansion and thus provide increased accommodation for students.
Once again he was embroiled in difficulties with the municipal
authorities.
A Madame de Gourgue died at Bordeaux in 1654. Under her
will she bequeathed 15,000 livres for foreign missionary purposes.
The queen regent, probably at the prompting of O'Scanlon, made
representations to M. de Pontac, president of the parlement de
Bordeaux, that the Irish college was engaged in missionary work
and was a fit subject to benefit under Madame de Gourgue's
bequest.[16] Anne of Austria wrote of the heroic and apostolic work
in Ireland of priests trained in the college of Bordeaux. She
suggested that the cost of erecting new college buildings be borne
by the missionary bequest. M. de Pontac was unmoved. He ruled
that the Irish priests and students in Bordeaux were not members
of any société des missionaires du clergé.
O'Scanlon was not yet at the end of his resources. He enlisted
the aid of Henry de Béthune, archbishop of Bordeaux. The archbishop's letter, dated 20 July 1661, was a model of tact.[17] Unlike
Louis XIV and the queen regent, he made no reference to the
happenings during the wars of the Fronde. Instead he gave a
summary of the historical circumstances leading to the foundation
of the college in 1603 : persecution in Ireland, and the determination by Irish priests to bring succour to their afflicted countrymen. He stressed that some priests, educated and ordained at
Bordeaux, had already suffered martyrdom. De Béthune declared
that the Irish priests and students had always given edification by
their spiritual standards and their scholastic achievements in the
study of philosophy and theology. He added a general exhortation
to the people of Bordeaux to give increased support to the seminary.

16. Bertrand, op. cit., 355 ff.
17. Recueil des mandements des archevêques de Bordeaux, t, i, 127,
quoted by Bertrand, op. cit., p. 357.

It seems that O'Scanlon was not only an enterprising superior but also enjoyed the esteem of the staff and students. He was continuously in office from 1648 to 1696.[18] He appears to have died or resigned in the latter year; Dr William Fleming was elected superior in September 1669.[19] Fleming re-opened the debate about the subsidy payable to the college.[20] He informed the king that the arrears now amounted to 10,000 livres. Moreover, a special levy of 3,000 livres on the suburban areas of the city, payable in instalments of 300 livres, had also been withheld. We have no knowledge of this special levy. Fleming pressed for payment. The *chambre des comptes* pleaded that it was on the verge of bankruptcy.[21] Fleming was dissatisfied and engaged M. Scève, a lawyer, to prosecute the Irish claims. At a meeting of the city council in March 1675 priority was sought for the subvention to the college but without success. Fleming had recourse to the king. The response of Louis was to send to M. Scève a résumé of the endowments granted to the Irish seminary.

There is no more evidence dealing with the transactions between the college authorities and the mayor and jurats of Bordeaux. Some settlement must have been reached. In 1766 Martin Glynn, superior, made a statement of the college revenues, to be quoted on a later page. He noted an annual payment of 300 livres by the hôtel de ville, arising from a capital sum of 10,000 livres.

Despite passing difficulties with the parlement de Bordeaux the college worked smoothly during *le grand siècle*. Three centuries later our generation will ask—who were the students and when were they ordained? As discovered in the departmental archives of the Gironde the lists of ordinations obviously are not complete and show wide gaps.

> John O'Connor, Cork, William Daniel, Emly, 1622; Richard Roche, Charles Fuohy, 1623; Donatus O'Connell, 1624; John Ryan, Cork, William MacCarthy, Ross, Diarmuid Horgan, Cork, Bernard Hennessy, Cloyne, 1625; Malachy O'Connell, 1626; William MacCarthy, —— Hourihan, John Fahy, Diarmuid MacCarthy, William Riordan, Cloyne, Daniel Bohilly, Thomas Kirwan, Cornelius Mehigan, Henry Skiddy, Boetius

---

18. Allain, *Inventaire sommaire des archives de l'archevêché de Bordeaux* (Bordeaux, 1893), p. 31.

19. *Ibid.*, p. 200.

20. 'Documents etc.', *Ir. Ecc. Rec.*, xlvii, March 1936, 330 ff.

21. 'Documents etc.', *ibid.*, xlvii, April-May 1936.

Egan, Charles MacCarthy, 1627; William Burke, James Pierse, Edmond FitzGerald, Felix MacCarthy, John Cronin, John Cogan, 1629; Daniel Desmond, Jeremiah MacSweeney, David Roche, Maurice Machulius (*sic*), Robert Cogan, 1630.[22]

Only in the closing years of the century do we find further records of ordination.[23]

Denis Enery, William Dundon, John Conway,[24] Mathieu Corbin,[25] Cornelius O'Kehir [O'Hare?], Limerick, Columban Morgan, Waterford, Thady MacCarthy, Aghadoe, 1694; John Coughlan,[26] Demetrius Moloney,[27] Cork, Eugene MacCarthy,[28] Ardfert, Moriart O'Brien, Killaloe, 1695; James Creagh, Limerick, Terence MacMahon, Killaloe, 1696.

Another occasion in the history of the college is documented and adds another list of students. With the publication of Pascal's *Provincial Letters* in 1656 the Jansenist controversy raged in widening circles. Alexander VII imposed a declaration of orthodoxy on collegiate bodies throughout France. On 10 January 1665 the academic staff of the college at Bordeaux signed the formulary. A copy is preserved in the departmental archives.[29] The signatories were :

Cornelius O'Scanlon	Raymond de Bourg
supérieur du séminaire	prêtre assistant,
Ricardus de Burgo	Cornelius O'Mihigan
prefectus studiorum	prêtre,
Morgan O'Mahony	Thomas Lacy
sacerdos et syndicus,	prêtre irlandais.

22. A.Dep. (Gironde), G 545. In 1624 the ordaining prelate was Cardinal de Sourdis, archbishop of Bordeaux; in 1626 Claude Gélas, bishop of Agen; the ceremonies took place in the Irish church of St Eutrope; in 1627 Henri d'Escoubleau de Sourdis, bishop of Maillezais; in 1629 Claude Gélas, bishop of Agen.
23. A.Dep. (Gironde), G 545. In 1694 the ordaining prelate was Louis d'Anglure, archbishop of Bordeaux.
24. Conway died in Bordeaux and was interred in the Irish church of St Eutrope on 29 December 1708, *état civil de St Projet,* archives municipales de Bx.
25. Corbin died in Bordeaux 16 October 1696, aged 30 years.
26. Coughlan died curé de Libourne on 2 December 1743.
27. Moloney is described as a native of Rosscarbery, Co. Cork.
28. MacCarthy is said to be the son of Demetrius MacCarthy and Brigid Scossard, Ratass, Co. Kerry.
29. A.Dep. (Gironde), G 899.

A list of the students for the same year is on record.[30] In 1665 the students addressed a memorial to Henry de Béthune, archbishop of Bordeaux, requesting that Dr O'Scanlon be retained as superior. The signatories were :

Thomas Rice	Gilbert Wall
Patrick Coman	Thaddeus Mahony[32]
John Costelloe	Thomas Connor
Maurice Roche	Robert Moore
Thaddeus Kennelly	Richard Barry
John O'Connor	Walter Huony (sic)
David Lacy[31]	

A final call-over of students at this period is found in the record of the election as superior of Dr William Fleming in 1672.[33] Present at the election were :

John Hannon—priest	Eugene O'Dulig—student
Hugh Conway—priest	John Cantillon—student
William Mahony—priest	Matthew Kennedy—student
Thady Rahelly—priest[34]	Paul Creagh— student
Denis O'Gorman—priest	Godfrey O'Daly—student[36]
Gilbert Brody—priest[35]	Denis O'Kenneally—student
	Thadie Cullen—student

30. Archives de l'archevêché, mandements, no. 17, printed by Bertrand, op. cit., p. 361.
31. On 12 April 1708 before the justices of the peace David Lacy, parish priest of Askeaton, Co. Limerick, gave surety for £200, Burke, Irish Priests in the Penal Times, p. 392.
32. Thaddeus Mahony was appointed superior of the college in 1684. He died curé de Cardan on 27 May 1702, état civil de Cardan, archives municipales de Bx.
33. A.Dep. (Gironde), G 886.
34. On 21 June 1714 at a general assizes and gaol delivery held at Tralee a warrant was issued against Teig Rahelly, parish priest of Kilcoman, Co. Kerry, Burke, op. cit., pp. 387-88.
35. On 21 March 1711 Gilbert Brody, parish priest of Kilmacduan, was lodged in the gaol of Ennis, Burke, op. cit., p. 400.
36. In accordance with the act for registering the popish clergy in 1704 Godfrey Daly declared his age as fifty seven years, that he was parish priest of Murhur and Knockanure, that he lived at Gorteromaganny, and that he had been ordained by the bishop of Bordeaux in 1678, J.C.H.A.S., no. 45, 1900, p. 60. On 2 April 1715 at a general assizes at Tralee it was stated that Godfrey Daly, priest, was deceased, Burke, op. cit., p. 383.

An incident, trifling in itself, throws light on the Irish scene in Bordeaux in 1687.[37] The canonical status of the priests of the college was questioned by the curé of Saint-Projet in whose parish the Irish seminary and community chapel were located. The burden of the curé's complaint was that the Irish priests were arrogating to themselves certain parochial functions such as marriages and funerals. Louis d'Anglure, archbishop of Bordeaux, by a decision dated 16 March 1687, upheld the parochial rights of the curé of Saint-Projet. The real significance of the incident is the strong likelihood that the priests of the Irish college were requested to assist at marriages of lately-arrived émigrés from Ireland. To them nothing was more natural than to seek the ministrations of Irish priests.

Although the seminary had now been established for three quarters of a century the harmony of the institution was not so far disturbed by the regional controversies that marred the early phases of other continental colleges. But Bordeaux was not to be an exception. In 1678 the Munster monopoly was challenged on the occasion of the election as superior of Dr William Fleming. We summarise Abbé Bertrand's narrative.[38]

Issues were sharpened in 1678 when Fleming, a Munsterman, was given a third period in office. The renewal meant a continuation of preference to the southern province in the admission of students. The non-Munster minority made protests but disciplinary action quelled the agitation. In the following years successive elections were marred by regional or provincial rivalries. In 1717 seven Irish bishops of dioceses outside Munster appealed to Armand de Bezons, archbishop of Bordeaux, to remove any restriction of entry on students from Leinster, Ulster, and Connacht.[39] The bishops asserted that the Munster dominance hitherto maintained was to the detriment of the faith in Ireland and was at variance with the college constitutions as embodied in the bull *In Supremo Apostolicae* of Paul V in 1618. The effective remedy was to withdraw the right of the students to elect a superior. De Bezons was asked to seek a ruling from Philippe d'Orleans, regent of France, or the Holy See. The sequel to the Irish bishops' memorial

37. Bertrand, *op. cit.*, pp. 365-66.
38. *Op. cit.*, pp. 367-72. The documents he consulted are in archives de l'archevêché, A.Dep. (Gironde) and in the archives du Grand Séminaire de Bordeaux.
39. MacMahon of Armagh, Byrne of Dublin, Fagan of Meath, Verdon of Ferns, Murphy of Kildare, De Burgo of Tuam, O'Rourke of Achonry.

was a decree by the *conseil d'état* on 16 March 1722 which declared that in future students from the provinces in Ireland must be accepted without discrimination. But there was no alteration in the system of election. Dr Andrew MacDonough of the diocese of Tuam was elected superior in 1729. Analysis of the voting figures shows that there were seventeen students from Munster, three from Leinster, one from Ulster, and three from Connacht. Obviously, the voting was not governed by regional loyalty. Nevertheless, some Munstermen made stormy protests. The vicars general of Bordeaux declared the election void. Somewhat ineptly they appointed Dr Ignatius O'Connor, an alumnus of the college and now of the parish of Saint-Rémi, Bordeaux, to act as superior. The aggrieved supporters of MacDonough sent a memorial to Louis XV. The final outcome was a decision of the *conseil d'état* on 26 March 1733 : the voting rights of the students were withdrawn and authority to nominate a college superior was vested in the archbishop of Bordeaux who thereupon appointed MacDonough. There are no further references to student restiveness.

3

THE EIGHTEENTH CENTURY

A review of Franco-Irish relations in the eighteenth century usually finds a major theme in the Irish brigades in the French service. For this popular perspective there are valid reasons. The story of the military achievements of our race has its own contagion. One readily recalls the stirring dedication to the Irish troops in France which prefaces the Abbé Geoghegan's *History of Ireland* (1758). At that time the regiments of Clare, Galmoy, Bulkeley, Dillon, and Walsh-Sarrant were adding lustrous chapters to French military history. One consequence of the flight of the Wild Geese and the later build-up of the Irish brigades was not apparent to MacGeoghegan : the social effects of the Irish military recruitment. Of the 480,000 Irishmen who enlisted in the French service during 1691-1791 many were accompanied by their families and other relatives.[1] Here was the beginning of human relationships of which there are visible traces in France today. French families who are conscious of remote Irish ancestry are legion.

1. Petrie, *The Jacobite Movement* (London, 1948), p. 103.

Hence the Jacobite exodus was the beginning of a deeper and more permanent penetration into French social life. Lart's *Jacobite Extracts from the Registers of St Germain-en-Laye* gives a detailed picture of expropriated Irish families grouped around the shadow court of the throneless Stuarts. The pattern was similar at Bordeaux, Rouen, St Malo, Nantes and Angers.[2] The permanent fruits of the Irish settlement must be estimated in terms of commerce and industry rather than in terms of military prowess. Logically, Belloc saw the mingling of French and Irish at all levels as the fusion of two cultures with profit to both.[3]

Especially at Bordeaux the exiled Irish quickly won a place in the economy. In the *état civil* or registers of the fourteen parishes of the old city one could trace the French expansion of Irish families whose names are still remembered in the Irish countryside : Lynches of Galway, Caseys of Limerick, Bartons of Tipperary, O'Byrnes of Cabinteely, Gernons of Louth, and the Clarkes of Dromantine.[4] Here and there in the modern city of Bordeaux one finds more obvious reminders in street names : rue O'Reilly, rue Quin, and rue Sullivan, which honours the memory of Marie Judith Sullivan, daughter of Daniel Sullivan, M.D., 'out of Munster', who allowed the municipality in 1775 to drive five streets through her demesne. And today one senses something of Ireland in the chateau Pichon-Longueville, residence of M. Edouard F. Miailhe, descendant of the Lynches and Burkes of Galway.

Inevitably, Bordeaux drew many of the expropriated landed families of Cork : Coppingers of Ballyvolane, MacCarthys Reagh of Kilcoe, Gallweys of Bantry, Powers of Clonmult, and Hennessys of Ballymacmoy.[5] The Cork families in Bordeaux had a chronicler in James Roche, the banker.[6] In the late evening of his life Roche unfolded the scroll of memory—teeming with names that surely were the tabletalk of the Irish college.

2. Hayes, *Old Irish Links with France.* On 11 April 1699 Mary of Modena, the exiled Stuart queen, thanked the archbishop of Bordeaux for his acceptance of eighteen Irish scholars. She also asked the archbishop to settle Irish priests in benefices under his jurisdiction, *Stuart Papers*, Letter Book, 217, cited in Burke MSS.
   3. Introduction to Hayes, *Ireland and Irishmen in the French Revolution.*
   4. E.g. marriage of Jean Lynch to Guillemette Constant on 26 November 1709, *état civil de St Projet,* Bordeaux, where Lynch is described as 'natif de Grand-Louay en irlande'.
   5. Burke, *Landed Gentry of Ireland,* ed. 1904; Trant MacCarthy, *The MacCarthys of Munster* (Dundalk, 1922), 161 ff.
   6. *Essays, Critical and Miscellaneous, Memoirs of an Octogenarian* (Cork, 1851).

In the middle years of the century the economic status of the Irish at Bordeaux was assured.[7] At one period membership of the chamber of commerce was almost one-fifth Irish. Daniel MacCarthy of the trading concern MacCarthy Frères was president in 1767. John Lynch was counsellor of the parlement de Bordeaux; his son, John Baptist Lynch, was mayor of Bordeaux in 1808, and was later created a count of the empire of Napoleon. Official recognition of another kind was accorded to the Irish families at the outbreak of the seven years war in 1756 : an order of exclusion against British subjects made exemption of the Irish.

Naturally, the Irish families foregathered in the Irish collegiate chapel of St Eutrope. In 1734, to cater for the growing colony, Mgr d'Audibert de Lussan, archbishop of Bordeaux, directed the priests of the college to preach a course of Lenten sermons to be attended by the Irish mercantile families.[8] He also arranged for a special Mass to be celebrated in the college chapel every Sunday at eleven o'clock. The usual evening devotions of vespers and compline were prescribed. St Patrick's day was honoured with a high Mass, followed by exposition of the Blessed Sacrament and a panegyric on the national apostle. A plenary indulgence could be gained by all who would visit the Irish church on that day.

Indirectly, we can see the effects of the Irish settlement on the college. Clearly, there was an increased influx of students after 1690. Extension of the college building in the rue du Hâ called for a heavy outlay but apparently Irish support was forthcoming. In 1696 Thaddeus O'Mahony, superior, purchased from François Morin a house and garden adjoining the college.[9] A debt of 10,000 livres was incurred but it was liquidated in 1717. Again, Daniel O'Dea, superior, made more structural alterations in 1739 at a cost of 6,300 livres. There was no consequent debt. Oddly enough, the only Irish benefactor whom we can find was an unnamed Irish priest on 6 October 1740. Other benefactors were the abbé of Faise and Madame Dulède, wife of a former president of the parlement de Bordeaux. At some unknown date M. de Possier made an outright gift of 8,000 livres.

Despite the absence of figures of enrolment we have evidence that the numbers of students showed a steady increase in the

7. R. Nevin, *La Colonie Irlandaise à Bordeaux au xviiie Siècle* (unpublished university thesis, 1962, U.C.D.).
8. Bertrand, *op. cit.*, 366.
9. *Ibid.*, 373-74.

eighteenth century. In the years 1694-1782 major and minor orders were conferred on seventy-three occasions of which we have records.[10] Frequently, the ceremonies took place in the chapel attached to the hospital of St André. In many instances the parentage, parish of birth, and diocese of the student are noted.[11] One meets delightful cameos of Irish history on 18 December 1756 and 15 March 1757 when John O'Brien, the exiled bishop of Cloyne, ordained Patrick Boylan and Peter MacNamara of Cloyne, Edmund Dennehy of Cork, and Denis Mahony of Kerry.[12]

Throughout the century the nexus with the diocese of Cork was maintained. Colman Sarsfield, of the Sarsfield's Court family, was one of the best-known priests in Cork during penal times.[13] He was ordained at Bordeaux in 1695 and was parish priest of St Finbarr's to his death in 1752. Randal O'Hurly, ordained at Bordeaux in 1742, was of the family that held Ballinacarriga castle, near Enniskeane, Co. Cork.[14] Another of the family, Timothy O'Hurly of Enniskeane, was admitted to the college in 1777. After ordination he was offered but declined a professorship in experimental science in the university of Bordeaux.[15] One of John Hogan's lesser-known sculptures is a mural monument to O'Hurly in the parish church, Kinsale. A better-known contemporary was Jeremiah Collins, dean of Cork and formerly prefect of studies at Bordeaux. John F. Maguire, first biographer of Father Mathew, has drawn a memorable portrait of Dean Collins.[16]

A feature common to all the Irish colleges in France, and more obvious at Bordeaux than elsewhere, was that of priests remaining in France after ordination. Why they should have decided not to return home has not so far been satisfactorily explained.

In 1653 Nicholas French, bishop of Ferns, complained to the Holy See that many Irish priests, ordained in the continental

10. A.Dep. (Gironde), G 543, G 547, G 548, G 770, G 914.

11. Printed in *Arch. Hib.*, xv.

12. A.Dep. (Gironde), G 547. O'Brien was appointed bishop of Cloyne in 1748 but most of his episcopate was spent in exile. He published his well-known Irish Dictionary at Paris in 1768. Cf. Brady, *Epis. Succ.*, ii, 99; O Cuilleanain in *Feilscribhinn Tórna* (U.C.C., 1947).

13. *Ir. Ecc. Rec.*, xii, May 1876, 346; Burke, *Irish Priests*, p. 381.

14. 'Some Account of the family of O'Hurly', *J.C.H.A.S.*, lxix, 1906.

15. Clancy, *Funeral Oration at the Obsequies of Dr Timothy O'Hurly* (Cork, 1828).

16. *Father Mathew* (Cork, 1865), p. 39, p. 51. Cf. MacCarthy Glas, *A Historical Pedigree of the MacCarthys of Gleannacroim* (Exeter, n.d., p. 198).

colleges, failed to return to Ireland. He suggested that an apostolic visitor should be sent to the seminaries to strengthen the infirm of purpose.[17] Edmund O'Reilly, archbishop of Armagh, was more emphatic in 1660. He urged the Congregation de Prop. Fid. to communicate with archbishops and bishops in Spain, France, and the Low Countries instructing them to ensure the return to Ireland of Irish priests in their dioceses.[18] In 1668 John Sullivan, a professor of theology in a Belgian abbey, submitted a report on the Irish pastoral scene to the Holy See. He stated that there were Irish priests in Belgium and France who were under an obligation to return to their native land. He added that although priests in Ireland lived in poverty 'it is better that the missionaries suffer bodily hunger than the people spiritual hunger.'[19] Shortage of clergy bore heavily on John Brenan, archbishop of Cashel. On 6 November 1687 he advised the Holy See that 'many priests of this kingdom who are in comfortable circumstances abroad do not care to return home although they were ordained *in titulum missionis.*'[20]

At present Irish and French sources of history do not allow an estimate of the number of priests who remained temporarily or permanently on the French mission. It is possible, however, to arrive at an approximation of the number of Irish clerics, most of whom were alumni of the college at Bordeaux, who served, temporarily or permanently, in the area now included in the department of the Gironde.

The following estimates are put forward with some diffidence. During the period 1655-1793 some 118 Irish priests served in various parishes of the archdiocese of Bordeaux. Of that number the obits of sixty-six are found in French sources.[21] In other words, they did not return to Ireland. The obits of fifty-four additional priests for the years 1684-1788 are found in the *état civil* of St Projet.[22] Hence we conclude that some 120 Irish priests during 1655-1793 remained permanently on the French mission. On the other hand, fifty-two find a fleeting mention in French records and

17. *Comm. Rin.*, v, 141 ff.
18. *Father Luke Wadding*, p. 203.
19. *Coll. Hib.*, nos. 6 and 7, 1963-64, 144 ff .
20. Power, *A Bishop of the Penal Times*, p. 86.
21. Cf. 'Irish Priests in the Gironde', *Arch. Hib.*, xv, pp. 107-124.
22. *Ibid.*, pp. 131-133. The hospital of St André where many priests died and the Irish church of St Eutrope, the place of burial, were in the parish of St Projet.

then completely disappear. We conclude that they returned to their native dioceses. Thus Andrew O'Sullivan of Cork was curé of Gastes for the year 1747-48 but a laconic note explains his departure to Ireland.[23] Doubtless, John Prendergast of Kerry, curé of Bayas during 1762, was similarly recalled to his diocese.[24] Another possibility cannot be excluded : not all who served in the parishes of Bordeaux were alumni of the college. Some may have been chaplains in the French service and then retired to a country parish. One such is noted : Jeremiah Mahony, who died at Soulac on 3 January 1737, was a former almoner or chaplain in the king's ships.[25] Nicholas Madgett of Kerry, appointed curé of Civrac in 1776, was ordained at the college of St Barbe, Paris.[26] Our estimates are in accord with the figures of Abbé Nicolai. He states that in 1748 there were thirty-nine Irish priests in the Gironde, in 1760 the number was eleven, in 1767 fifteen.[27] There is insufficient data to strike a ratio between overall alumni of the college and the number who remained in France.

At Bordeaux there were special circumstances that drew the young Irish priest. Firstly, the priests and students of the college enjoyed French citizenship under the grant of Louis XIV in 1654. Secondly, the large Irish colony with its social contacts encouraged the young men to regard France as their second homeland. Even in the academic sphere there was an Irish background : Joseph O'Halloran[28] and Edward Creagh,[29] Irish Jesuits, occupied chairs of philosophy and theology at the university of Bordeaux. Moreover, an Irish tradition had grown in many parishes. Thus the parish of Boyentran had a succession of Irish curés: John Harding of Cork (1696-1740),[30] Philip Shiel (1740-63),[31] and James Burke (1764-66).[32] Similarly, the parish of St Magne de Belin had four

---

23. A.Dep. (Gironde), G 774—'rappelé par son evêque en irlande'.
24. A.Dep. (Gironde), G 775.
25. A.Dep. (Gironde), E suppt. 3948. Cf. *Revue Catholique de Bordeaux,* 1890, p. 400.
26. A.Dep. (Gironde), G 771. Later Madgett was chaplain to Count James Fanning at Angers. He was accused as a secret British agent at the National Convention in 1795. Cf. Hayes, *Biographical Dictionary,* p. 196.
27. *Statistique du clergé girondin à Bordeaux au xviiie siècle* (Bordeaux, 1909), p. 70.
28. Hayes, *Biographical Dictionary,* p. 233.
29. A.Dep. (Gironde), G. 547.
30. *Ibid.,* G 769.
31. *Ibid.,* G 649.
32. *Ibid.,* G 777.

Irish curés successively during 1761-93 : Thomas Brooks, ——
MacManus, ——Howard, and Peter Stafford.[33] Certainly, during
the eighteenth century it was easy for the alumni of the college to
find an anchorhold in France.

4

SUPPRESSION

The conclusion of the seven years' war in 1763 saw France
crippled with an enormous national debt. In the economic slump
Irish prestige and commercial status at Bordeaux entered on the
first stage of decline. The college revenues dwindled in value; soon
there was distress. In 1766, Martin Glynn of Tuam, superior, supplied a statement of the institute's finances to Louis d'Audibert de
Lussan, archbishop of Bordeaux.[1] The annual income amounted
to 2,531 livres, about £105 in modern values, and this was the sole
source of maintenance for a community of thirty. In 1774 Glynn
decided to seek aid in Ireland, England, and Scotland. We infer
that an appeal to French charity would have been in vain. Armed
with letters of credence from Montdauphin, vicar general, he
made a personal approach to the Irish bishops and to the English
and Scottish vicars apostolic. The journey cannot have been
fruitless because urgent repairs to the college buildings were made
on Glynn's return.

Clouds were gathering on the distant horizons. Voltaire's formula
Ecrasons l'infâme was the herald of the impending storm. As the
ancien régime tottered to its fall Franco-Irish concord approached
its term.

33. Gaillard, *La Baronnie de St Magne* (Bordeaux, n.d.), ii, 85.

1. Annual allowance granted by letters patent of Louis XIV 1700 livres
   Annual payment from receivers of taxes—arrears on 4800
   livres due to college .... 96 livres
   Annual rent from property of the late M. Pichon—a
   bequest of an Irish priest in 1740 .... 60 livres
   Annual payment from hôtel de ville arising from the sum
   of 10,000 livres granted by Louis XIV in 1664 .... 300 livres
   Dividend from a bequest made by a former counsellor of
   the parlement de Bordeaux .... 100 livres
   Rent of a shop .... 275 livres

   Total 2531 livres

   Bertrand, *op. cit.*, p. 375.

At Bordeaux there was growing hostility to the Irish students. In 1774 Father Glynn addressed a long letter to Dr Charles Kelly, an Irish Dominican at Rome, describing the mounting indignities heaped daily on the students as they passed through the streets to perform their duties as gravediggers and funeral bearers :[2]

> The students are gathered to observe a rule which divides their time between study and exercises of piety. It is only thus that they can form themselves to the ecclesiastical state and render themselves worthy of carrying out the important tasks for which they are destined.
>
> How shall they apply themselves to this task? They are called every day, and many times in the day, to divers burials which take place in this big city and its suburbs. Scarcely ever can they be assembled for the exercises of the house. The divine office cannot be said in common; the hours of meals vary daily for the most part; they have to lose the lectures in the university; they can scarcely find time for study. The sad necessity of these occasions is that they are scattered through the streets and the squares of the city mingling with a low crowd which reviles and insults them. They can find no shelter where they can take refuge from the inclemency of the weather.
>
> Amongst the unfortunate students are sometimes found friends or scions of the first houses in Ireland who have the honour of belonging to the most distinguished people in the state and church and who in a foreign land have been reduced to this state for their attachment to the true faith.

Glynn resigned his office as superior in 1786 and was appointed canon theologian to the chapter of St André, Bordeaux.[3] His successor was Patrick Everard, a native of Fethard, Co. Tipperary.[4] Within a few years the Irish college, its superior and students, were swept away in the torrent of revolution.

On 2 November 1789 it was decreed that the property of the church in France should be confiscated; on 13 February 1790 all religious houses were suppressed.[5] On 28 October 1790 M. Chassey

2. Archives San Clemente, Rome, Codex 11.D. 106. The complete text is printed in *Arch. Hib.*, xv, 138-141.

3. Glynn was a native of Inisboffin, born of Denis Glynn and Hanora Hosty. He was ordained at Bordeaux on 3 April 1756, Bertrand, *op. cit.*, p. 376.

4. Patrick Everard was born in 1752. He was president of Maynooth college 1810-12, Healy, *Centenary History of Maynooth College*, p. 229.

5. Morse Stephens, *Revolutionary Europe*, pp. 69-70.

recommended to the National Assembly that Irish, English, and Scottish colleges should be retained subject to any future laws on education. Further acknowledgment of the extra-territorial character of the foreign seminaries was given on 14 June 1791 when non-French priests were exempted from taking the oath to the civil constitution of the clergy. The first actively hostile measure came on 30 August 1792 when the buildings and property of the colleges were placed under sequester. A year later, when Britain and the republic were at war, the National Convention declared that all the movable and immovable goods of the foreign colleges were state property and were to be placed in charge of the administrators of the national domains.

Although the oath to the civil constitution of the clergy was framed for Frenchmen it was later demanded of foreign priests. The Irishmen were divided. Some made an outright rejection, some through revolutionary zeal subscribed to the oath, others conformed with a hesitating belief in its lawfulness. The condemnation of the measure by Pius VI on 13 April 1791 gave them second thoughts; hence the retractions. From records of the revolutionary period we have made a partial reconstruction of the Irish *insermentés* (non-jurors) and *assermentés* (jurors).[6]

Insermentés	*Assermentés*
Martin Glynn, Tuam	James O'Flanagan, Galway
Patrick Everard, Cashel	Matthew Leyne, Kerry
Daniel Ryan, Cork	(retracted)
—— O'Dwyer, Cork	Alexander MacDonald, Dublin
—— O'Brien, Cork	(retracted)
Patrick Ryan, Cork	Myler Prendergast, Tuam
Edward Dennehy, Cork	(retracted)
Lucas Dignam, Dublin	Francis Lombard (retracted)
Peter Stafford	James Gleeson, Cashel
William Moore	Joseph Talbot, Killaloe
Peter Kirwan	Michael Coghlan
Thaddeus Murphy	James Burke, Killaloe
Thaddeus O'Kelly	John Hennessy, Cork (reconciled
Thomas Prendergast, Tuam	under concordat 1802)
Richard Byrne, Meath	George Jennings, Tuam
Richard Prendergast,	
Thomas Burke, Killaloe	

6. A.Dep. (Gironde), series L and Q. Cf. 'Irish Priests in the Gironde', *Arch. Hib.*, xv, 115 ff.

Girondist influence restrained excesses at the outbreak of the reign of terror in September 1793, but Robespierre planned a bloodbath for Bordeaux. Thither he sent Tallien, Carlyle's 'Pluto on earth', Ysabeau, and Baudot with their portable guillotines. Under the triumvirate the tempo of revolutionary fury was increased. The faubourgs were roused against the city : several Irish merchants were cast into prison—Thomas O'Byrne, Robert Murphy, John Woods, Nicholas Hennessy, Richard Gallwey, and James Roche. Every village and hamlet had its committee of public safety. Death stalked through the vineyards where so many Irish priests had parishes : St Emilion, Gujan, Castillon, St Germain du Puch.

Foreigners were now enemies of the republic! Their institutions must be destroyed. In the first week of October 1793 a mob invaded the college in the rue du Hâ. Dr Patrick Everard, the superior, was the object of special animosity : not only had he refused to subscribe to the oath but he was acting vicar general during the imprisonment of the archbishop, de Cicé. Everard fled from the pursuing rabble, was caught, but made his escape leaving a rent soutane in the hands of his captors. The fifty priests and students of the college were placed under arrest and imprisoned in the Orphelines, a former Carmelite monastery. Through the efforts of James Burke of Killaloe, a revolutionary zealot, they were released and placed on board an American ship bound for Ireland.[7]

Under Lacombe, 'the Robespierre of the Gironde', the *Commission Militaire* set up its tribunal in the college buildings. The most melancholy episode in the history of the college took place on 18 July 1794 when Martin Glynn, former superior, was arraigned within the precincts of his own *alma mater*. He was accused of refusing the oath and of aiding aristocrats, the enemies of the people, and condemned to death. Next morning he was guillotined on the grassy plot before the Fort du Hâ. James Roche of Cork, recently released, witnessed the scene. Later in his *Memoirs* he wrote that Father Glynn was done to death with revolting brutality. Two other Irish priests, Francis Dinety (*sic*) and James Cornelly, guardian of the Recollects at Boulay, were also imprisoned with Glynn but they escaped the guillotine. Dinety died in the hospital of St André; the fate of Cornelly is unknown.[8] A number of Irish

7. Bertrand, *op. cit.*, p. 391.
8. Manseau, *Les prêtres et religieux déportés sur les côtes et dans les îles de la Charente-Inférieure* (Bruges, 1886), 436-37.

priests, including Thomas Prendergast of Tuam, were placed on board an Irish ship *The Favourite Nanny* sailing for Bilbao.[9] On 23 February 1796 the former Irish college, now the property of the republic, was sold to Citoyen M. de Marmande for use as a tobacco factory; the price paid was 136,000 francs.[10] A similar fate befell the Irish church of St Eutrope. On 23 June 1796 it was acquired by Citoyen Jacques Chamblant for 21,000 francs for use as a saltpetre factory. The building was demolished in 1849. Today the site is occupied by the Magasin Plazanet, a furniture emporium. At the rear one may still see the walls, niches, and alcoves, once part of the church. The college buildings are still standing in the rue du Hâ—used as a garage and motor repair depot.

THE ABBÉ JAMES BURKE

One of the bizarre figures of the revolution in the Gironde was the Abbé James Burke.[11] Having won notoriety as a flaming revo-

9. *Revue Catholique de Bordeaux*, 1895, 348, 392.
10. The following is taken from an inventory of the sale of the college and its furnishings as submitted some years later to M. Mourré, president du bureau de surveillance des établissements britanniques en France, cited by Bertrand, *op. cit.*, p. 391.

1 Church of St Eutrope	21,000 fr.
chalices and vestiments	6,000 fr.
2 College buildings (in assignats)	136,000 fr.
3 College furniture	
(a) 53 beds at 300 fr.	15,900 fr.
(b) 4 servants' beds at 200 fr.	800 fr.
(c) 300 pair sheets at 30 fr.	9,000 fr.
(d) table linen, presented by Irish and French ladies	2,000 fr.
(e) table service, kitchen utensils	6,000 fr.
(f) roasting-jack, presented by M. Thomas Lynch, father of M. le Comte Lynch	1,200 fr.
4 Provisions in stock	
(a) 30 casks of wine at 300 frs.	9,000 fr.
(b) 1,000 bottles Medoc at 30 sols.	1,500 fr.
(c) Other items, silver lamp presented by Mesdames Dudon and le Berthon	7,200 fr.

Total 215,600 fr.

11. Burke was born in 1739 at Ennis, Co. Clare, of James Burke and Mary Gallery. He was ordained at Bordeaux in 1770. Thomas Burke, his brother, was also ordained in Bordeaux; he refused the oath, died at

lutionary he spent more than twenty years in a self-imposed penance—an endeavour to restore his *alma mater*. Success seemed to be within his grasp but finally eluded him. His story is a tragic and pathetic epilogue to the history of the college.[12]

At the outbreak of the revolution, James Burke, curé of St Jacques du Bec d'ambès, was in the forefront of the zealots. In the excess of his fervour he renounced his priesthood, took the oath to the civil constitution of the clergy, demolished his own church and the adjoining Ursuline convent, selling chalices and ciboria. He made common cause with a kindred spirit, Ysabeau, an apostate Oratorian and emissary of Robespierre. Together they rode the crest of the revolution. Burke, rich on plundered church property, settled down to the life of a farmer. In October 1793, when he heard that the priests and students of the Irish college were imprisoned, old loyalties and traditions were stirred. At least, he would save them. Burke hastened to Bordeaux and sought out his friend the sanguinary Lacombe whom he found presiding over the death-dealing tribunal in the college buildings. The macabre happenings within the hallowed walls struck Burke to the heart. He described the scene : [13]

> In the building were Lacombe, his family, the revolutionary committee—and the secret meetings. Thence he sent his lieutenants to spread terror abroad, brigandage and death! It was from that place that Moutardier, the lawyer, set out to preside over the revolutionary committee at Lesparre which sent to the guillotine many members of the most respected families. Bizat, the notary, drew up the lists of the prescribed. Challifour, the architect, arranged the ceremonies of the Feast of Reason where horses and asses were paraded in priestly vestments. Holy vessels were profaned in a way too terrible to describe, the effigy of the pope was burned. God was blasphemed while an ox was adored in the cathedral.

12. A considerable body of literature has grown about the strange figure of James Burke. Burke, *Burke a sauvé la maison de Bordeaux* (Bordeaux, 1806; *Copie de le lettre écrite par Monseigneur le Prince de Rohan* (Bordeaux, 1810); *Attestation de M. Ysabeau, ex-législateur* (Paris, 1811); Archbishop d'Aviau, *Notice sur le séminaire-collège des irlandais de Bordeaux* (Bordeaux, 1814); Burke, *A Son Altesse Royale Madame, Duchesse d'Angoulême* (Paris, 1817); Vivie and Escarraguel, *Monographie de la commune d'Ambès* (Bordeaux, 1867); Vivie, *Une Épisode de la Terreur* (Bordeaux, 1867); Vivie, *Le Curé de Saint Jacques d'Ambès pendant la Terreur* (Bordeaux, 1867).
13. *Burke a sauvé la maison de Bordeaux.*

The spirit of revolution died within Burke; his conversion was complete. He approached his friend Ysabeau who had just returned from the carnage at Cadillac and La Réole. Several years later Ysabeau told how Burke pursued him from place to place with the incessant cry : 'Save the lives of my countrymen held in the Carmelite prison; save the college where I was a student.'[14] Ysabeau was obliging. As we have told, the prisoners were released and put aboard an American ship bound for an Irish port.

In the zigzag course of the revolution Robespierre fell in July 1794 and with him succumbed Lacombe. Burke, another of the revolutionary old guard, was landed in prison. In the palais Brutus gaol in February 1796 he heard of the sale of the college buildings to Citizen de Marmande. The fell tidings were unbearable. Burke secured his liberty and forthwith began a tussle with Marmande to cancel the deed of sale. He succeeded through the good offices of the mayor of Bordeaux whom he described as 'le plus galant homme du monde.' The disillusioned Irishman now constituted himself a watchdog over the empty college. In 1803 by some leger-demain he was officially appointed caretaker with the right of residence. But he did not get vacant possession—the building was illegally occupied by a group of negroes and mulattoes. Having failed to remove the squatters by legal means Burke stripped the tiles from the roof. At length the elements compelled the intruders to depart. To meet any future threat the redoubtable caretaker made a search for the missing title deeds. He discovered intact the safe holding the precious documents. To the robber who had stolen the safe he paid five Louis d'or and a cask of wine !

The struggle to assert and preserve Irish rights was now begun in earnest. Burke was involved in legal actions against the muni-cipal authorities and against the *bureau de surveillance* charged with the care of British establishments in France. Then he was at loggerheads with Mgr d'Aviau, archbishop of Bordeaux.

As a result of the concordat between the Holy See and Napoleon in 1802 the French Church drew up a programme of reconstruction. M. Delort, chancellor of the diocese of Bordeaux, applied for legal permission to convert the former Irish college in the rue du Hâ to a French seminary. Burke took instant alarm and according to his own narrative ran to the magistrates' court and produced the title deeds of Irish ownership.[15] The application of the chancellor was

14. *Attestation etc.*, p. 2.
15. *Burke a sauvé la maison de Bordeaux*, p. 7.

refused. By now Burke was a celebrity in Bordeaux and was awarded an annual pension of 1,000 francs. His hope that the Irish students would return was unshaken. In preparation for that day he purchased three houses adjoining the college buildings. Prominent Franco-Irish figures lent their support to Burke's agitation for an Irish return. His petition to the ministry of the interior in 1814 was signed by Marshal MacDonald, the Duc de FitzJames, the Comte de Marcellus, and the Comte de Sèze. Comte de Lally-Tolendal, minister of state, whose Irish affinities were well known, made a powerful appeal to the minister of the interior in January 1815.[16] The petition was favourably received, but the escape of Napoleon from Elba in March of that year pushed the problems of the Abbé Burke into the background.

Meanwhile negotiations were afoot between Archbishop d'Aviau of Bordeaux and Dr Patrick Everard, former superior of the college and now coadjutor archbishop of Cashel. In a pastoral, dated 13 June 1814, the archbishop of Bordeaux commended the rehabilitation of the former Irish college to the newly-restored Louis XVIII.[17] He prayed that the seminary would be revived to serve the same purposes which gave it origin in 1603. During the final Napoleonic phase negotiations were necessarily slow but on 27 February 1816 Mgr d'Aviau in an optimistic mood informed Burke that the return of the Irish students was imminent. D'Aviau wrote : 'It would be a double consolation in my old age to see you share the excellent dispositions and apostolic labours of this venerable superior [Dr Everard].' But it was only wishful thinking. The Irish bishops were uncompromisingly hostile to any return.

Burke was undaunted. In 1817 he presented a powerfully-supported memorial to Marie Thérèse Charlotte, Duchesse d'Angoulême, daughter of the executed Louis XVI and protector of the ecclesiastical establishments in France. It was signed by several members of the British house of commons. The earl of Kenmare, Lord Trimbleston, Sir John Burke, and Sir Francis Gould added their names 'en notre qualité de délégués des catholiques d'Irlande.' The memorial stressed that many aged Irish priests in the Gironde were now dragging out their last years in poverty and

16. Lally-Tolendal was a grandson of Lally-Tolendal of Tullaghnadaly, Co. Galway, who emigrated to France in 1690. The Count Lally-Tolendal was a prominent supporter of Louis XVI and narrowly escaped death in 1789. He fled from France but returned after the restoration of the Bourbons.
17. *Notice sur le séminaire-collège des irlandais de Bordeaux.*

infirmity. They were buoyed with the hope that they would be allowed to end their days within the shelter of their beloved college. There was a simple eloquence in Burke's concluding words:[18]

> It is because your Highness has always been the hope and support of the afflicted Irish, deprived of help and deserving of charity that they hope that your Highness will deign by her powerful influence to compel the government to direct that the house at Bordeaux will be restored as soon as possible in accordance with its ancient statutes.

It was all in vain. Whatever the measure of sympathy forthcoming from the Bourbon rulers of France, the Irish bishops were adamant in their solicitude for the infant foundation at Maynooth. Another embarrassment was the sharp disagreement between dissident Franco-Irish groups and the Irish bishops concerning Irish educational foundations in France.

James Burke died in the college buildings in rue du Hâ on 13 April 1821, aged 82 years. In his will he declared his firm belief that some day the Irish students would return. He made provision for foundation Masses for the repose of his soul—to be celebrated in the chapel of the restored Irish college at Bordeaux.

From official records it is clear that Burke was never permitted to exercise his priestly orders.[19] Nevertheless, in the burial register of the cathedral of St André where the obsequies took place there is a marginal note indicating that James Burke was a priest.

The following is a list of the superiors of the college at Bordeaux 1603-1793. The sequence appears to be complete.

1   Diarmuid MacCarthy 1601-21.
2   Jacques Piers succeeded.[20]
3   Kilian MacCarthy elected July 1630.[21]

---

18. *A Son Altesse Royale, Madame, Duchesse d'Angoulême, protectrice des établissemens ecclésiastiques de charité et autres du royaume.*
19. A. Municipales de Bordeaux, *Registre des nominations, translations, et décès des prêtres du diocèse de Bordeaux de 1802 à 1827.*
20. Bertrand, *op. cit.*, p. 344.
21. A.Dep. (Gironde), G 886. In *C.S.P.*, 1615-25, nos. 732-33, MacCarthy is described as Eugene MacCarthy, abbé of Fermoy He was formerly superior of the college at Santiago.

4   Thomas Giraldin [FitzGerald] elected 20 June 1633.[22]
5   Kilian MacCarthy re-elected 1648.[23]
6   Daniel Murphy succeeded, ceased to hold office 15 November 1648.[24]
7   Cornelius O'Scanlon elected 17 November 1648; still in office 1665, re-elected 1661, 1665, 1669.[25]
8   William Fleming elected September 1669; re-elected 1675, 1678.[26]
9   Francis de la Hide [Hyde] elected 11 June 1682, resigned 28 August 1684.[27]
10 Thaddeus O'Mahony succeeded; still in office 1685.[28]
11 John O'Gorman elected 24 December 1687; still in office 1689.[29]
12 Thaddeus O'Mahony re-elected 1696.[30]
13 Maurice Leo [Leyne] elected 4 January 1717.[31]
14 Richard Rahilly elected 29 March 1726.[32]
15 Ignatius O'Connor elected April 1729.[33]
16 Andrew MacDonough appointed by archbishop of Bordeaux 1733.[34]
17 Robert Lacy succeeded; re-appointed 1736.[35]
18 Daniel O'Dea appointed 1736 and continuously to 1748.[36]
19 Cornelius Ryan appointed 1748 and continuously to 1759.[37]
20 Martin Glynn appointed 1766 and continuously to 1786.[38]
21 Patrick Everard appointed 23 February 1786.[39]

22. Allain, *Inventaire sommaire des archives de l'archevêché de Bordeaux* (Bordeaux, 1893), p. 199.
23. A.Dep. (Gironde), G 886.
24. Allain, *op. cit.*, p. 32.
25. A.Dep. (Gironde), G 889; Allain, *op. cit.*, p .31; Bertrand, *op. cit.*, p. 361.
26. Allain, *op. cit.*, p. 200; Bertrand, *op. cit.*, p. 345.
27. A.Dep. (Gironde) G 774; Bertrand, *op. cit.*, p. 345.
28. Allain, *op. cit.*, p. 133.
29. A.Dep. (Gironde), G 765, G 819.
30. Bertrand, *op. cit.*, p. 373.
31. A.Dep. (Gironde), G 819.
32. A.Dep. (Gironde), G 772.
33. Bertrand, *op. cit.*, p. 373.
34. *Ibid.*, p. 371.
35. *Ibid.*, p. 381. Lacy was consecrated bishop of Limerick on 23 February 1738 by Honoré-François de Maniban, archbishop of Bordeaux.
36. A.Dep. (Gironde), G 886.
37. A.Dep. (Gironde), G 774.
38. Allain, *op. cit.*, p. 138, p. 200; Bertrand, *op. cit.*, p. 383.
39. A.Dep. (Gironde), G 886.

Chapter Three

THE IRISH COLLEGE AT TOULOUSE 1659-1793

1

FIRST PHASE

In the context of the Irish colleges in France an old French jingle does not exactly reflect the pattern of history :

Paris pour voir
Lyon pour avoir
Bordeaux pour dispendre
Et Toulouse pour apprendre.

A priority not only in time but in educational eminence must be accorded to commercially-minded Bordeaux. Toulouse, city of St Dominic, despite its cultural prestige, was secondary in the sense that its first Irish settlement was an overspill from Bordeaux.

There were obvious reasons why Irish youths in the early seventeenth century sought and obtained education in the university towns of the Spanish Netherlands, France, and Spain. Toulouse, on the upper Garonne in the old province of Languedoc, does not fit easily into the geographical picture. There were few Irish ties with Languedoc. In another way, in a manner unique among the Franco-Irish foundations, the college at Toulouse staked a strong title to remembrance. Francis Moylan, bishop of Cork, and Abbé Henry Edgeworth, confessor of the ill-fated Louis XVI, bequeathed to posterity a testament of friendship—a collection of letters which we read today as the last strophes of the *ancien régime* and its meaning for Ireland.[1] The *Letters* have a wide and eager observation of humanity in travail. There are no contorted shadows, no despairing elegies. Half a century previously Moylan and Edgeworth shared the joyous optimism of youth at Toulouse. In the *Letters* are revealed the beauty and fitness of two noble souls standing firm when their world tumbled to ruin. After the orgy of massacres at Toulouse Moylan and Edgeworth thought of happier days in their beloved college and recalled old friends who had perished. Yet the very deformities of the France they loved were reasons for forgiveness. For both, Toulouse was enchanted ground.

1. Abbé Edgeworth, *Letters to his Friends* (London, 1818).

Materials relating to the college are now preserved in the archives départementales de la Haute-Garonne, Toulouse. From such sources it is possible to present a moderately detailed account of the foundation for the years 1659-1793. Strangely enough, there are no indications of the time and circumstances of the first Irish settlement. From another source, however, we learn something of the Irish arrival.

In the manifesto or pamphlet published by Father Diarmuid MacCarthy at Bordeaux in 1619, to which we have already made reference, the founder listed the names of some two hundred and fifteen priests, mostly from Munster, victims of edicts of expulsion from Ireland in 1604-11.[2] They sought refuge with MacCarthy and his community at Bordeaux. Not all could be accommodated there, and Cardinal de Sourdis arranged accommodation for the émigrés at Toulouse, Agen, Cahors, and Aux.[3] The stay in France was brief; most of them returned to Ireland eventually. Most likely, a small Irish nucleus, from which the college took origin, remained at Toulouse. The earliest document of Irish interest preserved at Toulouse is a copy, dated 15 September 1645, of the 1623 brief of Urban VIII permitting the Irish continental colleges to promote students to the priesthood on the sole title of a mission in Ireland.[4] Clearly, young Irishmen were then receiving education at Toulouse.

Ware's account of the origin of the college has inherent probability.[5] He says that the seminary was founded in the reign of James I of England. The institution was without endowments but existed on casual charity. In 1660 on the occasion of the marriage of Louis XIV to the Infanta of Spain the court of France was residing at Toulouse. The Irish in the city sent a petition to the queen mother pleading for support. Anne of Austria, doubtless with happy memories of the Irish intervention at Bordeaux during the rebellion of the Fronde, readily acquiesced. She declared herself the foundress of the college, to which she granted the royal titular *Sainte-Anne-le-Royale*. In addition she prevailed on Louis XIV to issue a patent of foundation allowing an annual income of £60 from the royal revenues.

In fact, the letters patent had been issued by Louis XIV in December 1659.[6] There was parity of privileges with the seminary

2. See p. 93.
3. Cahors was merged with Toulouse in 1731.
4. A.Dep. (Hte-Garonne), G 427.
5. *Works* (ed. Harris 1745), ii, 255.
6. A.Dep. (Hte-Garonne), G 428.

at Bordeaux, and both colleges shared the rights of French citizenship. No special constitutions or statutes were formulated; instead, the statutes of the foundation at Bordeaux were declared valid for the new seminary at Toulouse. In later years the omission to draft special statutes was the source of much unhappiness.

Early documents show the small college in action. The number of students seldom exceeded twelve, drawn from the dioceses of Cork, Cloyne, Ross, and occasionally from Kerry. Down to the closing years of the seventeenth century the foundation was almost entirely the preserve of youths from Cork and Kerry. The students were required to take the usual oaths to abide by the college rules and to return to the Irish mission after ordination.[7] Some of them attended lectures at the university of Toulouse. Maintenance apparently depended entirely on an annual grant of 1,200 livres payable from the *gabelle* or salt tax of Languedoc. Probably for this reason the municipality exercised some form of statutory control. Thus at an early unspecified date the mayor of Toulouse appointed M. de la Fond, canon of the cathedral of St Etienne, and M. de Merville, vicar general and canon of St Sernin, as official visitors charged with superintendence of administration. At some unknown date benefactions were made to the college by a Madame Leary, Madame d'Allies, M. Pierre de Reynes, and M. Dulé.

The emerging picture of the college is of a large house at the junction of rue Valade and rue Labastide (now rue Pargaminières) in the parish of St Pierre-des-Cuisines. The building had a porticoed entrance, a verandah, and a spacious garden adjoining the Ursuline convent grounds. The Irish college enjoyed another distinction : it was the first of many seminaries to be founded at Toulouse.[8]

We find the first mention of a superior in 1659—Denis O'Riordan of Cork. In the following year he was succeeded by Daniel MacCarthy, also of Cork. Here follows the earliest list of the college community. They are the signatories to a statement of domestic accounts on 11 December 1661.[9]

---

7. Cf. Boyle, 'The Irish Seminary at Toulouse', *Arch. Hib.*, i.
8. Other seminaries were: le séminaire du diocèse, rue Valade, 1684; le séminaire de Saint Charles du Languedoc, 1684; le séminaire de la mission, congrégation de Saint-Lazare; séminaire de Notre Dame de la Dalbade.
9. A.Dep. (Hte-Garonne), G 428.

Daniel MacCarthy, superior
Constantin Egan, priest
Terence MacSwiney, priest
Bernard MacSwiney, priest
Christopher Creagh, priest

William Barett, student
John Coyne, student
Patrick Gould, student
Cornelius Leyne, student
Richard Ronan, student
Maurice Power, student

Extant statements of quarterly accounts and the *registre de réception des séminaristes* furnish us with a partially complete record of the college personnel during the years 1664-94.

1664[10]
Giles O'Sullivan, priest
Charles Delea, student
John O'Brien, student
Callaghan MacCarthy, student
Thady Sullivan, student
Denis Delea, student

1665[11]
Richard Grandon, priest
Denis Comyn, student
Jeremiah O'Riordan, student
Diarmuid O'Riordan, student
Daniel O'Leary, student
Barry MacSwiney, student
Denis MacSwiney, student

1671[12]
Moriarty Kelleher, priest
Cornelius O'Brien, student
Robert Barry, student
James Barry, student
John Houlihan, student
Diarmuid O'Sullivan, student
Eugene Delea, student

1674[13]
Florence O'Mahony, priest
Jeremiah O'Riordan, student
Alexis O'Leary, student
John Barrett, student

Admitted to the college 1684-94[14]

Cornelius O'Brien, Cloyne
Diarmuid O'Mahony, Aghadoe
Denis O'Mahony, Aghadoe
Anthony Creagh, Limerick[15]
Edmond MacSwiney, Cork

Edmond Delea, Cork
Jeremiah Creedon, Cork
John Barry, Cork
Cornelius O'Mahony, Cork
William O'Connell, Cork

10. *Ibid.*
11. *Ibid.*
12. *Ibid.*
13. *Ibid.*
14. A.Dep. (Hte-Garonne), G 428
15. A student from Limerick was unusual but a marginal note states that Creagh was the nephew of Peter Creagh, bishop of Cork.

Patrick Burke, Cork   Diarmuid Cronin, Cork
Maurice Ronayne, Cork   William O'Riordan, Cloyne
Daniel MacSwiney, Cork   Edmond Delea, Cloyne
Modeste MacSwiney, Cork   Daniel O'Connor, Aghadoe

In a college working within narrow limits of revenue it is not surprising to learn that one of the besetting problems was the provision of *viaticum* or expenses of young priests returning to Ireland. To raise funds for this purpose Joseph de Montpézat, archbishop of Toulouse, addressed a pastoral letter to the people of the city. An undated copy has survived.[16] From internal evidence we believe that the pastoral was written about 1683. The document, which we quote in full, sets in perspective the generous sympathy of a French archbishop for an Ireland then in the harrowing aftermath of the Titus Oates plot.

By the providence of God it is clear that the Irish nation will never forsake our Holy Mother the Church even though the enemy of man's salvation during these last centuries has done all in his power to choke with the bad seed of heresy the good seed which our Heavenly Father has sown in that land, and persecution has been so cruel and relentless that no one could make profession of the Holy, Roman, Catholic, and Apostolic religion without forfeit of life, honour, and possessions.

It has pleased the Divine Goodness to inspire several of their priests and seminarists to seek refuge in certain towns of France and amongst them, Toulouse. Having been cordially received here with Christian charity they have made such progress in theological studies as to become fit candidates for ordination. Of these, a great number from time to time have returned to their native land where by their help and encouragement as soldiers of the Lord they have striven to repair the ravages of heresy. Many of them having borne witness to the Faith by the shedding of their blood have ensured that in spite of persecutions it can still be said that the kingdom of Ireland has remained faithful to the Catholic Faith.

Nevertheless, it seems that the seminary which under my jurisdiction they have established in this town is so badly in need of funds that some of the students having completed

16. *Ibid.*, G 427. Joseph de Montpézat de Carbon was archbishop of Toulouse 1675-86.

their studies as far as the priesthood find that there is no money available to pay for their journey or for secular clothes to disguise themselves (*pour se déguizer*) or for other priestly needs (*quelques ornements sacerdotaux*). Consequently, they are obliged to remain here in France to the great loss of their motherland. We have verified these reports very carefully by going through the state of the finances of the seminary. We found there three priests who simply through lack of funds were prevented fulfilling their vocation. As a remedy, they have suggested that through a collection sufficient money might be gathered to give the necessary help. Therefore, we now pray and exhort all faithful Christians to receive kindly those whom we appoint to make the said collection this year. Herewith they have permission to afford the collectors such alms and assistance as can be given; the alms could not be put to a better purpose. They are not so much for the help of a neighbour as for the advancement of God's cause, rescuing those who have fallen away and confirming those who have remained faithful. It is all for the glory of God.

Evidence of response to the archbishop's appeal is a note recording the departure to Ireland of two priests, Aneas O'Leyne and Anthony Garvan, on 17 April 1683.[17]

Notwithstanding the carefully-phrased optimism of the archbishop's pastoral there was grave official concern for the seminary. A spirit of restiveness seriously interfered with the routine of. student life. There were strange happenings at Toulouse.

The adaptation or modification of the constitutions of the college at Bordeaux to serve the foundation at Toulouse was an unhappy decision. Triennial elections of a superior by the students was a feature common to most continental colleges. At Toulouse, however, there was a quarterly audit and approval of college accounts that had no basis in the Bordeaux constitutions. The quarterly meetings provided a forum for critical and insubordinate elements, but serious rivalries accompanied the elections of college superiors. The details which follow are taken from a group of documents bearing the title, inscribed by a later hand : *Piéces produits par l'archevêque de toulouse pour justifier son autorité dans le séminaire des irlandais*.[18]

17. A.Dep. (Hte-Garonne), G 427, pièces détachées.
18. A.Dep. (Hte-Garonne), G 428. Some of the documents are illegible.

In 1663 John Coyne was elected superior in succession to Daniel MacCarthy. The election was confirmed by Charles-François de Bourlemont, archbishop of Toulouse. The first outbreak of student dissent took place at the election in 1669 of Coyne's successor. The archbishop took immediate action and requested M. Raymond de la Fond and M. Antoine de Saint-Laurans, vicars general, to investigate and report on the disorders in the Irish college. The inquiry took place in the great hall of the archbishop's palace, 2 May 1669. The entire college personnel was present : John Coyne, Callaghan MacCarthy, Germain O'Riordan, Denis Comyn, Thady Casey, priests; Charles Dulan, Barry MacSwiney, Denis MacSwiney, Moriarty Queally, Daniel O'Leary, Robert Barry, students. The proceedings were opened with the singing of the *Veni Creator Spiritus* to implore the divine guidance. Then the vicars declared their duty—to discover and remedy the causes of the recent scandals. Although the vicars' report to the archbishop runs to nine folios we cannot discover the precise nature of the scandals beyond the repeated statement that there were grounds for complaint against certain students. The final verdict was that Daniel O'Leary, Barry MacSwiney, and Robert Barry were the ringleaders of the disturbances. They were removed from the college and sent to the French seminary at Carmaing. Germain O'Riordan and Callaghan MacCarthy were suspended from their priestly functions for one month and declared permanently ineligible to hold office in the college. A period of severe fasting was imposed as a penance on the students. The recommendations of the vicars are more informative. They suggest a reinforcement of discipline and specifically (a) regular attendance at lectures, (b) regular hours of study, (c) unauthorised visits by outsiders to be prohibited, (d) students must not leave the college unless with the superior's permission, (e) the superior is directed to give a spiritual conference every evening.

Apparently, the assertive young Irishmen were not overwhelmed by the vicars' report. In 1671, despite the declaration of ineligibility by the vicars, Germain O'Riordan was elected superior. Moreover, in 1676 a superior (unnamed) was forced to resign by dissident students; his place was taken by a student who had not yet received first tonsure, in other words, a layman. The archbishop again intervened and appointed Maurice O'Keeffe.

One finds it difficult to trace the sequence of events at this stage but the succession of Jean Baptiste Michel de Colbert to the see of

Toulouse marked a new phase in the history of the college.[19] In order to calm current unrest the new archbishop resolved to draw up statutes to meet the special character of the seminary. The first draft was completed in 1694.[20]

In a lengthy preamble the archbishop drew his text from Luke X, 2 : *The harvest indeed is great but the labourers are few.* Then follows a reproach of the students for their 'pestilential quarrels and controversies'. De Colbert summarised the primary purpose of the Irish foundation at Toulouse and stressed the implication of ordination to the priesthood on the sole title of a mission in Ireland. His analysis of the student rivalries was based on Luke XXII, 24 : *And there was a strife among them which of them should seem to be greater.*

He emphasised in Pauline language the need to promote the mystical body of Christ. There was depth of feeling for Ireland in the archbishop's prayer : may the God of patience and comfort grant to the people of your homeland priests according to his own heart!

There were fifty statutes in all. In the light of reforms the first was the most significant. The supreme director and superior of the college was the archbishop of Toulouse : from his decisions there was no appeal either to an ecclesiastical or to a civil court. Students were required under oath to accept this principle. The trouble-laden quarterly meetings to approve accounts were abolished but the new statutes were never approved. A special ordinance, dated 20 February 1694, stated that henceforth the appointment of a college superior was reserved to the archbishops of Toulouse.[21] This was confirmed by letters patent issued by Louis XIV in April 1695. Accordingly, on 1 June 1696, de Colbert named Florence MacCarthy superior of the seminary. Modeste MacSwiney, the dispossessed superior, refused to accept the ruling. On the following day M. Raby, vicar general, made a visitation of the college and reported unfavourably.[22] He disclosed that of the twelve students only six lived in community, the others lodged in private houses in the city. There had been a grave dereliction of duty by the superior, MacSwiney; he had not slept in the college for one night during the previous three years! In these circumstances the arch-

19. A.Dep. (Hte-Garonne), G 427, pièces diverses. Jean Baptiste Michel Colbert de Villacerf was archbishop of Toulouse 1693-1710.
20. A.Dep. (Hte-Garonne), G 427.
21. A.Dep. (Hte-Garonne), G 427.
22. *Ibid.*, procès-verbal de visite du séminaire par M. Raby.

bishop repeated the dismissal of MacSwiney and nominated Florence MacCarthy.[23] MacSwiney was obdurate and decided to refer the dispute to the civil law courts. He cited the archbishop juridically to appear before the Parlement de Toulouse. The summons was declared invalid by the Parlement of Paris.[24]

When Florence MacCarthy's term of office ended in 1699 Louis XIV acted somewhat injudiciously. By lettres de cachet of 14 July M. de Lamoignon, intendant of the province of Languedoc, was instructed to obtain from the students a panel of candidates from which a superior would be selected.[25] The archbishop selected William O'Sheehan. Once again MacSwiney intruded himself on the foundation, whereupon O'Sheehan withdrew to the Jesuits at Paris. There was another intervention by the king : MacSwiney was ordered to quit the college for good. A decree of the *conseil d'état*, dated 24 July 1699, nominated a superior who had no immediate connection with the seminary—Timothy O'Brien of the diocese of Cloyne, professor royal of the faculty of theology at the university of Toulouse.[26] Under Dr O'Brien's firm guidance the college entered on a period of peace.

Reviewing the documentation of the student turbulence during 1669-1699 one is at a loss to indicate the basic causes of the insubordination. We are not told in precise terms 'the grave disorders and continual insolences at all times.' The report of Canons Raymond de la Fond and Antoine de Saint-Laurans in 1669 comes nearest to objectivity. The visitors charged the students with lack of diligence in study, irregular exits from the college, and with excessive meetings with outsiders. The disorders in that year must have been grave when two students were committed to the archiepiscopal prison *de l'Ecarlate,* a fourteenth-century fortress.

Again, the *procès-verbal* of M. Raby in 1696 returns to the theme of insubordination. The juridical rights of the archbishop of Toulouse are ponderously vindicated in a long but uninformative memorandum. Nor does a statement of the Marquis de Chateauneuf, secretary to the council of state, bring us any nearer to the radical causes of the discontent.[27]

23. *Ibid.,* letters de nomination de supérieur du séminaire.
24. The parlement de Toulouse was incorporated with the Parlement de Paris, cf. Thiers, *History of the French Revolution* (Edinburgh, 1883), p. 280.
25. A.Dep. (Hte-Garonne), G 427.
26. *Ibid.*
27. *Ibid.*

We may eliminate regionalism. Twelve young men from Cork and Kerry had no reason to be agitated by provincial jealousy. Most likely, the student restiveness found a cause in the popularity or lack of popularity of a particular superior. And the tasks of a superior were demanding. For example, Maurice O'Keeffe, the superior in 1677, was also curé of Fadouas, some miles from Toulouse. Similarly, Modeste MacSwiney had parochial responsibilities in 1696. Supervision of the seminary and pastoral duties devolving on one man were not calculated to achieve efficiency. Another consideration may not be omitted—the general character and fitness of the students. It can be argued that lack of control by Irish bishops was a severe handicap. A student was admitted to the college without adequate reference to character and antecedents. Promotion to holy orders on the sole title of a mission in Ireland sometimes had manifest disadvantages.

The verdict of an anonymous French writer of the last century will be generally accepted. Referring to the rule which required a superior to give an account of his stewardship to the students he says that the occasion established a kind of republic in the seminary, and for young people who were enthusiastic and natural lovers of independence it was, if not the main cause, at least a motive for the disorders which afflicted this valuable institution for many years and almost brought about its ruin.[28]

2

THE EIGHTEENTH CENTURY

When the secular clergy of Ireland registered in 1704 the following stated that they had been ordained at Toulouse : *Cork*—Owen O'Keeffe, Duhallow (1679); *Kerry*—Teige Leyne, Ferness (1684); Aneas Leyne, Kilcolman (1678); Owen Dunlea, Kilcommon (1688); *Limerick*—Darby O'Brien, Ballinard (1694); Darby O'Connor, Ballingarry (1680).[1] The number is surprisingly small. One won-

28. 'Ce dernier article établissait dans le séminaire comme une espéce de république, et devint, pour une jeunesse ardente et naturellement amie de l'indépendance, sinon la première cause, du moins l'occasion des désordres qui, pendant longues années, desolèrent cette précieuse institution, et faillirent en amener la ruine.' *Mémoires historiques et chronologiques sur les séminaires établis dans la ville de Toulouse* (Toulouse, 1852), p. 14.

1. *Ir. Ecc. Rec.*, xii, May 1876.

ders how many of the alumni of Toulouse elected to remain in France.

In the opening years of the century Europe was convulsed with the war of the Spanish succession. Franco-Irish military co-operation was seen on the battlefields of Blenheim, Ramillies, Oudenarde, and Malplaquet. Reinforcements of Irish regiments in the French service brought a steady inflow of Irish youth. One is tempted to speculate whether any of the young men turning away from military lustre found their way to one or other of the Irish colleges, but no such evidence is found at Bordeaux or Toulouse. The tide of war left Toulouse untouched but surely the college was an Irish rendezvous when the regiment of Berwick was posted to Languedoc in 1705 to suppress the Camisard or Huguenot revolt in the Cevennes.

During this period the college was continuously under the direction of Dr Timothy O'Brien of Cloyne. In 1720 he resigned and returned to Ireland where he was appointed parish priest of Castlelyons, Co. Cork.[2] Not a single record has survived to tell us of his efforts to promote peace and progress in the college. We do not know the name of his immediate successor.

Jean-Louis de Balbis-Berton de Crillon, appointed archbishop of Toulouse in 1728, lost no time in focusing his zeal on the Irish college. He nominated Peter Daly as superior.[3] He also introduced a period of probation for Irish youths before they were formally admitted as students. The first record of probation contains the names of Thaddeus MacCarthy, Ross; David Barry, Kerry; Daniel O'Leary, Cork; Simon Quin, Cloyne.[4] The vexed question of rules and statutes was still unsolved and the new archbishop set his hand to the task. Letters patent over the name of the youthful Louis XV in 1730 directed the archbishop and M. de Bernage de St Maurice, intendant of justice, police, and finances in the province of Languedoc, to devise rules and statutes for the better administration and control of the seminary.[5] In the decree the king recalled the solicitude which his great-grandfather, Louis XIV, had always entertained for the college. Certainly, there was no official intent to minimise its Irish character and purposes.

2. In later years O'Brien won considerable distinction as a religious controversialist. He died in 1747. Cf. Smith, *History of Cork,* ii, 302.
3. A.Dep. (Hte-Garonne), G 427.
4. *Ibid.,* cf. Boyle, 'The Irish Seminary at Toulouse', *Arch. Hib.,* i, 126.
5. *Ibid.*

The King being informed ... that the Irish seminary (established in the city of Toulouse) which has never had special rules, has been governed up to the present partly according to the statutes formerly drawn up for a similar foundation in the town of Bordeaux and that the said statutes being unsuitable in several ways for the aforementioned seminary at Toulouse, this has led to great drawbacks which have caused considerable dissensions between the seminarists and their superiors. As a result of not being governed by more suitable rules this establishment has not produced all the good expected of it for Religion and His Majesty, wishing to follow the views of the King his great grandfather and to carry out to the latter's pious intentions to the best of his ability—the King sitting in council has commanded and commands the Archbishop of Toulouse and M. Bernage de Saint-Maurice, Intendant of justice, police, and finance in the province of Languedoc whom His Majesty has appointed and appoints for that purpose, the state of the seminary of Sainte-Anne, established in the town of Toulouse for the education of Irish priests, will be looked into and that all rules and statutes necessary for the proper administration and control of the said establishment will be drawn up by them; however while waiting for these rules to be made His Majesty has commanded and commands that the archbishop of Toulouse will appoint as superior of the aforesaid seminary the person whom he will consider fit to carry out the duties of the post. His Majesty wishes the Irish in the aforesaid seminary to obey all orders which the commissaires deem necessary to give in order to carry out the present edict. For this purpose the commissaires are given complete power and jurisdiction.

Within a year the work was completed. Archbishop de Crillon gave his personal approval to the new statutes in a decree issued at Nîmes, 3 February 1731.[6] For some unknown reason the usual endorsement by the *conseil d'état* was not forthcoming. The transfer of de Crillon to Narbonne in 1740 seems to have suspended further consideration of the affairs of the Irish seminary.

Archbishop de la Roche-Aymon (1740-53), de Crillon's successor, returned to the subject at some later date. He had misgivings about

6. A.Dep. (Hte-Garonne), G 427.

de Crillon's draft statutes. He believed that the civil authority was given too wide a scope for interference in the spiritual direction of the college. Hence de Crillon's thirty-five statutes were reduced to twenty-four.[7] We do not know why a delay intervened but, apparently, Father Francis O'Hea of Ross, superior of the college, took the initiative in submitting the statutes to the Holy See. On 31 August 1753 Benedict XIV issued a brief of approval. The letters patent of Louis XV endorsing and authorising the statutes were communicated to O'Hea in 1754.[8]

There is no obvious reason for such protracted preoccupation with the rules of a college containing less than a score of students. Perhaps there were antagonisms and a clash of authorities at a higher level. If more evidence were extant we might discover that the college at Toulouse was the scene of a minor encounter between Gallicanism and the supreme authority of the Holy See.

With the exception of the documents we have mentioned very little has survived relating to the internal history and student enrolment during this period. For example, we do not know how long Peter Daly, appointed in 1728, held office.[9] There is no mention of his successor. From other sources, however, we learn that Donal Dineen of the diocese of Cloyne was superior in 1748-1751.

Dineen was a character of more than passing interest. He was a close friend of the poet, Liam Rua Mac Coitir of Castlelyons, who sent copies of his poems to Toulouse.[10] A fuller picture is found in the papers of the Oliphants of Gask, a Scottish Jacobite family.[11] After the defeat at Culloden in 1745 the Oliphants, father and son, fled to France. In 1748 they stayed at Toulouse. In his diary, under 29 May, Laurence Oliphant notes that he and his son had 'dined in the Irish seminary with Mr Dineen and Mr O'Hay [O'Hea], the two principal masters.' During the following years letters were exchanged between Dineen and the Oliphants. On 20 October 1751 Dineen disclosed to the younger Oliphant that

7. *Ibid.*, the printed copy is in the form of a broadsheet.
8. *Ibid.*, extract des registrés de parlement de Toulouse.
9. Under his will Dr Peter Daly bequeathed 20 livres turnois to provide prizes for students who won distinction in the college, Boyle, *The Irish College at Paris*, p. 121.
10. O Foghludha, *Cois na Cora* (Baile-atha-Cliath, 1937), p. 15; cf. O Ceallaigh, *An Sagart*, Earrach, 1968, p. 8.
11. Cunningham, 'The Irish College at Toulouse', *J.C.H.A.S.*, lxxiv, 219, 1969.

because of strained relations with his colleague O'Hea the archbishop had removed him from office as superior and had appointed
O'Hea in his stead. In a subsequent letter Dineen made known his
wish to obtain a French benefice and sought an approach by the
Oliphants to the authorities on his behalf.

At this point we meet one of the most informative documents
relating to the college—O'Hea's ledger or book of acocunts. From
this source we are able to present a close-up view of the seminary
and its working conditions at a time when the *ancien régime* was
drawing to a close.

FRANCES O'HEA (1751-66)

O'Hea began his administration with something of a flourish.
On the first page of the college ledger he inscribed his name and
birthplace in Co. Cork.[12]

> *Compte de la receitte et de la depense qui seront faites par
> moi François O'Hea pretre Docteur en Theologie natif de
> Little Island, Diocese de Ross Carbery, Comté de Cork en
> Irlande pour le seminaire des Irlandois de Toulouse á com-
> mencer ce vint et deuxieme Jour de Janvier mil sept cens
> cinquante et un auquel Jour J'ai eté chargé du gouvernement
> et de l'administration du dit seminaire.*[13]

Under his direction the college entered upon its most memorable
and progressive period. Although he succeeded to a burden of debt
he gradually achieved solvency. He seized the opportunity of turning to profitable account the popularity of the foundation with the
citizens of Toulouse. Accommodation was given to French boys for
the purposes of secular education. In 1758 the number of French
students was almost the equivalent of the Irish enrolment. Their
quarterly pensions of 78 livres were a welcome addition to the
college revenues.[14] In addition to the half-yearly grant of 598

12. A.Dep. (Hte-Garonne), G 427. The ledger is without cover, 46 cms
x 37 cms, pp. 181.
13. The ruins of the O'Hea home may be seen at Kilkieran, Little
Island, near Rosscarbery, Co. Cork.
14. E g. 18 avril 1753: *de M. Lesbordes conseiller au parlement pour le
second quartier de la pension de son fils et pour chandelles a lui fournis
depuis le 14 novembre—82 livres.*

livres from the *gabelle* or salt tax O'Hea notes recurring receipts from the estates of Dame Cecile de Casauban, M. Camboulas, and some unspecified payments from M. de Puyvert, president of the parlement de Toulouse.

We see O'Hea at his daily work. Payments were made to masons and carpenters for repairs to doors, windows, chapel, and portico. A new wall was erected dividing the college garden from that of the Ursulines next door. There was a constant thought for the students' welfare. Purchases of bed and table linen are recorded. Normally the students paid for firewood and candles but sometimes the necessaries were provided by the superior. Outlay on food is stated : naturally, the heaviest item was bread : 411 livres for less than five months. Dr Duford drew payment of 12 livres for attendance to the sick for an unnamed period. Payment was made to the neighbouring Ursuline sisters for decoration of the college chapel for the feast of St Patrick, 1756. An extern teacher was employed to teach the students mathematics and handwriting. There is a touch of humour when O'Hea notes the salary to the college cook. He writes the name by which the lady was known to the students—La Verdura ! On 6 April 1755 O'Hea had an alms for 'some wandering Irishmen'.

As a man from Carbery in West Cork the superior did not miss the historic antecedents of Charles MacCarthy who entered the college on 11 July 1752. The young man was of the illustrious MacCarthy Reagh family, lords of Carbery, now expropriated and living in Toulouse.[15] The first link in a long chain of history was forged when Mr Robert Edgeworth paid fees on behalf of his sons, Robert and Henry Edgeworth.[16] Forty-one years later Abbé Henry Edgeworth standing on the scaffold in the Place de Louis XV saw the head of Louis XVI roll from under the guillotine. Irish contacts were valued by O'Hea : he noted his own journey (undated) to Montpellier to visit Charles O'Brien, viscount Clare, marshal of France, and hero of Fontenoy. We are able to fill a gap in the wanderings of John O'Brien, the exiled bishop of Cloyne. O'Brien

---

15. The family was ennobled as Counts of the French empire by Louis XVI. The last of the MacCarthys Reagh died at Toulouse in 1906. Hayes, *Biographical Dictionary*, p. 169; *Sermons of the Abbé Nicholas MacCarthy* (Dublin, 1848), p. xvii.

16. 24 septembre 1752 : *de M. Robert Edgeworth pour 17 pagelles de bois a bruler et demi-pension pour ses deux fils, Robert et Henry—126 livres.*

stayed in the college as the guest of O'Hea from 22 September to 31 October 1765.

In one important respect O'Hea's ledger fails us. Rarely does he write the christian name of a student and more rarely the Irish diocese to which he is attached. We have extracted the names of some fifty students; the date in parentheses is the record of the young priest's departure to Ireland.

1751

M. Lynch[17]
M. Houlihan
M. King
Charles Hart, Ross[18]
Stephen O'Sullivan
M. Byrne
M. Lombard
M. Dugan
M. Carney

1752

George Mahony (22 Feb. 1755)
M. Leary
Edmond Barry, Cloyne
   (24 May 1752)
Daniel Nolan (11 May 1757)
William Lombardy[19]
John Copinger (9 July 1752)
Edmond Fitzgerald

1753

David Barry
M. Craggs
M. Sexton

1754

Daniel Collins
M. Kelly
M. Davis
Jeremiah O'Daly, Cork
M. Donovan (7 July 1754)

1755

Simon Quin[20]
Denis Daly
Michael Murphy
Thady MacCarthy
   (11 April 1758)

1757

M. O'Cridan
M. Brady (30 May 1754)

17. Described as an American.
18. Later parish priest, Castlehaven, Co. Cork, d.1781, cf. Holland, *History of West Cork and the Diocese of Ross* (Skibbereen, 1949), p. 323.
19. A doctor of medicine from Cork who spent 1739-43 in the college.
20. Appointed co-adjutor bishop of Cloyne 1779, Brady, *Epis. Succ.*, ii, 100.

1760	1761
Charles O'Brien, Cork	M. O'Fahy
M. O'Brien (brother of above)	M. MacLoughlin
William Callanan, Cork	Robert MacCarthy, Cork[21]
	M. O'Kelly-Farral[22]
	Nicholas Madget
	John Madget (brother of above)
	M. Falvey
1763	**1765**
M. Gould	M. O'Keeffe
M. Cleary	M. Deignan
M. Reddan	M. Desmond
James Cotter	M. Morgan
	le petit Edwards

At Toulouse, as in other Irish continental colleges, there were priests who failed to return to Ireland. On 20 December 1752 William O'Meara, bishop of Ardfert (1743-53), informed O'Hea of the earnest wish of the Irish bishops that the college at Toulouse should send to the Irish mission field priests imbued with apostolic zeal. On the other hand, the increasing intake of French students was slowly changing the character of the seminary. A Franco-Irish figure, Arthur Richard Dillon, was named archbishop of Toulouse in 1758. On 13 October 1761 he formally conferred the status of a French diocesan seminary on the Irish college.[23] Too few years remained for this radical decision to have permanent effect on the essential purposes of an Irish foundation.

Entries in O'Hea's ledger cease in 1766; nothing more is known of him. Elsewhere we discover the surname only of his successor —Dower. In 1767 Frederick Augustus Hervey, earl of Bristol, visited France.[24] The colleges at Bordeaux and Toulouse were included in his itinerary. Hervey was impressed by all that he had

21. Last superior of the college, appointed 1771.
22. This student's pension throughout his course was paid by Arthur Richard Dillon, archbishop of Toulouse.
23. A.Dep. (Hte-Garonne), G 427. The decree is a printed document, and the last amongst the Irish historical materials at Toulouse. Arthur Dillon was the brother of Colonel James Dillon who fell at Fontenoy. In modern Toulouse the Franco-Irish archbishop is commemorated by the cours Dillon which leads to the Hotel Dieu and the Pont-neuf.
24. Harvey was appointed Protestant bishop of Derry in 1768. Lord Bristol, his brother, was viceroy of Ireland in 1766. Cf. Lecky, History of Ireland in the Eighteenth Century, ii, 78, 359 ff.

seen at Bordeaux.[25] At Toulouse he was received by the superior.
Doubtless, Dower was aware of Hervey's liberal views on religious
toleration. In a letter to Hervey, dated 9 August 1767, the superior
hopefully developed the theme of toleration.[26] The letter is signed
in French fashion with the surname only—Dower, superior of the
Irish seminary at Toulouse. In 1771 he was succeeded by Robert
MacCarthy of Cork who was fated to be the last superior of the
college.

Arthur Richard Dillon's successor in the see of Toulouse was
Etienne-Charles de Lomenie de Brienne (1763-88), one of the last
political prelates of France. In 1787 as chief minister of Louis XVI
de Brienne was given the task of warding off national bankruptcy.
He could not have succeeded where Necker and Calonne had failed.
New taxes added to the growing discontent; thus the archbishop of
Toulouse became the symbol of the venality and corruption of a
decaying *régime*.[27] In August 1788 de Brienne was driven from
office but not before he had enriched himself with 800,000 francs of
church revenues.[28] At Toulouse the position of the college was
not made easier by the fact that it was a beneficiary of the hated
salt tax.

In the Irish seminary, as in the other Irish foundations in France,
there was no cause for alarm with the outbreak of revolution in
1789. In the summer of 1790 the position at Toulouse worsened.
In July Robert MacCarthy, superior of the college, wrote to
Francis Moylan, bishop of Cork, telling of ominous happenings.
All the seminaries in the city were closed save the Irish college.
Although as yet there was no direct interference with the community the priests and students were obliged to wear the republican
tricolour in their buttonholes and a cockade in their hats. The
building next door, presumably the suppressed Ursuline convent,

25. '*Je confesse n'avoir pas vu de collège irlandais aussi propre, aussi
bien meublè, et dans lequel les élèves soient aussi bien instruits que dans
votre maison de Bordeaux.*' Harvey to Archbishop de Cicé of Bordeaux,
quoted by Bertrand, *op. cit.*, 380.
26. Public Record Office, Belfast, D 1514/9/70. Dower wrote: *None,
I dare say, can contribute more to your glory than to quell, if possible
religious divisions and hatred, to prove inward peace and union, to recall
numbers of expatriated children to their native soil to serve their king and
mother country.*' We are grateful to Rev. J. Walsh, Maynooth College, for
the reference.
27. Carlyle, *The French Revolution* (London, 1891), 61 ff.
28. Thiers, *The History of the French Revolution*, p. 6; McManners,
The French Revolution and the Church (London, 1969), p. 16.

was converted to a barracks holding some 800 volunteers who hurled insults across the dividing wall. MacCarthy added that the future was heavy with peril : 'everyone here expects, and in a short time, a change. The few fear it and tremble.'[29] More news of Toulouse reached Cork in the Abbé Edgeworth's letter to Moylan in March 1792 : churches were closed, clergy who had refused the oath to the civil constitution were in prison, anarchy now prevailed. The abbé's letter of November 1792 brought heavy tidings : Père Gagnières of the church of St Francis de Sales and Père Neullou, friends of former days, had perished.

In August-October 1793 the Jacobins were triumphant. The immunity and extra-territorial character of the Irish colleges were no longer recognised. At Toulouse Robert MacCarthy, superior of the Irish community, was among the proscribed but he escaped to Spain in disguise. There were nine students : six of these, Tracy, O'Meara, Cotter, Murphy, and two brothers named MacCarthy, were arrested. The three others, Rice, Rafferty, and Rochford, evaded capture for a time but were eventually apprehended. For a time all were held prisoners in the former convent of St Catherine, Toulouse. Finally, they were repatriated in November 1794.

On his return to Cork Robert MacCarthy was appointed vicar general and director of the young institute of the Presentation Sisters founded by Nano Nagle. He died 29 January 1814.[30]

Under a provision of the peace treaty between Britain and France in 1815 claims for losses of Irish property included 36,725 livres for the seminary at Toulouse.

Today nothing remains of the former Irish college. The bui'-dings at the junction of rue Valade and rue Labastide were pulled down in 1857.

29. Abbé Edgeworth, *Letters to his Friends*, p. 51. In his diary, now preserved in Mount Argus, Dublin, John Kavanagh, a student of the college in the period prior to the outbreak of the revolution, noted his forebodings—note in Burke MSS.

30. 'On Monday last the remains of Dr Robin MacCarthy were committed to a specially prepared tomb in the North Parish chapel. The funeral was attended by most of the Catholic priests of the city and county of Cork. The deceased gentleman was connected with the MacCarthys of Springmount in this county. Early in life he went to France to prepare himself for the ministry. Later he became head of the college at which he studied at Toulouse. The French revolution, that hotbed of all the angry and destructive passions of our nature, was at war with all that was amiable, respectful and good, soon drove Dr MacCarthy from that country. He was received in Cork under Dr Moylan's pious and hospitable roof which he never quitted until his death.' *Cork Freeholder*, 4 February 1814.

The following is an incomplete list of the superiors of the Irish college, Toulouse, 1659-1793. We indicate merely date of election or appointment.

1 Denis O'Riordan, Cork, 1659.[31]
2 Daniel MacCarthy, 1661.[32]
3 John Coyne, 1664.[33]
4 Germain O'Riordan, 1671.[34]
5 Maurice O'Keeffe, 1671.[35]
6 Maurice O'Keeffe, 1677.[36]
7 William Cheriton, 1684.[37]
8 Modeste MacSwiney, 1694.[38]
9 Florence MacCarthy, 1696.[39]
10 William O'Sheehan, 1699.[40]
11 Timothy O'Brien, 1699.[41]
12 Peter Daly, 1728.[42]
13 Donal Dineen, 1748.[43]
14 Francis O'Hea, 1751.[44]
15 —— Dower, 1766.[45]
16 Robert MacCarthy, 1771.[46]

31. Compte des receptes, G 428.
32. Ibid.
33. Procès-verbal of election, G 428.
34. Registre des déliberations, G 428.
35. Ibid.
36. Procès-verbal of election, G 428.
37. Registre de réception des séminaristes, G 428.
38. Procès-verbal de visite du séminaire par M. Raby, vic. gen., G 427.
39. Ordonnance de Mgr de Colbert, G 427.
40. Lettres de cachet de Louis XIV, G 427.
41. Arrêt du conseil d'état, G 427.
42. Nomination du supérieur par Mgr de Crillon, G 427.
43. Cunningham in J.C.H.A.S., lxxiv, 219, 1969.
44. Compte de receitte par François O Hea, G 427.
45. P.R.O. Belfast, D 1514/9/70.
46. MS. Annals, South Presentation Convent, Cork.

Chapter Four

THE IRISH COLLEGE AT LILLE 1610-1793

1

FOUNDER: FRANCIS NUGENT

The Irish college at Lille must be fitted into a category different from that of the other Irish continental institutes. It was the only training-ground of secular priests founded and maintained by an order of regular priests, the friars minor Capuchin. While regionalism or provincial exclusiveness was at times a live issue in many colleges, the problem was invariably solved. But from the foundation of Lille seminary in 1610 to its suppression in 1793 only students from Meath and the dioceses of Leinster were received. In other words, the college was an enclave of the pale. A partial explanation of this restrictiveness lies in the character and background of the founder.

Francis Nugent was born in 1569,[1] the second son of Sir Edward Nugent, of Ballybrenagh or Walshestown, Co. Westmeath, and his wife, Margaret O'Conor of Offaly.[2] The Nugents, barons of Delvin, despite their long Anglo-Irish ancestry, had succeeded to the lore, dinnsheanchus, and traditions of the bardic schools.[3] How much the confluence of the two racial streams and cultures was evident in the life of Francis Nugent is difficult to assess. His deepest sympathies, however, always reached out to the Catholics of the pale. In later years, he spared no effort to defend his pre-occupation with the dioceses of Leinster.

In 1582 Nugent was sent to the continent for education.[4] After a short period of study at Pont-à-Mousson in Lorraine he entered the university of Paris.[5] About this time he had thoughts of the priesthood but deferred making a decision. Later he was enrolled as a student at Louvain, where he gained a master's degree. He remained for a year as lecturer in the *pédagogie du Faucon*.

1. He was given the name Lavalin at baptism; Francis was his name in religion.
2. O'Connell, *Historia Missionis Hibernicae Fratrum Minorum Capuccinorum,* f. 12v; Archbold, *Historie of the Irish Capucins,* p. 1.
3. Martin, *Friar Nugent* (London, 1962), p. 4.
4. O'Connell, *Historia,* f. 13r.
5. Brevis et vera relatio de ortu et progressu Provinciarum Rhenanae et Coloniensis Fratrum Minorum Capuccinorum, *Analecta Capuccinorum,* xvi, 1900, pp. 250-55, 276-83.

At Paris and Louvain Nugent became keenly aware of the strong impetus of the Catholic counter reform. The most recent development in the Franciscan order, the friars minor Capuchin, was in the vanguard of the Tridentine movement.[6] On 4 October 1591 he was received into the Belgian province of the Capuchins, taking the name of the saint of the day, Francis of Assisi. He was ordained priest at Mons in 1595 by Louis de Berlaymont, archbishop of Cambrai.[7]

Nugent's varied talents were soon recognised. He filled responsible posts in the Low Countries, France, Italy, and later in the Rhineland. But he had an overriding ambition compared to which all his other activities were secondary, namely, to introduce the Capuchins to Ireland. In 1606 he was appointed to the friary at Lille. Here he beheld a familiar picture—groups of young Irishmen, victims of the Irish scattering.[8] Soon his constructive genius was devising plans to meet their needs. While the establishment of the Irish Capuchin mission was his major objective he saw that a college for Irish youths at Lille could be an ancillary aid of real value. High hopes were born when by apostolic brief, dated 29 May 1608, Paul V gave formal approval to send Capuchin missionaries to England, Scotland, and Ireland. For Nugent, however, there were yet many mountains of difficulty. It was futile to visualise a mission to Ireland or anywhere else without missionaries. He made the first move when he sent three Irish students to the Capuchin friary at Paris.[9] Such a measure was only a makeshift arrangement and could not serve the long-term policy of building an Irish Capuchin mission. While he was contemplating a more positive organisation he was ordered in 1610 to make a Capuchin foundation in the Rhineland.

By this time plans for the college at Lille were well advanced. Nugent's absence in the Rhineland did not impede progress; Christopher Cusack, president of the Irish colleges in the Low Countries, undertook to make final arrangements with the civic authorities. Meanwhile Nugent was not idle. In 1611 at Cologne he gathered a group of eight Irish students to form an Irish missionary

6. The Capuchin reform of the Franciscan Order was instituted in 1526 by Matteo di Bassi of Urbino, Cuthbert, *The Capuchins* (London, 1928), ii, 325 ff.

7. Archbold, *Historie,* pp. 2-4.

8. O'Connell, *Historia,* p. 39.

9. Archbold, *Historie,* p. 73.

nucleus.[10] Trials and disappointments dogged his path. He was charged, probably with justification, with having more thought for Ireland than for the Rhineland. Moreover, Cologne was not a suitable training centre for Irish Capuchin aspirants. The problem was solved when Father Cyprianus Van Antwerpen, provincial of the Belgian Capuchins and deeply sympathetic to Ireland, offered the Capuchin friary at Charleville, near Sedan, to serve as a regular Irish novitiate. In 1615 Nugent returned from the Rhineland, free to give full rein to his energies in the service of his native land.[11]

The salient details of his remaining years may be briefly told. In 1624 he visited Ireland disguised as a Flemish merchant. In 1627 he was invited to accept the archbishopric of Armagh, but declined.[12] Inevitably, his unique qualities were prized by the Holy See. On several occasions he was entrusted with diplomatic negotiations but such European prominence was unsought. He died on 16 May 1635, aged 66 years. He was interred before the high altar in the Capuchin friary, now the *palais de justice,* Charleville.

In recent years an appreciation of Nugent by a contemporary fellow-Capuchin has come to light. A Latin text acquired by the National library of Ireland bore the signature of its first owner— Francis Nugent.[13] Under his name was written in a contemporary hand :

> This was the Rev Father Nugent, the first Irishman, to enter the Capuchin Order at Brussels in Brabant, A.D. 1591. When he wrote this his name with his own hand he was Master of Arts and Public Professor in the University of Louvain.
>
> I have heard personally a learned man, a doctor of medicine at Musonium [Pont-à-Mousson] in France thus speak of our Francis : such and such of your order I know to be most eloquent and excellent preachers, but I know of none who could be better versed in the more difficult questions of theology than Fr Francis, the Irishman. And he added : I think your Fr Francis from Ireland is one of the four most learned men in the world.[14]

10. Martin, *op. cit.,* p. 108.

11. Archbold, *Historie,* p. 3; *Comm. Rinn.,* i, 366.

12. Brevis et vera Relatio, *loc. cit.*

13. *Sermones D. Guarrici Abbatis Igniacensis* (Lovanii, 1555).

14. The above is in the handwriting of Nicholas Archbold, the Capuchin historian (d.1650), Bieler in *The Irish Booklover,* xxx, no. 5, 1948.

2

LILLE COLLEGE : FIRST PHASE 1610-1700*

When Nugent was appointed vicar of the Capuchin friary at Lille in 1606 two factors spurred him to action towards the foundation of a college. Firstly, he deemed it a duty to make provision for the disorganised groups of young Irishmen in the town. He described them as 'sheep without a shepherd or a sheepfold.'[1] Secondly, a decision taken in 1607 to limit the intake of Leinster students at the seminaries at Douai and Antwerp seemed to him to be an unjust discrimination. His hand was strengthened when Father Michael Angelus, procurator general of the Capuchins, in a circular letter from Rome, dated 17 June 1609, appealed to all provinces contiguous to England and Ireland, i.e. Flanders, Paris, Lorraine, and Lyons, to extend educational facilities to young men from Ireland.[2] Cusack, by reason of his official position as overseer of the colleges, was privy to Nugent's designs. In fact, for reasons to be explained, Nugent was glad to act through Cusack. Although the Capuchin friar drew the blueprints Cusack made formal application in 1610 to the mayor and corporation of Lille. The *requete* was worded with care :

> Christopher Cusack, president of the Irish seminaries in the Low Countries, humbly points out to your worships that for many years large numbers of poor Irish students have been living in this town, sometimes together and sometimes here and there. May it please your worships to allow a house for their lodgment ...

With relentless logic he elaborated the reasons for the foundation :

1 The Irish endure a hard exile for their fidelity to the faith.
2 It is fitting to make application in Lille which received the faith in former times from Irish missionaries.
3 The erection of the college would be a spiritual alms.
4 Antwerp, Tournai, and Douai do not regret the Irish colleges in their towns.

---

*In the following pages the Troyes transcripts will be cited as *T.T.* Lille college transcripts will be cited as *L.C.T.* See introduction on sources for history of Lille college.
1. O'Connell, *Historia*, p. 39.
2. *Ibid.*

5 The Irish will not be burden to the townsfolk; they will maintain themselves.

6 The Irish in Lille will show virtue and learning as already manifested by the [Irish] Jesuits.

Reception by the mayor and corporation was friendly and Cusack lost no time in pressing home his petition to the Archduke Albert and the Infanta Clara Isabella, viceroys of the Spanish Netherlands.[3] They were reminded of the service rendered to Spain by Irishmen. At the present time there was a strong Irish presence in the land : some were students, others soldiers in whose regiments there were Irish chaplains. Cusack urged that standards of holiness and virtue amongst Irish religious and priests were a source of edification to the populace.

All went well. The corporation of Lille approved the erection of an Irish college on a site, covering 200½ verges, at the junction of rue du Plat and rue de la Vignette adjoining the Capuchin friary.[4] Letters patent were issued by the viceroys at Marimont on 19 November 1610.[5] The seminary was thereby an accredited educational institution and granted all the exemptions, privileges, and immunities accorded to similar institutes.

It will be noted that in the negotiations leading to the establishment of the college Nugent's name was not mentioned in the legal preliminaries; he remained an anonymous figure in the background. This fact coupled with his absence in the Rhineland during 1611-15 almost led to the loss of the foundation.

Anonymity was forced upon Nugent. As a friar of a mendicant order he could not acquire personal property. For the same reason and as a foreigner he was precluded from obtaining legal title to real estate. Of course he provided the necessary funds. Canon Dilenus of St Pierre's, Lille, held in trust three thousand florins which Nugent had collected from friends in Ireland and in the Low Countries.[6] For the rest the friar depended on intermediaries. A much-titled and decorative figure, Don Jean de Robles, count d'Annapes and baron Billy, governor of Lille and captain-general

3. 'Lettre d'envoi de la requete de Christophe de Crisac au conseil prive a Brussels, 1610', *L.C.T.*, i, 45.

4. 'Mandement accordant l'amortissement pour le nouveau seminaire de Lille', *L.C.T.,* i, 43. A verge was the equivalent of a rood.

5. 'Lettres d'amorissement des Archducs pour le terrain de la rue de la Vignette a Lille', *ibid.,* 15.

6. 'Letter of Nugent to the bishops of Meath and Leinster 20 April 1622', *L.C.T.,* i, 55.

of the garrisons at Lille, Douai, and Orchies, conducted the actual negotiations with the corporation of Lille—on behalf *'de quelques personnages Hibernois'*.[7] Apparently, no questions were asked about the unnamed Irish individuals. John Morel, a wealthy burgess and a friend of Nugent, attached his name and signature to the title-deeds. Another co-operator was Romain Fruit, a merchant of Lille, who acted on the authority of the archbishop of Liège but whose function is obscure.[8] Obviously, Nugent had implicit trust in his friends.

Some time after the friar's departure to the Rhineland John Morel began to cause difficulties. As possessor of the legal title he arrogated to himself the rights and privileges of a primary founder. A spirit of rivalry generated friction between himself and Fruit. Fruit's services were easily dispensed with but for cogent reasons Morel could not be eliminated. Not only was he the legal owner of the college building but he was the trustee of Irish funds; in addition he had promised to endow six burses. To make confusion worse Morel died in the early weeks of 1614. Under his will he bequeathed property in the parish of St Sauveur, Lille, to the Augustinians but the college passed to his daughter Marguerite. As her father's heir-in-law she presented the Irish college to the Augustinians.[9]

Nicolas Stassart, provincial of the Augustinians, eagerly grasped the opportunity to make a foundation at Lille. In April 1614 he sought the approval of Maximilian Vilain de Gandavo, bishop of Tournai, who had episcopal jurisdiction over Lille. Stassard promised to maintain the Irish character of the college.[10] The bishop wisely withheld his approval.[11] Nothing daunted, on the strength of a title in civil law, Stassard with an armed escort took forcible possession on 20 November 1614. Such was the chaotic state of affairs confronting Nugent on his return to Lille in 1615.

At once he plunged into the task of salvaging his college and vindicating Irish rights. The only course open to him was to seek redress in the law courts, but his dilemma was painful. He had to convince the court that he, Father Francis Nugent, Irish Capuchin, was the rightful owner of the institute. At the legal hearing

7. 'Titres de propriete et amortissement pour la maison de Lille, 1610', *ibid.*, 5.

8. 'Statement by Nugent on the parts played by Canon Dilenus, Count d'Annapes and Romain Fruit, 1618', *ibid.*, 35.

9. 'Agreement between executors of Morel and the Augustinians, 25 April 1614', *ibid.*, 71.

10. 'Petition of Stassart to the bishop of Tournai', *L.C.T.*, i, 65.

11. 'De Actis Vicariatus Tornacensis', *ibid.*, 77.

Christopher Cusack gave sworn testimony.[12] The purpose of his evidence was to segregate the college at Lille from the other Irish foundations in the Low Countries. He disavowed personal responsibility for the Lille foundation : that was rightly Nugent's. Don Jean de Robles corroborated Cusack's evidence, revealing the identity of 'a certain Irish personage' who was the prime mover in the foundation.[13] De Robles declared that Morel's claim to a personal title of ownership was spurious : the seizure by the Augustinians was an invasion of Irish property. After a lengthy hearing the *conseil privé* at Brussels gave its verdict on 27 November 1618.[14] The rights of Nugent were upheld and vindicated; the Augustinians were ordered to surrender the college before the following Easter. In 1634, a few months before his death, Nugent recalled his struggle : 'I, unworthie, got by Our Lord's favour means for the like dedes, with all decencies of our state . . . and still to God the honor.'[15]

Now that legal issues were clarified Nugent set about organising the internal affairs of the college. He was dissatisfied with the administration and perturbed lest his restriction of entry to students of the pale should be overruled.

An odd feature of the Lille foundation was that neither Nugent nor any other Capuchin friar ever acted as superior of the college; the post was always filled by a secular priest. At the foundation in 1610 Cusack was named superior but the demands of the other Irish seminaries allowed him little time in Lille. With the consent of Nugent Laurence Sedgrave took charge of administration, and continued in office for several years after Nugent's return to Lille. Despite the friar's efforts to provide revenues the foundation entered upon a lean period in 1622. In 1625 John Roche, bishop of Ferns, in a report to the Holy See painted a gloomy picture of the Irish continental colleges.[16] He stated that Lille college had scarcely any means of support. As Nugent surveyed the resources of his foundation he found grave fault with Sedgrave's administration : funds intended for the exclusive use of the seminary at

12. *L.C.T.*, i, 161-62. Curiously, he signed his name 'Christopher *Crisac*.'
13. *Iibd.*, 241.
14. 'Sentence du conseil privé contre les Augustins et les heritiers de Morel', *ibid.*, 39; 'Arret de la cour de Bruxelles 27 novembre 1618', *ibid.*, 269.
15. 'A Declaration for Deathe, 1635', *ibid.*, 223.
16. *Arch. Hib.*, xxii, 148.

Lille had been diverted to prop the colleges at Douai and Antwerp.
There was vexation of spirit in Nugent's complaint in 1628 to
Martin Lalor, Sedgrave's successor :[17]

> If I doe resolve to make use of a fitt instrument Mr
> Sedgrave is to give a solide account of two or three hundred
> pounds sterling but I hope still his conscience will move him
> ennough and if the President [Cusack] with him had followed
> my advise he had never been displaced from Douai.

These were harsh words but Nugent was more emphatic. He
charged Sedgrave, and by implication, Cusack, with the misdirec-
tion to Douai of sixteen hundred florins that were raised for the
sole support of Lille college.[18] Surprisingly, he adds that some of
the funds were given to Captain Thomas Preston.[19]

One cannot help thinking that Nugent was unjust in his strictures. Sedgrave, Cusack, and Nugent himself, were palesmen and
regarded the supply of priests to the dioceses of the pale as a
primary need. In the 1620s, as we have seen, the Irish seminaries
in the Low Countries were in an impoverished state. Indeed the
college at Antwerp was closed for a short period. Cusack and
Sedgrave saw no reason why Lille college should be regarded as a
separate unit : in the last analysis all the foundations served a
common cause. Moreover, Nugent did not have statutory authority
to withdraw his college from the overall jurisdiction of Cusack.
Hence, Sedgrave, and presumably Cusack, felt justified in using
Nugent's resources to ensure the survival of the seminaries at
Douai and Antwerp.

Ultimately, the difficulties were solved and harmony reigned once
more. Whatever the divergences of opinion among themselves
Cusack and Nugent remained fast friends. Shortly before his death
Cusack paid generous tribute to the Capuchin.[20]

> I have had a letter from F. Francis Nugent desiring me to
> write to your R. that you would agree that Martin Lalor should
> govern the seminarie at Lille whom I hear to be a very honest

17. 'De la premiere cause a traiter contre Mons Laurent Sedgrave',
T.T., iii, 185.
18. 'A copie of R. father Francis Nugent fundator of the Irish Colledge
in Lille to the then prefect Mr Martin Lalor', *L.C.T.*, i, 213.
19. Afterwards General Thomas Preston of the Irish Confederate wars.
20. 'Cusack to Sedgrave, 2 October 1622', *T.T.*, iii, 143.

man though to me unknown, which request I see no reason you refuse and do beseech you to give the good father what contentment you can for his virtue deserves the same though we have had bickering with him many tymes.

Nevertheless, Nugent had learned a lesson. Problems of administration were minor irritations compared to the transcending necessity of limiting the intake of the college to students from Meath and the dioceses of Leinster. In 1614 regional rivalry provoked disturbances at Cusack's own foundation at Douai. Doubtless, the experience had mellowed his ideas on provincial exclusiveness. An undated and unsigned fragment in Nugent's handwriting may have been intended for Cusack's reading :[21]

There be some very disposed for broyling the howse of Lille and saing that it should doe with the rest of the colledges for common use. Remember you, that if any suche doe make demands it be answered.

Pressure was building up against the narrow regionalism of Lille college. In 1626 Nicholas Aylmer, president of the seminary at Douai, urged the Holy See to remove the Capuchin control at Lille and to unite the college with his own.[22] Di Bagno, nuncio at Brussels, was asked to investigate the position. He advised Cardinal Ludovisi, protector of Ireland, that in the present state of economic stress at Douai the union would not be expedient, but that the proposal would be considered at a later date.[23] In 1631 Bonaventure Magennis, the Franciscan bishop of Down and Connor, was more forthright. He complained to the Holy See that the colleges at Lille and Antwerp were not observing due equality in admitting students from the provinces of Ireland. He called for an examination of the situation in both seminaries by Di Bagno, the nuncio, and the bishops of Tournai and Antwerp.[24]

Nugent was constrained to justify his principles. The restriction of entry at Lille was a subject on which he had already written trenchantly.[25] The decision in 1607 limiting the intake of Leinster

21. *L.C.T.*, i, 229.
22. *Coll. Hib.*, no. 10, 1967, p. 43.
23. *Ibid.*, p. 42.
24. *Ibid.*, p. 37.
25. 'Letter to the Irish bishops, 1622', *L.C.T.*, i, 55; 'Letter to Martin Lalor, 1628', *ibid.*, 213.

students at Douai and Antwerp rankled in his mind. From an anonymous *mémoire*, written about 1630, we learn that the consequent rejection of Anglo-Irish youths gave shape in 1608 to his plans for Lille seminary.[26] Of necessity he relaxed the restriction when a youth from a part of Ireland outside Leinster sought admission in the hope of joining the Irish Capuchins. In 1634 Nugent prepared a memorandum entitled *'Mementos for the understanding of my severall doings'*. It held the friar's *apologia*:[27]

> Lille Howse, which by authenticall memories, not only was founded for youthes of Meeth and Leynster but also for som others chosen by me with an ey to there vocation to our order . . .

'Authenticall memories' were altogether inadequate. Nugent had no option but to secure maximum legal validity for the reservations to be observed in his foundation. The limitation in favour of the pale must needs be included in the constitutions of the college. He made a preliminary approach to Julius Stravio, nuncio at Brussels. As a result, Bertrand Verman, canon of the collegiate church of St Pierre, Lille, made a visitation of the institute. The outcome of his report was a decision in 1634 by Maximilian Vilain, bishop of Tournai, giving canonical effect to Nugent's request.[28] Thus fortified the friar looked for a ruling from the civil law. On 13 November 1634 the magistrates' court at Lille gave legal validity to the application that none but students from Meath and the dioceses of Leinster be admitted to the seminary.[29] The restrictions of entry were accepted by the Holy See on 20 July 1636 when Urban VIII by apostolic brief approved the motives and principles governing the Irish Capuchin college at Lille.[30]

Nugent must have been concerned about the judgment of posterity. He placed a signed declaration in the hands of Fathers Joseph, Bonaventure, and Luke, Irish Capuchin brethren at

26 'Raisons pour lesquells le P. François Hybernois capucin a procure un college pour les 2 provinces de Media et Lagenia', *ibid.*, 167.

27. *T.T.*, iii, 145. So O'Connell explains Nugent's views, *Historia*, pp. 42-44.

28. 'Correspondence avec les eveques de Tournai', *L.C.T.*, i, 117, 119, 131.

29. 'Ordonnance du Magistrat de Lille', *ibid.*, p. 113.

30. *Bullarium Ordinis FF. Minorum S.F. Francisci Capucinorum*, v, f. 281; *Notitia Historica S. Francisci Capucinorum Hiberniae* (Rome, 1859), p. 24.

Charleville, setting forth at length his concern for the dioceses of
the pale; the dioceses of Munster being the objects of his aver-
sion.[31] Before his death in May 1635 he had the comfort of knowing that his two objectives had been realised : the Capuchin
missionaries were established in Ireland and the pastoral needs of
Meath and the dioceses of Leinster were the sole concern of the
foundation at Lille.

As a corollary to the canonical recognition of the college in 1634
Maximillian Vilain, bishop of Tournai, drew up a formal body of
rules and constitutions.[32] Administration of the temporalities was
vested in four provisors, two priests nominated by the bishop of
Tournai and two laymen appointed by the corporation of Lille.
The provisors met monthly to approve accounts submitted by the
bursar. Along with the other Irish foundations in the Spanish
dominions the college was granted a state subvention but with the
passing years payment became less certain. The disadvantage was
partly offset by the fact that the Capuchins, a mendicant order,
were permitted to quest. As at Bordeaux, the students acted as
municipal funeral bearers and gravediggers thus adding to the
common fund. There is evidence that occasional support came
from Leinster.[33]

One wonders why there was sudden concern in 1650 in the Irish
continental colleges for proficiency in the Irish language. Perhaps
it was in anticipation of the Cromwellina *régime,* when hazardous
pastoral conditions in Ireland made an assured knowledge of Irish
imperative. Cardinal Carafa sent a memorial to the Holy See
urging that a knowledge of their native language be mandatory on
all students in the continental seminaries. The Congregation de
Prop. Fid. decided in 1650 that for the future a knowledge of the
Irish vernacular was a pre-requisite for entry into any of the
colleges.[34] An exception was made in the case of students from
those areas in Leinster where Irish was not the vernacular. Despite

31. 'Declaration of Fr Nugent, 30 November 1634', *L.C.T.,* i, 165.
32. Printed by Peter de Racha, sub bibliis aureis, Lille, 1635.
33. Cogan, *The Diocese of Meath* (Dublin, 1874), iii, 671. On the
occasion of his visit to Ireland in 1624 Nugent was given £1,000 for Lille
college by Luke and Thomas Plunket, merchants of Dublin. Nugent set the
sum at interest in the *mont de Piété,* Burssels. In 1632 the place and
circumstances of the capital investment were the subject of a lawsuit in
which the verdict was awarded to Nugent, Archbold, *Historie,* p. 55,
O'Connell, *Historia,* 364 ff.
34. Acta S. Cong. 1648-50, vol. 10, no. 23.

the close affinity between Lille seminary and the dioceses of
Leinster the students recognised the need for proficiency in the
native language. The custom was introduced of speaking only
Irish on certain days of the week. In 1764 the custom was cited as
evidence when the question of compulsory Irish at Lille was a
subject of acute controversy.

Under such auspices and notwithstanding a chronic lack of
resources a small but constant flow of priests went out from Lille
to the dioceses of Leinster. In 1640-43 the Capuchins were again
on the defensive. Complaints were made at Rome concerning the
spiritual standards and discipline of the students. A letter, dated
18 March 1640, from Father Joseph Corbally, guardian at Charleville, to the bishop of Tournai, refuted the criticisms.[35] His testimony was endorsed by an undated memorial to the bishop, signed
by the entire community of the college.[36] The bishop investigated
the charges and found that they were without foundation.[37]
The Holy See was completely satisfied and in 1648 directed that
the status quo at Lille must be maintained.[38] When Nicholas
French, bishop of Ferns, surveyed Cromwellian Ireland in 1653 he
named Lille seminary as a fruitful source of zealous workers in the
Irish mission field.[39] In 1671 Father Luke Nugent, the Capuchin
commissary general, gave an estimate to the Holy See of the prestige attached to the foundation : many heroic preachers of the
gospel had departed from Lille to Ireland. Their incredible suffer-
ings were the means of bringing salvation to many souls.[40] But in
1671 vast political changes involving the college were taking place
in the Low Countries.

The Spanish Netherlands, that strange anomaly of European
history, fell an easy victim to French expansionism. By the treaty
of the Pyrenees in 1659 France gained nearly all the territory of
Artois. In 1668 French Flanders, including Lille and Tournai,
came under French rule. Ten years later by the treaty of Nymegen
Franche-Comté, Cambrai and what was left of Artois, were
absorbed into the dominions of Louis XIV. Although the term
Spanish Netherlands continued to have a geographical meaning to

35. The guardian at Charleville to the bishop of Tournai', *L.C.T.*, i, 139.
36. 'Priests and students to the bishop of Tournai', *ibid.*, 141.
37. *Ibid.*, p. 143.
38. Arch. de Prop. Fid., scr. rif. nelle Congregazioni Generali, vol. 417,
f. 323.
39. *Comm. Rin.*, v, 142 ff.
40. Arch. de Prop. Fid., scr. rif. Irlanda, vol. 429, 3 augusti 1671, no. 15.

1713, for practical purposes the Spanish Netherlands with their traditions of Irish heroism and culture ceased to exist.

Absence of comment in the documentation of Lille college leads us to think that the transfer from Spanish to French rule was a painless process and may not have been unwelcomed. The change-over, however, gave an opportunity to powerful interests who were opposed to the narrow provincialism governing the conduct of the foundation at Lille. In 1678 Capuchin control was challenged by an Ulsterman, Dr Patrick Maginn, abbot of Theulay, in the diocese of Langres, and first almoner to Catherine of Braganza, wife of Charles II of England. Maginn was prominently associated with the Irish college, Paris. Supporting the protest were Canon Gregory Joyce, St Gudule's, Brussels, a native of Galway, and James Talbot, former superior of the college at Antwerp. Maginn addressed a *mémoire* to Louis XIV.[41] Summarily, he reminded the king how harmful to Ireland were racial divisions : the Capuchins at Lille perpetuated old antagonisms that were injurious not only to Ireland but to education. Boys who had completed the study of humanities in Lille seminary were not permitted to begin studies for the priesthood for no reason other than that they were not natives of Leinster.

Strangely enough, the provisors of the college, not the Capu-chins, entered the lists in defence. In a counter memorial, a lengthy document covering seventeen folios, addressed to M. le Pelletier, intendant of justice, police, and finance in Flanders, member of the *conseil d'état,* the memorialists recapitulated the history of the college and Nugent's rigid concern for the pastoral needs of Meath and the dioceses of Linster.[42] They added that at Bordeaux and Toulouse there was a frank unwillingness to accept students who were not natives of Munster. There is no further reference to the episode. Evidently, Louis XIV was unmoved; the status quo at Lille was not altered.

Within a few years the effects of war, political upheaval, and frontier adjustments were felt in all the Irish foundations. The days of the Spanish subsidies were over. Even the trickle of support from Ireland ceased. In 1681, Sebastiano Tanari, inter-nuncio at

41. 'Mémoire de l'abbé de Theulay contre les capucins irlandois', *L.C.T.,* i, 187; 'Lettre de l'abbé de Theulay', *ibid.,* 209.

42. 'Mémoire contre l'abbé Patrice de Theulay au sujet des privilèges des provinces de Lagenie et Medie du collège de Lille, 29 octobre 1678', *L.C.T.,* i, 189.

Brussels, submitted a report to the Holy See.[43] At Louvain, the Franciscans, the Dominicans, and the Pastoral college, where there were eight students, were all in the deepest penury.[44] In French Flanders the picture was of growing poverty. Tanari wrote that Douai college, holding nine students, had lost all its funds in the recent wars. Soon the eight students at the college at Tournai would be devoid of maintenance. The plight of Lille college was not so alarming: it had an enrolment of twenty-four students and an annual income of 330 *scudi,* supplemented by the students' earnings as gravediggers. As yet, no debt had been incurred. The Holy See, through Tanari, made liberal disbursements of alms. It seems clear that support from Rome saved the foundations from extinction during the critical years.[45]

An upheaval of another kind befell the Irish Capuchins. In 1685, by decree of Louis XIV, they were transferred from their friaries at Charleville and Sedan to friaries in Bar-sur-Aube and Vassy in Champagne. Hitherto contact between Irish missionary head-quarters at Charleville and Lille was easy. But at Bar-sur-Aube and Vassy, more than a hundred miles south-east of Paris, communication with Lille was less certain, and consequently, less effective. In the early years of the eighteenth century the Irish Capuchins almost lost control of the college.

3

LILLE COLLEGE : SECOND PHASE 1700-93

When Charles II of Spain died in 1700 succession to his crown and empire passed to Philip of Anjou, grandson of Louis XIV. The Princes of Austria were rival claimants. In 1701 the Grand Alliance of Austria, the empire, the Dutch provinces, and England was formed against France. In the following year half Europe was locked in the war of the Spanish succession. For a decade French English, Dutch, Spanish, and German troops marched and counter-marched in the *arène militaire* or cockpit of Europe. In 1713 with the peace of Utrecht and the withdrawal of the Dutch garrison

43. *Coll. Hib.,* no. 3, 1960, pp. 80-81.
44. Charles II of Spain (1665-1700) made amends. In 1688 he directed that the grant due to the college of St Anthony, Louvain, be paid punctually. In 1695 he ordered a substantial payment of the arrears amounting to 30,000 crowns, *Wild Geese in Spanish Flanders,* p. 479.
45. Cf. *Spic. Oss.,* ii, 285, 347.

from Lille under the treaty of the barriers the Irish Capuchins in distant Bar-sur-Aube and Vassy were at last able to take stock of their college. They found much that was disquieting.

In broad outline, in the havoc of the recent wars when administration rested with the provisors, Irish control of the seminary was reduced to a minimum. In 1690 the provisors, without prior consultation with the Capuchins, appointed James Dempsey as superior. He was advanced in years and utterly incompetent. The *de facto* superior was a layman named Bonnier who with his wife lived in the college. He had omitted for many years to keep a record of accounts and there was evidence of misappropriation of college funds. That was not all. Lille was a stronghold of Jansenism. Seraphim Manier, priest of the church of St Maurice, Lille, used the seminary as an *entrepôt* for the dissemination of Jansenistic literature in Flanders.

Nothing was done hastily. In 1720 Father Bonaventure Donnelly, assistant-provincial of the Irish Capuchins, formally removed Dempsey from office. The lay provisors of the college refused to accept the decision and made ready to contest the issue of Capuchin control in the law courts.[1] The hearing in the magistrates' court was fixed for 5 December 1720.

We do not propose to enter into the details of the evidence presented at the magistrates' court at Lille.[2] The debate ranged over familiar ground. The provisors argued their case on the grounds that Cusack, not Francis Nugent, was the founder of the college in 1610. Cusack never claimed the rights now put forward by the Capuchins. Donnelly based his defence on the interpretation of the decision by the magistrates on 13 November 1634 by which statutory effect was given to the purpose of Lille college. This included the right to nominate superiors and students. The court ruling precluded forever any departure from its terms. The magistrates gave their decision on 11 February 1721 : the rights of the Capuchins to govern and regulate the seminary were upheld.[3] Forthwith Father Donnelly nominated a new superior—Michael

1. 'Defense pour les proviseurs seculiers du college des pauvres estudians hibernois a Lille, 5 decembre 1720', *L.C.T.*, ii, 11.
2. 'Presentement by Donnelly to the mayor and corporators of Lille', *L.C.T.*, ii, 29; 'Statement by Donnelly to the mayor and council of eight citizens of Lille', *ibid.*, 35; 'Memoire pour le R. P. Donnelly', *ibid.*, 55; 'Another mémoire in favour of Donnelly', *ibid.*, 63.
3. 'Copie de la sentence des Messrs Magistrats de Lille rendue 11 fevrier 1721', *ibid.*, 93.

Kinnin, a native of Leix, *licencié* in law of the university of Paris.
For more than a year nothing happened. But another Irish defeat of Jansenism was not to go unchallenged. The two lay provisors, acting independently of the ecclesiastical provisors, moved to contest the decision of the lower court at Lille in the supreme court of Flanders. *Lettres de relief d'appel* permitting the introduction of the case were sent by M. Beequet on behalf of the king on 12 September 1722.[4] Father Philip Kennedy, the newly-appointed superior of the Irish Capuchins, was called upon to defend not only Capuchin rights at Lille but the existence of the college.[5] At a time when the Irish Catholics were bearing the brunt of the penal code the continental colleges were more vitally important than ever. The pastoral contribution of Lille seminary to the dioceses of Leinster must be maintained.

Before the appeal of the provisors was heard in the supreme court of Flanders Kennedy made a dramatic move. On behalf of the Irish Capuchins he sent a long memorandum to Louis XV.[6] We give a translation of a few paragraphs :

To the King

Sire

Philip Kennedy, custos of the Irish Capuchins of Bar-sur-Aube, humbly presents on their behalf that in 1609 and 1610 Father Francis Nugent, superior of the Capuchins then at Charleville, founded a college at Lille for students who were natives of the provinces of Leinster and Meath in Ireland, to train them and render them fit for the ecclesiastical state in order that they might repel the invasion of heresy in the said provinces. Towards this end the zealous Father collected funds among his relatives and Catholic nobility of Leinster. He obtained letters patent from the Archduke Albert, then sovereign of the Low Countries. The Count d'Annapes, governor of Lille, and M. Morel, burgess of the same city, lent their names to facilitate the purchase of the necessary land for building. Christopher Cusack, priest and president of all the Irish

4. 'Lettres de relief d'appel en faveur des proviseurs du college de Lille, 12 septembre 1722', *L.C.T.*, ii, 163.
5. Philip Kennedy, place of birth not known, was received into the Capuchins in 1696. He was elected superior in 1721, 1723, re-elected 1731. He died at Bar-sur-Aube 1736.
6. *L.C.T.*, i, 109. The manuscript in the dep. archives, Troyes, is dated only 1723.

students in the Low Countries, was appointed prefect, being the choice of Father Nugent. He [Cusack] undertook on 19 October 1611 an obligation by which he bound himself and his successors to retain the prefecture under Father Nugent and his successors.

Then follows a summary of the legal proceedings in 1634 and 1678 forced on the Capuchins to safeguard their rights at Lille.

Then it happened that, with the approval of the King, the Capuchins were transferred from Charleville to Bar-sur-Aube. Profiting by their [the Capuchins] absence and the perilous times of war, the provisors established some prefects in the college without consulting the Capuchins. The circumstances of the time did not permit the revocation of such acts and the Capuchins gave their approval to the prefects as persons qualified for the charge of the college and students. But at the time the Dutch held a garrison at Lille. The provisors upset the established order of the foundation by depriving the prefect of his authority and introducing this man Bonnier, a native of Flanders, as sub-prefect and bursar. With his wife he dissipated a great part of the college funds. Add to this, the fact that M. Magloire,[7] dean of the collegiate chapel of St Pierre, Lille, attempted to make the college common to the other provinces of Ireland.

Having given a summary of the proceedings in the lower court at Lille in 1720 Kennedy continued :

The provisors hope that poverty will prevent the Capuchins in the task of sustaining an expensive lawsuit at Flanders. The college archives are in the possession of the provisors; the Capuchins can produce only a few statements made by magistrates. The process causes the utmost confusion to the college, tending to its ruin by overwhelming costs.

The Custos [Kennedy], therefore, has recourse to the king to whom the Irish Capuchins appeal against the flagrant injustice of the provisors who have tried to arrogate to themselves a right directly contrary to the fundamental purposes of

---

7. In the present context the name is written as above. But in the sentence of the court it appears as Maguire which seems more probable.

this college and its time-honoured observances. It is unreasonable to expect that inhabitants of Lille could be competent judges of the qualities required of a prefect or of students who are destined to discharge priestly duties in Ireland. Wherefore His Majesty is humbly supplicated &c.

There was a protracted hearing of the appeal in the supreme court at Douai. Little purpose is served by examining the extensive documentation of the proceedings.[8] The verdict was given on 21 January 1724.[9] The appeal of the provisors was rejected; the decision of the lower court at Lille on 11 February 1721 was confirmed. Costs of the appeal were placed on the college.

Judging by modern legal standards the decision in 1724 by the supreme court of Flanders should have conferred on the Capuchins an immunity to further questioning of their rights at Lille. But it was not so. In 1764 came the final challenge, not from French interests, but from the bishops of Leinster whose dioceses the college was founded to serve. At first sight, the position seems paradoxical, but on closer observation one realises that much deeper issues were involved. In a sense, all the Irish continental colleges were on trial in 1764.

From the historical perspective the legal action by the Irish bishops must be seen as part of the running-down process of the continental college movement. In the middle years of the eighteenth century Irish Jacobitism, the bugbear of the Protestant ascendancy, was dead. There were signs that religious toleration was not too far off. One of the most cogent proofs was that in 1750

8. 'Statement of the ecclesiastical provisors in support of the lay provisors, 29 October 1722', *L.C.T.*, ii, p. 171; 'En la cause des proviseurs des hibernois en la ville de Lille', undated, *ibid.;* 'Plea in bar of the lay provisors, 7 May 1723', *ibid.,* p. 161; 'Mémoire pour les proviseurs au sujet de la nomination du prefet tendant a prouver la nullite de la declaration du 19 [recte 13] novembre 1634', *ibid.,* p. 189; 'En la cause du R. P. Custode des capucins irlandois au convent de Bar-sur-Aube, 21 octobre 1723', *ibid.,* p. 139; 'Plea in bar of Fr Philip Kennedy, 7 May 1723', *ibid.,* 'Reflection pour le reverend Pere Custode des capucins irlandois', undated, *ibid.,* p. 125. Added to the documentary evidence produced by the provisors were relevant extracts from a college register (now lost) entitled 'Livre contenant la recueil des titres de la fondation, de la creation et progres du seminaire ou college des hibernois a Lille'. Annexed to this is a copy of the *Conditiones quibus praefectus Collegii studiosorum Hybernorum Insulis tenebitur se conformare.*

9. 'Sentence de la cour du Parlement de Flandres, fait a Douay 21 janvier 1724', *L.C.T.*, ii, 201.

every diocese in Ireland had its bishop in undisturbed possession of his see. To the bishops it was obvious that the conditions that gave origin to the continental seminaries in the previous century had passed; the extra-canonical privileges vested in college superiors were now working to the detriment of ordinary episcopal jurisdiction and procedure as visualised by the council of Trent. The time was opportune to regularise the affairs in the colleges abroad. That the Furlong legal episode at Lille was a *cause célèbre* is evident from the voluminous testimony presented to the court, evidence submitted by Irish bishops and ecclesiastics, Irish scholars from Louvain, superiors and students of other Irish foundations, officers and chaplains of famous Irish regiments in the French service. Finally, there is an element of incongruity in the spectacle of a French court adjudicating on a topic that still provokes animated discussion : compulsory Irish.

Since 1741 there was growing criticism among bishops and clergy of the privilege enjoyed by the continental colleges of ordaining students to the secular priesthood on the sole title of a mission in Ireland.[10] At Lille the anomalies were most striking. Here a regular order of mendicant friars with missionary headquarters in France received and promoted students to the diocesan clergy without consultation with or canonical authority from the bishops of the dioceses concerned. In a letter, dated 7 January 1764, Dr Owen Geoghegan, vicar general of Meath, stated his objections very incisively.[11] Writing to David Flood, acting superior at Lille, he charged the Capuchins with a refusal to receive students nominated by Dr Augustine Cheevers, bishop of Meath (1756-78). Geoghegan added that the exercise of Capuchin rights at Lille had not been helpful : if contentious matters could be settled the college, now almost empty, could be of immense benefit. An undated copy of a *mémoire* by Patrick Fitzsimons, the newly-appointed archbishop of Dublin, and his suffragans, set forth the uneasiness felt by the bishops of Leinster.[12] Briefly, the bishops were turning critical eyes on the foundation whence came many of their priests. In 1764 the opportunity came of contesting the procedure at Lille.

It will be remembered that in 1650 the Holy See ruled that a knowledge of the Irish language would henceforth be mandatory

10. Cf. *Col. Hib.*, no. 8, 1965, 78 ff.
11. *L.C.T.*, iii, 317.
12. 'Mémoire pour l'archeveque de Dublin et les eveques ses suffragants', *L.C.T.*, iii, 431. Fitzsimons was appointed to the see of Dublin, 20 Sept. 1763.

on all students entering the continental seminaries.[13] An exception was made of students from areas of Leinster where Irish was not the vernacular. In 1764 the position was changed : the bishops of Leinster contended that a knowledge of Irish was a primary pastoral need in their dioceses.

In 1763 Father Augustine O'Kelly, assistant to the Commissary of the Irish Capuchins, appointed Father Peter Furlong, a native of Killinick, Co. Wexford, superior of the college at Lille. The bishops impugned the appointment on the grounds that Furlong lacked competence in the Irish language and, therefore, was unfit to train and educate students for the dioceses of Leinster. The four provisors, acting as agents of the archbishop of Dublin and the vicar general of Meath, presented their case against the Capuchins in the magistrates' court at Lille. On 1 March 1764 a verdict was given in favour of the Capuchins.[14] At once the provisors lodged an appeal with the supreme court of Flanders; *lettres de relief d'appel* were issued by the court on 10 March.[15] The supreme court sitting at Douai was asked to decide a question of fact : was a knowledge of Irish a pastoral necessity for priests in the dioceses of Leinster? We give a summary of the evidence.[16]

On behalf of the appellants M. Vincent submitted written testimony by Dr Fitzsimons, archbishop of Dublin,[17] Eugene Geoghegan, vicar general of Meath, and Anthony Nowlan, parish priest of Fuldamore [Tullamore?].[18] The Irish language was not merely useful but absolutely necessary. The archbishop stated that even in Dublin confessors could not discharge their pastoral duties unless they were proficient in Irish. Bernard Brady, regent of the Irish Dominicans in Louvain, made his testimony in Irish, translated into French for the court : any view expressed against the neces-

13. Acta S. Cong. de Prop. Fid., 1648-50, vol. 10, no. 23.
14. 'Certificate in favour of Fr Peter Furlong, signed by Cardon, de Beaufrenez, Leroy, de Willermont on behalf of the mayor and magistrates of Lille', *L.C.T.*, ii, 253.
15. 'Lettres de relief d'appel autorisant les proviseurs &c', *L.C.T.*, iii, 369.
16. Cf. 'Compulsory Irish in France', *J.C.H.A.S.*, lviii, no. 187, 1953.
17. Fitzsimons to David Flood, acting prefect at Lille, 26 April 1764', *L.T.C.*, iii, 349; 'Copie ou traduction de la lettre de sa Grandeur Monseigneur l'Archeveque de Dublin', *ibid.*, p. 347.
18. 'Declaration by Eugene Geoghegan and Antoine Nowlan, 30 March 1764', *ibid.*, 345.

sity of the Irish language is a calumny.[19] Hugh MacMahon, president of the Pastoral college, Louvain,[20] and Stephen Taylor, Dominican of Louvain, were in agreement.[21] Taylor recalled his student days at Lille when the young men spoke only Irish on Tuesdays and Thursdays in order to gain proficiency. The testimony of Anthony Fitzsimons, rector of St Anthony's, Louvain, was written in Irish and was translated into French for the court : Irish was essential for the instruction of poor Irish Catholics; English was the language of commerce.[22]

M. Vincent cast his net widely to collect evidence. He assembled the views of officers and chaplains of famous Irish regiments in the French service : Clare's regiment in garrison at Philipville,[23] Bulkeley's regiment encamped at Rocroy,[24] Rothe's regiment in garrison at Bouchain.[25] They were unanimous in their opinions : the Irish language was as necessary for a priest in Leinster as in any other part of Ireland. Henry Shee, officer in Clare's regiment, gave personal testimony that he had spent twenty-two months in Lille college : the common language of the students was Irish.[26] The final submission came from the college : eleven students, natives of Dublin, Wicklow, Kildare, Meath, and Westmeath, presented a signed assurance to the court that proficiency in the Irish language was essential for the discharge of pastoral work in Leinster.[27]

In his rebuttal of the provisors' evidence, M. O'Faral, advocate for the Capuchins, adduced the written views of Francis d'Evreaux, superior of the Irish (Lombard) college, Paris, David Henegan, doctor of the Sorbonne and prefect of studies in the said college : English is the vernacular of the province of Leinster : in the Irish college, Paris, lectures in theology and scripture were delivered in English.[28] Randolph MacDonnell, priest of the diocese of Dublin, doctor of the Sorbonne and examiner at the Irish college, Paris, corroborated : the Irish language was no longer the mother tongue

19. *Ibid.*, 27 April 1764, 341.
20. *L.C.T.*, iii, 337.
21. *Ibid.*, p. 343.
22. *Ibid.*, p. 339
23. *Ibid.*, p. 333.
24. *Ibid.*, p. 335.
25. *Ibid.*, p. 429.
26. *Ibid.*, p. 334.
27. *Ibid.*, p. 353.
28. *Ibid.*, p. 377

in Leinster.[29] A supporting view was expressed in a memorandum signed by eighteen students.[30] Robert Galvin, Patrick Doran, and Thomas Connell, priests of the diocese of Meath, sent written testimony : in Leinster clerical conferences and preaching were always conducted in English, never in Irish.[31] But they would do violence to their consciences if they asserted that a knowledge of Irish was not useful on the Irish mission.

On 10 May 1764 the court gave judgment in favour of the Capuchins; the appointment of Peter Furlong was upheld.[32]

The bishops persevered in their efforts. In 1766 they addressed a petition to the bishop of Orleans stating that if they were given control of the college they would furnish twenty students annually.[33] That the Capuchins were aware of the threat appears in a letter (undated) written by Father Norbert Shee, superior at Bar-sur-Aube, to the Duc de Choiseul, first minister of state under Louis XV.[34] But there was no reason for Shee's apprehensions. Few years remained for the college at Lille.

Father Furlong ceased to administer the seminary in 1776. In that year Father Patrick Geoghegan sought the appointment. His letter, dated 10 October, to Father Norbert Shee at Bar-sur-Aube, was optimistic.[35] He was ready to extricate the college from its present difficulties :

> Since I wrote to Father MacDermot[36] we had a great many regulations in this unfortunate house. I believe you know that the students were provided with cloaths, linnen, shoes, stockings, by the community. The only chance [charge] in this expense, they only get bread and small beer for breakfast. Three who came with me from Ireland are obliged to return

29. *Ibid.*, p. 379.
30. *Ibid.*, . 375.
31. *L.C.T.*, ii, 299.
32. 'Extrait des registres de la cour de Parlement, 10 mai 1764', *L.C.T.*, iii, 481.
33. Archives Communales de Lille, C 622, d. 12, cited in Burke MSS.
34. 'A son Excellence Monseigneur le Duc de Choiseul, Ministre de la Guerre a la Cour', *L.C.T.*, iii, 481. The letter appears to have been written in 1766.
35. *Ibid.*, 627.
36. Father Bartholomew MacDermot was a member of the Capuchin community at Bar-sur-Aube.

wich is better than to see them exposed to greater expenses than they can well afford.

This and several other circumstances contribute very much to the misery into wich a superior sees himself plunged without any possibility of relief.

Now, my dear Sir, I just take the liberty of asking you in a familiar manner, do the reverend fathers think it convenient to give me a nomination or not? If not, I beg you to press them as I am uneasy about a place where I suffer too much in seeing honest peoples' children distressed without hope of being able to redress their situation, neither do I refuse it as by being legally nominated. I have a certainty wich is necessary, I beg you will act for a person who is with the greatest sincerity.

Geoghegan secured his nomination; he was the last superior of the college. No documentary evidence has survived to tell of the last phase of the seminary. A pre-revolutionary review of all the Irish continental colleges gives the smallest enrolment at Lille—eight students.[37]

There was an Irish admixture when the revolution reached flashpoint on 14 July 1789. Did Joseph Kavanagh, an Irish cobbler of Lille, lead the attack on the Bastille?[38] Certainly, Irish figures were involved in the tragic happenings at Lille. In April 1792 General Theobald Dillon, a native of Dublin, advanced from Lille to meet the invading Austrians. Through a misunderstanding Dillon's troops believed that they had been betrayed and fled in panic. Dillon was hacked to pieces by the populace in the streets of Lille.[39] In the following year the college was engulfed in the torrent of revolution.

When compensation was claimed for Irish losses under the peace treaty of 1816 Lille college was valued at 20,000 francs. The buildings were demolished in the early years of the present century. The site in rue de la Vignette, Lille, is now occupied by houses.

---

37. Healy, *Centenary History of Maynooth College*, app. x, p. 696.

38. Hayes cites a contemporary pamphlet, *Exploits glorieux du célèbre Kavanagh, cause première de la Révolution Française*, cf. *Biographical Dictionary*, p. 132.

39. Thiers, *The History of the French Revolution*, p. 90.

SUPERIORS AND STUDENTS

The following list of superiors has been extracted from the sources noted.

Christopher Cusack, 1610
Laurence Sedgrave, 1614[40]
Martin Lalor, 1628[41]
James Dempsey, 1640[42]
Christopher Cusack, 1647[43]

John Egan, 1682
Charles Dempsey, 169C
Michael Kinnin, 1721[44]
Peter Furlong, 1763[45]
Patrick Geoghegan, 1776[46]

Only fragmentary lists of students' names are found. The following were admitted or were in residence at the dates noted.

1628[47]
Patrick Lynch
William Cunegan

Dominick Roche

1633[48]
James Achy, Meath
George Nasson, Connacht
Matthew Duff
Laurence Plunket
Parrat (*sic*) Ledwich

Barnaby Faral
Felix Faral
Peter Daly
Robert King
William Nugent

1634[49]
Nicholas French

40. 'De Actis Vicariatus Tornacensis, 1614', *L.C.T.*, i, 79.

41. 'A copie of R. father Francis Nugent, fundator of the Irish Colledge in Lille to the then prefect Mr Martin Lalor, 1628', *ibid.*, 213.

42. 'Father Joseph Corbally to the bishop of Tournai, 18 March 1640', *L.C.T.*, i, 139.

43. Christopher Cusack, Patrick Dempsey, John Egan, and Charles Dempsey (*infra*) and their dates of election are mentioned in the submissions of the provisors to the supreme court of Flanders, 1724, *L.C.T.*, ii, 189.

44. 'Nomination comme prefet de Michel Kinnin, 1721', *ibid.*, 17.

45. 'Certificate in favour of Fr Peter Furlong, 1764', *ibid.*, 253.

46. 'Geoghegan to Norbert Shee, 10 October 1776', *L.C.T.*, iii, 627.

47. 'Sedgrave to Nugent, 10 July 1628', *T.T.*, iii, 213.

48. 'Mementoes for the understanding of my severall doings (Nugent), 1633', *ibid.*, 145.

49. Acta S. Cong. de Prop. Fid. 1634-35, vol. 10, f. 19. French was bishop of Ferns 1646-78.

1643[50]

John Callaghan, priest, Munster
William Quealy, priest, Limerick
John Casey, priest, Westmeath
Peter Fay, priest, Westmeath
Maurice Cross, priest
James Archbold, priest
Thomas Barnewall
James Fitzgerald
James Kennedy
Christopher Wesley
Richard Dorner
Christopher Cusack

William Barnewall
William Walsh
James O'Brien
Martin Conor
Nicholas Swesty
Constantine O'Neill
Edward Wesley
Edward Gunther
Patrick Dempsey
Dominick Walsh
Edward Walsh
Edmund Bilgi (sic)

1650[51]

Gerard Faral, priest
Thomas Dalton, priest
John Lyredan, priest
George Barnewall, priest
John Balt, priest
Thomas Sweetman
Daniel Carroll

John Sarsfield
Peter Flood
Martin Lalor
Thaddeus Doherty
Richard Behan
Richard Faral
William Bathe

1678[52]

George Barnewall, priest
Gerald O Faral
John Syvedam [Sweetman]
Daniel Carroll
Peter Flood
Thaddeus Dempsey
Richard Faral

John Biet, priest
Thomas Dalton
James Dillon
John Sarsfield
Martin Lalor
Richard Behan
William Bath

50. Signatories to a protest by students against false charges, 1643, *L.C.T.*, i, 143.
51. Signatories to a petition to the bishop of Tournai asking the appointment of William Becham as superior, Arch. départementales, Lille, cited in Burke MSS.
52. Signatories to a petition requesting the bishop of Tournai to ensure the appointment of a Leinsterman as superior, *L.C.T.*, i, 153.

1691[53]

— Russell
— Dowdall
— Murphy
— Roche
— Moore
Christopher Dempsey
Nicholas Dempsey
Bartholomew Dempsey
Laurence Dempsey
— Archdeacon
— Peppard

Richard Foster
James Foster
— Toole
— Nelan
— St Leger
—Faye
— Hickey
— Plunket
— Neville
— Gilfoyle
— Duigan

1760-64[54]

Mr MacDermot
Thomas Wildon
Thomas Dowling
James Power
John Ledwige
Thomas Daly
Philip Farral
Edward O Brien, Palmerstown
Christopher Wogan, Kildare
Patrick Geoghegan, Westmeath
Patrick Hevey, Meath
Michael Betagh, Westmeath

Peter Keogh
John Sheridan
Gerald O Faral, Westmeath
Michael Caffry, Westmeath
Delany Major
Delany Minor
Patrick Dowling, Leix
Denis Clark, Kildare
James Callan, Dublin
James MacEvers, Westmeath
James Doran, Leix.

1769

— Delany[55]   Thomas Geoghegan[56]

53. List of students attending courses in the Jesuit college at Lille.
54. Nominations to the college by Father Robert Shee, *L.C.T.*, iii, 569.
55. Nephew of M. l'Abbé Moore, chez Madame la Comtesse de Laurag-
nais, rue de l'universite, Paris, *ibid.*, 571.
56. Son of Murtagh Geoghegan and Catherine Dolly [Daly], born
Durrow, 1754. Captain Mathias Geoghegan of Bulkeley's regiment demanded a free place in the college for his nephew. Father Peter Furlong
replied on 10 November 1768 to Father Robert Shee: 'I can assure you,
as I did in my last that the provisors and I would desire with all the veins
of our hearts [to]]receive as many subjects as you would desire, were the
revenues able to support them. You ought to be the more easily persuaded
of my sincerity on this point in that I have had [students] to the number
21 and the house is vastly indebted at my entrance.' *Ibid.*, 571.

1771
— Wettan[57]   — Reynolds
— Brynn [Byrne]
1773
James Whelan[58]

In the rawness and ugliness of revolution there was no longer a place in France for Irish educational endeavour. For the Irish bishops replacement of the suppressed foundations abroad must be on Irish soil : in the bright light of toleration all things seemed possible. Gardiner's bill of 1782 allowed Catholics to conduct schools, and the penal statutes forbidding parents to send their children overseas for education were repealed. The relief bill of 1793—Pitt's own handiwork—was a generous measure of religious and political freedom. The loss of the colleges might yet be turned to gain.

Nevertheless, 1793 was a year of dilemma for the bishops. Prior to the revolution most of the future priests of Ireland were in the seminaries in France.[59] A solution must be found quickly. In the

57. A statement of income by the bursar noted the receipt of 900 livres in payment of pensions by the above students, *ibid.*, 553.

58. Son of Denis and Mary Whelan, born Dublin 1762. Because of his youth he was admitted to study humanities, *ibid.*, 575.

59. The following is an undated pre-revolutionary survey of the continental colleges:

Paris	Masters	Students
(a) Collège des Lombards ...	4	100
(b) Collège du Cheval Vert ...	3	80
Nantes	3	80
Bordeaux	3	40
Douai	2	30
Toulouse	1	10
Lille	1	8
Total in France	17	348
Louvain	2	40
Antwerp	2	30
Salamanca	2	32
Lisbon	2	16
Rome	2	16
Total on the continent	27	478

Report by Andrew Dunne, 5 April 1808, secretary to the trustees of the Royal college of St Patrick, Maynooth, to James Trail, under secretary in the civil department of the Chief Secretary's office, Dublin castle—Healy, *Centenary History of Maynooth College*, app. x, p. 696.

present circumstances there was an imperious need for some form of state recognition of clerical education in Ireland.

A preliminary step was to set forth to the Holy See the grievous consequences of the suppressions in France. This was the theme of a letter signed by nine bishops on 5 December 1793 to Cardinal Antonelli, prefect of the Propaganda congregation.[60] A gentle hint was given that a proposal to the Dublin parliament was contemplated. A month later, Archbishop Troy of Dublin on behalf of the bishops of Ireland addressed a memorial to the lord lieutenant, the earl of Westmoreland.[61] The bishops begged his excellency's recommendation of a royal licence to secure funds legally towards the erection of an establishment for the training and education of priests. Despite the negative reception by Westmoreland the bishops persevered at a higher level. A bill was drafted in January 1795 at the direction of Earl Fitzwilliam during his brief term as lord lieutenant. The measure was introduced to parliament on 24 April by Pelham, chief secretary, and was rapidly passed through all its stages. On 5 June the royal assent was given to 'An Act for the better Education of persons professing the Popish or Roman Catholic religion'.[62] So the Royal College of St Patrick, Maynooth, came to life with an annual grant of £8,000. The warnings of Burke went unheeded; the bishops judged that they had won a victory for the Church and the Constitution.[63] They were the children of light!

Understandably, the texture and pattern of the new college was French. The first enrolment between June and December 1795 numbered forty students, almost all of whom had been driven from France by the revolution. Recruitment of the professorial staff was French : Delort of the university of Bordeaux, Aherne, fellow of the Sorbonne and formerly professor of philosophy in the university of Paris, Delahogue, fellow of the Sorbonne, Abbé Darré, and Anglade of the university of Paris. The obvious continuity

60. Healy, *op. cit.*, app. ii, p. 659.
61. *Ibid.*, app. i, p. 657.
62. *Ibid.*, app. vi, p. 666.
63. 'Be well assured that they never did and that they never will consent to give one shilling of money for any other purpose than to do you mischief. If you consent to put your clerical education, or any other part of your education under their direction or control then you will have sold your religion for their money.' Burke to Hussey, 17 March 1795, *Correspondence of the Rt. Hon. Edmund Burke*, iv, p. 298.

with the lost colleges in France—even the use of French in the community—drew scathing criticism.[64]

The French mists soon faded. An abounding life filled the new buildings that quickly grew around the house of John Stoyte, sometime steward of William Robert, second duke of Leinster and twenty-first earl of Kildare. Here was the hope for the future.

64. Cox's *Irish Magazine,* April 1808.

Chapter Five

THE FATE OF THE IRISH ENDOWMENTS

In the early weeks of 1795 France, says Thiers, 'returned with intensity of feeling to pleasurable enjoyments and to the refinements of civilisation.'[1] The National Convention gave serious thought to the tasks of reconstruction. Evidence of returning sanity was a decree of the newly-formed directory on 24 November 1795 demanding a restoration of their property to the former Irish, English, and Scottish colleges. Yet nobody had any idea of the extent or limitations of such a formidable undertaking.

Decrees of sequestration accompanied the closure in 1793 of the Irish foundations at Nantes, Douai, Lille, Bordeaux, and Toulouse. A similar fate befell the older institution in Paris, the collège des Lombards. Probably because it had paid the *contribution mobiliaire* the college in rue du Cheval Vert had the benefit of a temporary exemption. Suppression also was the lot of the English college in rue des Postes, Paris, the Scots college in the quartier St Victor, the secular, Franciscan, and Benedictine houses at Douai, the Liège academy, St Anthony's, Louvain, along with nine communities of English nuns.[2] Whenever the question of compensation would arise the claims would be heavy.

In Ireland there was a stirring of the national consciousness of losses sustained. As early as 1791 the bishops appointed Dr John Baptist Walsh of the diocese of Killaloe, superior of the Lombard college, and Abbé Charles Kearney, superior of the seminary in rue du Cheval Vert, as their official agents in France.[3] In particular, their duty was to keep a careful watch on the extensive Irish property, movable and immovable, then under threat. The agents were given little chance of exercising their responsibility; both were imprisoned in 1793. After his release in 1795 Walsh set to work but soon the bishops had misgivings—Walsh was too pliant an instrument of the French.

Although the bishops were careful not to make any statement of policy, there was widespread belief that their intention was to repatriate Irish educational funds. Franco-Irish elements and the

---

1. *History of the French Revolution,* p. 519.
2. The Benedictines of Ypres, Cambrai, Dunkirk, Paris, the Poor Clares of Gravelines, Dunkirk, Aire, and the Augustinianesses of Paris and Rouen.
3. Kearney was a native of Cashel, Co. Tipperary. He was involved in 1793 in a plot to effect the escape of Louis XVI. Camille Desmoulins saved Kearney from the guillotine, Hayes, *Biographical Dictionary,* p. 135.

United Irishmen émigrés were ready to offer strong resistance to the proposal. Then came intervention by Napoleon Bonaparte. As First Consul, Napoleon supported plans to re-open the channels of education. A move by the Prytanée or university of France to harness all educational foundations and revenues had his support. Nonetheless, he was sensitive of the blow to French prestige with the departure of foreign students. An Irish re-emergence in the educational sphere would be welcomed. Meanwhile, the Irish bishops took steps to forestall any invasion of Irish rights by appointing Dr Peter Flood, former superior of the Lombard college, Paris, and now president of Maynooth, as their accredited agent to negotiate with the French government. Flood's association with the new foundation at Maynooth gave firm basis to the belief that the bishops intended to repatriate Irish funds. But Walsh was not so easily thrust aside; he secured his own nomination as administrator general of British foundations in France.

With the signing of the peace of Amiens and the proclamation of the concordat with the Holy See in 1802 tensions between the Church and Bonaparte were relaxed. Flood made a diplomatic move to safeguard Irish interests when he suggested a union of all former Irish foundations and their revenues in the surviving college in rue du Cheval Vert, Paris.[4] Walsh rightly divined that this was a deliberate move towards transferring Irish funds to Maynooth.

Flood's suggestion to unify all the former Irish foundations in one college commended itself to Napoleon. On 17 October 1802 he decreed the union of the seminaries at Antwerp, Louvain, Lille, Douai, Nantes, Bordeaux, Toulouse, and the former English and Scots colleges, in one institution—the college in rue du Cheval Vert, Paris. The federated institute was entitled *Le Séminaire-collège des Irlandais, Anglais, Écossais réunis.*[5] Walsh, distrusted by Irish claimants to confiscated property, was named superior.[6] His assistants were Henry Parker, O.S.B., and Casimir MacNulty, *ci-devant* Capuchin of the Irish community at Vassy. Control and administration were vested in a *bureau de surveillance* of which the chairman was the archbishop of Paris. The latest innovation

---

4. Cf. *Louvain Papers,* ed. Jennings (Ir. MSS. Comm., 1968), p. 597.
5. Maynooth College, MS. Calendar of Long Papers.
6. 'Luke Bellew of Douai to James Cowan, O.F.M., Louvain, 13 May 1803', *Louvain Papers,* p. 597. To mark the federation Walsh proposed to strike a medal engraved: *Hiberni, Scoti, Angli pro fide et literis in Gallice hospites.*

was wholly unacceptable to the Irish bishops but Archbishop Troy's protest on 6 January 1803 was ignored.

Little success attended the new venture. There were no incoming students from Ireland or indeed from anywhere else. Walsh felt justified in handing the college over to Abbé Fontanel as a school for French boys. When Napoleon realised that his plan was far from realisation he made another effort. In August 1805 as part of a scheme of reorganisation he gave the institute a new constitution[7] and threatened that if Irish students did not avail themselves of the facilities offered he would disburse the revenues amongst Franco-Irish families. But the outbreak of war with England, Austria, and Russia delayed further developments. To keep the institute going and the burses viable Walsh admitted young laymen, students of law and medicine, officer cadets of the lycée Napoleon, all of Franco-Irish parentage.[8] The draw on the college funds was heavy but heaviest on the Irish. A statement of accounts, dated 17 March 1807, noted Irish revenues of 75,000 francs.[9]

At length it was borne in on Napoleon that a revival of the Irish colleges in any form must be sponsored by some prominent Irish figure acceptable not only in France but also in Ireland. Dr Bartholomew Crotty, superior of the Irish college at Lisbon, was known to be in favour of an Irish educational restoration in France.[10] In 1806 Lisbon was occupied by French troops under the command of General Junot who as former ambassador to Portugal was on terms of friendship with Crotty. Junot invited Crotty's participation in Napoleon's plan of revival. A suggestion was made, probably by Walsh, that the Irish students at Lisbon should be transferred to Paris, thus establishing a strong Irish nucleus. The rectorship was offered to Crotty. When details of the latest move by Bonaparte reached the Irish bishops their reaction was vehement. At a special meeting of the trustee-bishops of Maynooth held in Dublin on 24 January 1807 Napoleon's proposals were repudiated and Crotty was warned that ecclesiastical censures would fall

7. MS. Calendar of Long Papers, 32. Cf. *Louvain Papers,* 611.
8. See Appendix 2.
9. 'Extract from the minutes of the *bureau de surveillance*', Calendar of Long Papers, p. 68.
10. Crotty was born in Clonakilty, Co. Cork, 1769. He was appointed superior of Lisbon college in 1801, and president of Maynooth college in 1813. He died bishop of Cloyne in 1846.

on all Irish participants. The bishops were emphatic in their statement :[11]

> We feel it our duty to declare in the most unequivocal terms our reprobation of such attempts to seduce the youth of your house; and we are determined to use the authority vested in us in order to prevent even the possibility of excuse on the part of the students of our respective dioceses who might attempt to accept of that insidious offer.

One fact was now crystal clear : the Irish bishops were resolutely opposed to any revival of Irish educational effort under the auspices of Bonaparte. In France, failure of the plan for the federated college was placed to the discredit of Walsh. In July 1808 he was removed from office as administrator-general of British foundations in France; his successor was Richard Ferris, doctor of law and theology, canon of Amiens, a fanatical supporter of the Napoleonic *régime*—and the evil genius of the Irish in France.[12] The bishops in Ireland were powerless. Ferris, however, addressed a pamphlet to the Catholics of England, Scotland, and Ireland : *État actuel des Établissements et Collèges britanniques conservés en France et dans les Pays-Bas autrichiens.*[13] He charged Walsh, his predecessor, with maladministration and peculation and warned the Irish bishops that legal and other difficulties forbade the transfer to Maynooth of Irish funds held in France. Bonaparte had little time to consider Irish affairs; he was heavily committed to the Peninsular war.

With the fall of Napoleon in March 1814 the trend of events in France bore a more favourable complexion for the Irish bishops. Negotiations with a restored Bourbon, Louis XVIII, would be more amiable. Dr Paul Long, parish priest of Coolock in the diocese of Dublin, was sent to Paris to present Irish demands.[14] The new French government was conciliatory; Ferris was dismissed and Long appointed administrator of British foundations. The Napoleonic *bureau de surveillance* was abolished and a *bureau*

---

11. Healy, *op. cit.*, p. 398.
12. Ferris was a native of Tralee, Co. Kerry. He forsook his priesthood and married. He served as quarter-master in Napoleon's army of the Rhine. He is said to have been a secret agent of Pitt, Hayes, *op. cit.*, p. 87.
13. Calendar of Long Papers, p. 19.
14. Long's commission was signed by Archbishop O'Reilly of Armagh, Archbishop Troy of Dublin, Archbishop Bray of Cashel, Beresford, lord mayor of Dublin, Wellington, British ambassador in Paris.

gratuit was established comprising Franco-Irish figures. In September 1814 Long achieved another diplomatic feat when he persuaded the government to repeal the federating decrees of 1802 and 1805. Henceforth the Irish college in rue du Cheval Vert would be recognised juridically and historically as a purely Irish foundation. Thus encouraged, Long began to restore the clerical character of the college. Meanwhile, Ferris continued his pamphlet campaign against the Irish bishops. Dr Murray, coadjutor archbishop of Dublin, arrived in Paris to lead a new effort in the restoration of Irish property.

Dr Murray made no secret of his purposes—to secure the repatriation of Irish funds. Formidable opposition was raised by Irish officers in the French military service. On 24 December 1814 a memorial was presented to the ministry of the interior bearing the signatures of fifty-five distinguished Franco-Irish officers, some of them veterans of the former Irish brigades, whose names were deeply inscribed in French military history.[15] The memorialists deplored the attempts by Dr Long 'to obtain a new administration for the purpose of transporting these foundations to Ireland, to apply them to the college of Maynooth.' They urged that such a course would be a nullification of the founders' intentions. Why endow such an establishment as Maynooth 'a stranger to us?' There were approving voices among the United Irishmen. Miles Byrne, the doughty veteran of the '98 insurrection in Wexford and comrade of Robert Emmet, heaped contempt on the proposed transference of Franco-Irish funds and endowments to a country where Catholic emancipation was still denied:[16]

> It appeared strange to see the bishops attempting such a transfer before they had any hopes of emancipation. To be sure it was one way of shewing their devotion to their taskmasters, to deprive the Irish rebel and exile of the means of having his son well educated in France, in the event of another war between the two countries.

Napoleon's escape from Elba in March 1815 cut short the arguments. During the Hundred Days Long was obliged to return to

15. Among the signatories were: Maréchal Duc de Tarente MacDonald, Le Comte O'Shée, Lieut. Général O'Mahony de l'Ordre de St Louis, Lieut. Général Daniel O'Connell, Lieut. Général Dillon, MacSheehy, doctor of the king's quarters, MacMahon, chief of the medical department of Paris, cf. O'Connell, *The Last Colonel of the Irish Brigade*, ii, 322.
16. *Memoirs of Miles Byrne* (Dublin, 1907), p. 269.

Ireland—and Ferris was reinstated. Following the final overthrow of Bonaparte at Waterloo an allied army occupied Paris. Terms of peace now included a war indemnity for accumulated losses to British property since 1793. On 20 November 1815 a treaty was signed between Britain and France under which the French government accepted the obligation to make compensation for losses of British property during the years of revolution and war. The Irish college foundations and their endowments fell into the category of British losses. Talk of restoration and repatriation of funds was now meaningless; Irish demands on France must henceforth be stated in terms of compensation. At once Dr Long returned to Paris to prepare the presentation of Irish losses. So the struggle for the Irish endowments entered upon its second phase.

In Paris the machinery was set up to hear all claims for compensation as set forth under the ninth article of the treaty of November 1815. A mixed commission of French and English members was established to examine relevant documents. Within the time prescribed and in the approved form Dr Long presented the Irish case. The statement of claim included a valuation on immovable and movable property, arrears of revenues, misappropriation, and reimbursement of capital. Among the Long papers one finds itemised claims, e.g. the value of burses centralised in the college in rue du Cheval Vert is 51,619 francs.[17] An undated MS. without title estimates the revenues of the colleges at Douai, Louvain, Nantes, Bordeaux, Toulouse, and Lille as £13,860-8-4.[18] A complete statement of Irish claims was made in 1857 by the minister for Public Instruction: a figure of almost two and a half million francs.[19]

Before official consideration was given to Long's statement of losses a series of political manoeuvres placed obstacles in the way of the Irish, English, and Scottish claimants. On 17 September 1817 an *ordonnance du roi* decreed that henceforth all foreign colleges were subject to the French government. The decision was obviously directed against the college in rue du Cheval Vert—the only extant foundation—where Long in his efforts to restore the clerical character of the seminary had dismissed lay burse holders.

17. MS. État des revenus des Bourses Irlandaises, noted in the Calendar of Long Papers, p. 52.
18. *Ibid.*
19. Quoted by Boyle, *The Irish College in Paris,* pp. 74-75. Ward estimated the Irish colleges claims at more than £80,000, *The Eve of Catholic Emancipation* (London, 1912), iii, 130.

The *bureau gratuit* in charge of foreign foundations was abolished and a new body was set up which included the irrepressible Ferris. To counter the ill-effects of the decree Dr Poynter, vicar apostolic of the London district, Dr Paterson, coadjutor vicar apostolic of Edinburgh, and Dr Murray, coadjutor archbishop of Dublin, went to Paris and had audience of Louis XVIII. The king was sympathetic but unhelpful. Murray stated the fundamental reasons for the Irish claims.[20]

> The Irish establishments were acquired by Irishmen out of their own money—that they are destined exclusively for the Irish and according to the titles or acts of foundation those who nominate to the burses are either the Bishops of Ireland or with their approbation the relatives of the founders, that these Bishops have been in the peaceable enjoyment of this property until the Revolution; that Buonaparte misused the said property by allowing it to be enjoyed by persons not entitled to it, and particularly when he placed it under the control of the superintending Board, the members whereof may perhaps be neither Catholics or even Christians, that the power of recalling superiors given to the Minister of the Interior is unjust and dangerous; that these establishments were never confided by the founders to the administration of the French government but that the Catholic Bishops of Ireland are the natural and exclusive administrators of these establishments.

Refusal by the French government to surrender vital documents relative to the colleges' claims brought strong protests from Poynter and Paterson. At length M. Lainé, minister of the interior, requested the observations of the *bureau gratuit*. In a long memorandum the *bureau* reviewed the historical and juridical status of the colleges in the French economy. An entirely new issue was raised, namely, what competence had the bishops of Ireland, England, and Scotland? Emphasis was laid on the fact that the founders of burses acted without reference to bishops. There was no pretext for the assumption that the burses or the funds were ever at the disposal of any foreigner. The burses must be regarded as religious institutions similar to all colleges and communities which the munificence of French kings or the piety of the faithful had endowed for religious purposes in the kingdom of France.

20. Cork diocesan archives, Murphy Papers.

Clearly, the Irish bishops were targets for French obstructionists. Although Ferris was excluded from the *bureau gratuit* some months later (18 January 1819) one must suspect his hand in the following *exposé*.[21]

> These foundations established in France for the express purpose of withdrawing British subjects from the influence of their own government in matters of religion could not be kept too much disengaged from that influence and it was supposed that they would be more secured from it under the protection of French prelates and under the protection of the King of France than under the superintendence of prelates residing in Great Britain who must always depend more or less upon English authority. But if it was upon any foreign power it was still more essential to the dignity of the King of France that no other authority but his should give superiors to houses which existed by his permission. All discipline being by its own nature under the safeguard of the magistrate and consequently under the authority of the Prince, he can of course allow of none that does not emanate either directly or indirectly from himself. It is manifest besides that foreign prelates could not without great inconvenience have a right to send into France as administrators men suspected by their own government or dangerous for the government of the King.
>
> In short, it must be acknowledged that houses filled with young strangers and governed arbitrarily by strangers who acknowledge no other superiors than foreign prelates must present a spectacle very incompatible with the dignity of the Throne and perhaps not very well suited to the safety of the country. Our Kings have permitted that young British ecclesiastics should be educated in France, but they never intended that by a privilege which no community ever yet enjoyed these same young men and their superiors should form in the state a sort of republic quite independent of every religious control and of every civil authority.

For the diocese of Cork because of its traditional associations with the colleges at Bordeaux and Toulouse nomination to burses

---

21. *Ibid.*, Murphy Papers, no. 12: Observations presented to the Minister of the Interior by the Gratuitous Board of Administration for British establishments conformably to his desire signified in his letter of 31 January 1818.

formerly attached to these seminaries but now included with the endowments at Paris was of crucial importance. Since the days of Bonaparte the *bureau gratuit* exercised the sole right of nomination. Bishop Murphy of Cork (1815-47) challenged the procedure when he nominated a student named O'Hea, a native of Ross diocese, to the Callanan burse, a foundation in favour of Cork diocese formerly held at Toulouse. M. Mourré, president of the *bureau gratuit,* in letter to Bishop Murphy on 10 June 1818, summarily rejected the nomination on the grounds that O'Hea was a native of Ross, not of Cork diocese.[22]

Meanwhile, the Franco-British commission dealing with claims made little progress. Bickering among the members was a constant irritant. In addition, there was an overwhelming French anxiety to get rid of a foreign army of occupation. Finally, a new convention was signed by the two countries on 25 April 1818 which put an end to the mixed commission. An agreement was reached whereby the French government allocated a sum of seventy million francs bearing a perpetual annunity of three and a half million francs payable to British commissioners. All claims and awards were no longer a French responsibility; such matters were now in the competence of the British government.

Anticipating a complex situation, Father J. B. Kinsella, at the request of the Irish bishops, went to Paris to survey the prospects of Irish claims. Two letters from Kinsella in 1822 exposed the weakness and uncertainties of the Irish case.[23] Legal documentary proofs of ownership of movable and immovable goods were lacking. There were insufficient legal proofs concerning origins and investments of the burses. Moreover, the suppressed colleges were not corporate institutions in law. In other words, titles of ownership to property and revenues passed from superior to succeeding superior. In the absence of such legal instruments Kinsella was pessimistic as to the success of Irish claims in London.

In April 1819 under a special act of the imperial parliament statutory powers were vested in three commissioners to adjudicate upon all British demands for compensation. The stage was then set in London for the third phase of the fight to recover Irish losses.

Religious claims were placed last in the lists for hearing. By 1823 some 900 claims had been examined and 505 had been liquidated

22. *Ibid.*
23. *Ibid.,* nos. 13a and 13b.

⌄ 𝔧0 per cent of their value.[24] Confronted with the magnitude of the religious claims the commissioners realised that they would be faced with a deficit even if the ultimate awards were only a partial liquidation. A decision was made to regard the English claims for the colleges at Douai, St Omer, and the seminary at Paris as a general precedent or test case; remaining Irish, Scottish, and English applications for compensation must stand or fall with the Douai award.[25] When Dr Poynter, vicar apostolic of the London district, declared his difficulty in procuring documentary evidence from France the commissioners waived the necessity for such proofs.

On 19 January 1824 the Douai claim was rejected. The commissioners held that the original purposes of the colleges at Douai, St Omer, and Paris were in conflict with British law, and, therefore, were illegal institutions. In the second place, the foundations for which compensation was now sought were French, not British, institutes and as such did not come within the terms of the ninth article of the treaty between France and Britain in 1815 nor within the limits of the convention of April 1818.

Sir James Mackintosh, M.P., an eminent jurist, advised an appeal to the privy council. On behalf of Dr Poynter and other English appellants Mackintosh assembled proofs that the colleges at Douai, St Omer, and Paris had always been recognised in Britain and France as British institutions whose personnel was entirely British. Judgment was given on 25 November 1825 by Lord Gifford, president of the privy council.[26] The appeal failed for two reasons :

(a) While it was recognised that the colleges mentioned were British in origin and supported by funds derived from Britain it was clear from the status accorded to them in French law that they were French, not British, corporations.

(b) The colleges owed their existence to purposes inconsistent with British laws. In the treaty compacts between Britain and France it was not visualised that such institutions could be subjects for compensation.

24. Ward, op. cit., iii, 141.
25. For Douai the claim was £45,000, St Omer £20,300, the college in Rue de Postes, Paris, £22,000, Ward, op. cit., iii, p. 128.
26. Knapp, Reports of Cases argued and determined before the Judicial Committee of His Majesty's Most Honourable Privy Council, 23 ff.

Encouraged by the confirmation of their own decisions by the privy council the commissioners published a notice in the *London Gazette* on 31 January 1826 eliminating the presentation of further Roman Catholic cases for compensation.

Obviously, such high-level judgment on what was regarded a test case was based on a parity between English and Irish claims. Yet such a parity either in law or in fact did not exist. On these grounds Dr Long resolved to state the Irish case in an appeal to the privy council.

Daniel O'Connell, M.P., conducted the appeal, assisted by counsel, Mr William Witham of Gray's Inn and Mr Michael Quin. O'Connell denied the parity between English and Irish foundations in France. The legal attitude to the Catholic Church was different in each country. In contrast to England, the secular or diocesan clergy had always been tolerated in Ireland, celebration of the Mass was never a capital offence, the relieving statutes had always been more liberally interpreted. The description of the Irish colleges at Paris, Nantes, Douai, Lille, Bordeaux, and Toulouse as French corporations was at variance with facts; they were not corporations at all. Ownership and title passed from préfet to succeeding préfet. The Douai decision bore no relevance to the Irish claims.

Sir John Leach, master of the rolls, gave judgment on 27 February 1832.[27] He held that a study of French law governing the status of the Irish colleges left no doubt that they were French corporations. While he dissented from the view expressed by Lord Gifford in 1825, namely, that the colleges in France existed for purposes inimical to British interests, the other factor was clear. The Hon. Thomas Erskine, chief judge of the bankruptcy court, concurred with the judgment.

Notwithstanding the adverse decisions of the privy council Dr Patrick MacSweeney of the diocese of Cork, Long's successor in the Irish college, Paris, was ready to resume the struggle. The fourth phase, however, was in France.

Revolution again in 1848 but with a difference. A bourgeois triumph made Louis Napoleon president of the French republic. The president was conscious of support from the Catholics, clergy and people, and was inclined to hearken to a plea from Dr

27. Knapp, *op. cit.*, The Case of the Irish Roman Catholic colleges in France: the Rev. Paul Long v. the Award of the Commissioners for Liquidating British claims on France, s.a. 1832.

MacSweeney to re-consider the Irish claims for the loss of colleges and endowments. Perhaps Lacordaire's panegyric on Daniel O'Connell in Nôtre Dame on 10 February 1848 gave the French people a new awareness of Ireland.

Fittingly, the initiative came from France. Archbishop MacHale of Tuam, Bishop Denvir of Down and Connor, and Bishop Cantwell of Meath were invited to Paris to meet a French commission of inquiry. The membership of the French commission helped create a favourable atmosphere : M. Leon Sibour, vicar general of Paris, M. Louis Buquet, representing the archbishop of Paris, and M. Isodore Goschler, superior of the Collège Stanislas, Paris, representing the minister for Public Instruction. Numerous sessions were held in the Irish college, Paris, during September 1849. The findings of the commission were presented to the minister for Public Instruction by the archbishop of Paris.

They were never made public. An anonymous pamphlet, clearly of French authorship, was put into circulation in Paris : *Mémoire sur les fondations Irlandaises en France*.[28] It gave unqualified support to the Irish demands, alleging that hostility in influential quarters prevented the restoration of Irish property as recommended by the commission. The *Mémoire* gave biting comments on the French expropriation of Irish funds.[29] The sum of 159,000 francs had been alienated to date !

At intervals during the following years Irish representations were made at Paris but with no effect. Hopes faded in 1870 when Napoleon III and his army capitulated to the Prussians at Sedan. Bearing the humiliation of defeat and a war indemnity of 200 million pounds France forgot Irish claims.

All was not yet over. In 1870 Father Thomas MacNamara, the Vincentian superior of the Irish college, Paris, with the support of the marquis of Clanricarde, resolved to make a final appeal to the British house of commons. Thus the last act in the struggle for the Irish funds and endowments was in London. On 8 May 1871 a meeting took place in the Westminster Palace hotel, London, attended by four Irish bishops and members of the Irish parliamentary party, at which steps were taken to seek a review of Irish

28. Copy in library, St Patrick's college, Maynooth.
29. '... ce qui constituait une véritable prodigalité, sans precédent, non-seulement dans l'histoire du collège, mais même dans celle des établissements nationaux de France les plus en renom et les plus richement dotes, soit que l'on considére le montant de l'indemnité, soit que l'on calcule les années réelles des services', *Mémoire*, p. 20.

claims. A petition, signed by fifty members of parliament, was laid before Mr W. Gladstone, prime minister and first lord of the treasury, urging the government not to oppose a motion calling for a select committee.[30] On 9 May 1872 Mr Serjeant Sherlock moved for a production of the correspondence between the treasury, the earl of Dunraven and the marquis of Clanricarde regarding the Irish demands. The commons directed the printing of the correspondence. At length, on 30 April 1875 Mr Isaac Butt, member for Limerick, moved at Westminster that a select committee be appointed to consider submissions from the Roman Catholic bishops of Ireland.

In his speech Mr Butt reviewed the background of the decision in 1832 by Sir John Leach, master of the rolls.[31] The question of compensation turned upon a point of fact : was the Irish college, Paris, a French or a British institution? He summarised the proofs that the college and its assets were owned and controlled by British subjects. Leach's judgment in 1832 found that the college was a French institution and for that reason not entitled to compensation. Mr Butt assured the house that the judgment contradicted evident facts.

(1) The property and endowments of the college were always in the hands of Irishmen and under their control. Neither the French government nor the French bishops administered Irish foundations.

(2) A decree of the National Assembly in 1789 recognised the immunity and extra-territorial character of the college.

(3) Irish priests in the college were exempted from the oath to the civil constitution of the clergy.

(4) When the French government decreed the confiscation of British-owned property in 1793 the Irish colleges and foundations were included.

(5) The mixed commission set up under the treaty of 1815 accepted and registered Irish claims and set aside the sum of £67,000 to meet the demand.

Mr Butt asserted that there was a residue in the treasury arising from the settlement made by the French government under the convention of 1818. He argued that he had made a *prima facie*

30. Boyle, *The Irish College in Paris*, p. 100.
31. Hansard, *Parliamentary Debates*, third series, vol. ccxxiii, 1916 ff.

case for a re-examination of the Irish claims by a select committee. The O'Conor Don, member for Roscommon, supported the motion. Sir S. H. Northcote, chancellor of the exchequer, moved the rejection of the motion. He stated that the machinery of law set up in 1818 was adequate to meet all claims on their merits. The judgment in 1825 which covered the Irish case was tested before the privy council again in 1832 and rejected. To admit the motion now before the house would be equivalent to placing a duty on the commons to pass judgment on the acts of the privy council—a course wholly unconstitutional. Mr Newdegate, member for Warwick, spoke against the motion. On a division Mr Butt's proposal was defeated by 116 votes to 54.

That a considerable sum of money remained in the treasury when the 'British Subjects Indemnity Fund' was wound up in 1826 is beyond doubt. Various estimates have been made.[32] From time to time payments were made out of it for public projects in England such as the erection of Marble Arch in 1851.[33] This allocation was later refunded. Ward quotes the tradition that the residue was expended partly in payment of the debt on Brighton Pavilion and partly in furnishing Winsdor castle.[34]

International honour was not entirely tarnished. The independent Belgian government established in 1830 readily acknowledged its obligations arising from former Irish educational foundations. The trustees of Maynooth college receive annually the now somewhat depleted revenues of Irish endowments administered by the provincial commission of Hainault, the archiepiscopal seminary of Malines, and the provincial commission of Brabant.[35] Thus, burses founded by Irishment in the seventeenth and eighteenth centuries to be held in Irish continental colleges have their nominees today in Maynooth college.

32. An anonymous pamphlet printed in Paris in 1870 states that in 1842 an inquiry lasting four days found that the residue amounted to £482,752-6-8, *A Brief Statement of the Claims of the Irish College, Paris, on the British Government in virtue of treaties with France*, printed by Cusset et Cie, rue Racine, Paris.
33. Donnelly, *Short Histories of the Dublin Parishes* (C.T.S., 1915), p. 28.
34. *Op. cit.*, iii, 149.
35. In recent years compensation has been paid for English Catholic losses in Spain. In 1767 Charles III expelled the Jesuits and confiscated the colleges at Madrid and Seville. In 1965 the Director-General of the Spanish finance ministry paid to the English college at Valladolid eight million pesetas (£42,000) in compensation for property confiscated in 1767.

IRISH EDUCATIONAL FOUNDATIONS IN FRANCE

1

BURSES

In the index room of the library, St Patrick's college, Maynooth, is a collection of materials, printed and in manuscript, relating to the Irish statement of claim for confiscated property, endowments, and revenues. There is no record of receipt of the papers but clearly they were assembled by Dr Paul Long, superior of the Irish college, Paris, and administrator of Irish foundations in France. It is most probable that after Long's death in 1837 the collection of documents was deposited in the library of Maynooth college. In 1950 the materials were calendared by the Rev. Joseph Kelly. In addition to consulting the MS. calendar I have been given. access to some original documents.

Internal evidence shows that the materials were used in the presentation of Irish claims to the French and British commissioners. Despite the decision in 1826 of the British commissioners to regard the rejection of the English Douai claim as a precedent for a refusal to hear the Irish case, there was an appeal to the privy council; Dr Long was the appellant. Presumably, the Irish claims were based upon the same documentary evidence.

IRISH BURSES

As we have seen, in 1802 all Irish educational foundations were concentrated in the surviving college in rue du Cheval Vert, Paris. Unfortunately, the Long papers throw little light on the distribution of burses among the other colleges in pre-revolutionary times. In MS. *État des revenus des bourses Irlandaises* we find a state- of the eighteenth century.[1] The omission of reference to earlier foundations underlines the lack of documentary evidence that had an adverse effect on the Irish statement of claim.

---

1. MS. calendar no. 41.

Munster

Diocese	Burse	Foundation date	Value
Cloyne and Ross	MacKenna[2]	1760	
	John O'Brien[3]		
Kerry	Moriarty[4]	1753	
	O'Connell[5]	1775	
	MacDonough[6]	1780	
	Aherne[7]	1748	
	Moore (2)[8]	1761	
	Malone[9]	1784	
Cork	Henegan[10]	1774	
	The Poor of Macroom		
	Duff O'Brien		
	O'Crowley[11]	1774	
	Callanan[12]	1779	
Cashel	O'Meagher[13]	1774	
	Butler[14]	1777	
	Lanan	1731	
	O'Carroll	1724	
Limerick	O'Hanrahan[15]	1781	
	O'Keeffe[16]	1704	
	MacCarthy[17]	1729	
Waterford	Connery	1761	
Killaloe and Kilfenora	O'Molony[18]	1702	
	Murray[19]	1761	22786 frs.

2. Matthew MacKenna, bishop of Cloyne (1767-91).
3. John O'Brien, bishop of Cloyne (1748-67).
4. Denis Moriarty, bishop of Kerry (1703-20).
5. Thaddeus O'Connell, M.D.
6. James MacDonough.
7. Eugene Aherne, P.P., Lixnaw.
8. Richard Moore, canon of Senlis, and Gerald Moore, canon of Montpellier.
9. John Malone, P.P., Castleisland.
10. David Henegan, Irish college, Paris.
11. Jeremiah O'Crowley, burse was transferred from Poitiers.
12. Claudius Callanan.
13. Mrs John O'Meagher, burse transferred from Poitiers.
14. James Butler II, archbishop of Cashel (1774-91).
15. John Hanrahan, P.P.
16. Cornelius O'Keeffe, bishop of Limerick (1720-37).
17. Tadhg MacCarthy Rabagh, bishop of Cork (1726-48).
18. John O'Molony, bishop of Killaloe (1671-98), Limerick (1698-1702).
19. Bartholomew Murray, M.D.

Leinster

Diocese	Burse	Foundation date	Value
Dublin	Fagan[20]	1733	
	FitzHerbert[21]	1763	
	Byrne[22]	1766	
	Austin	1728	
	Walsh	1732	
	O'Rorke[23]	1779	
	Burke		
Kildare	Rouse[24]	1781	
	Walsh	1715	
	MacCarthy		
	MacCormack[25]	1748	
	Duffy		
Meath	Plunket[26]		
	Barnewall		
Ardagh and Kilmore	Brady[27]	1774	
	MacCabe[28]	1761	
	Farelly (2)[29]		7819 frs.

Ulster

Diocese	Burse	Foundation date	Value
Clogher	MacMahon[30]	1714	
	Duffy[31]		
	O'Neill[32]	1751	
	MacCabe		
Down and Dromore	Maginn[33]	1682	
	Barnewell		
Armagh	Bannan[34]	1755	4838 frs.

20. Luke Fagan, archbishop of Dublin (1729-33).
21. William FitzHerbert.
22. Patrick Byrne, P.P., Wicklow.
23. Griselle O'Rorke.
24. Philip Rousse, P.P., Kildare.
25. Robert MacCormack, P.P., Carbery.
26. Abbé Plunket, College de Navarre.
27. Abbé John MacBrady, Tours.
28. Alexander MacCabe, P.P., Gartilitragh.
29. Farelly Brothers.
30. Arthur MacMahon, canon of the cathedral church, Cassel, Flanders.
31. Patrick and Bernard Duffy.
32. Henry O'Neill, curé de Fontaine le Rivière.
33. Abbé de Theulay, Langres.
34. Andrew Bannan, P.P., Disart.

Connacht

Diocese	Burse	Foundation date	Value
Tuam	Brown[35]	1788	
	Lynch[36]	1711	
	Old Priests		
	Flynn[37]	1754	
Galway	Chapter of St Nicholas		
Elphin	Daly[38]	1785	
	Stafford[39]	1781	
	Plunket[40]	1785	
Clonfert	Merrick[41]	1733	
Achonry	Morevanagh[42]	1716	3901 frs.

2

ALIENATION OF IRISH ENDOWMENTS

In the absence of Irish students the Napoleonic *bureau gratuit* in 1807 nominated young laymen, sons of Irish émigrés, to the burses. The lay burse holders were students of law, and medicine, and officer-cadets at the *lycée Napoleon*. In his statement of claim for compensation Dr Long supplied the names and personal details of the students who were educated on the strength of alienated Irish funds. The following is taken from a handwirtten document entitled : 'Liste des boursiers placés dans les Établissements Britanniques par Bonaparte jusqu'au ler novembre 1816'.[43]

Name	Birthplace	Admission	Designation
Corbet	Paris	1.10.1807	distinguished in French army; father a soldier

35. Nicholas Brown, Royal chaplain.
36. James Lynch, archbishop of Tuam (1669-1714).
37. Davil Flynn, Chaplain to James III.
38. Michael Daly, priest of Paris.
39. Thomas Stafford, superior, Lombard college.
40. John Plunket, collège de Navarre.
41. James Merrick, provisor, Lombard college.
42. Bernard Morevanagh, chaplain to Irish brigade.
43. MS. calendar no. 45.

Barker	St Germain	1. 8.1807	son of refugee officer because of rebellion, lost an arm in invasion of Ireland
St Leger	Paris	1. 8.1807	officer in French army
Lewins, Laurence	Dublin	1.10.1807	father sent to Ireland, returned, a teacher
Walsh, Theobald	Paris	15.11.1807	unknown
O'Shee	Paris	1.10.1807	son of Irish officer in Fr. service
O'Hegarty, James	Dublin	1. 1.1808	idem., in regt. of dragoons
Wall, Thomas		1. 1.1808	Idem.
O'Ryan	Munster	1.16.1808	native ot Kerry, medical student
Durham	Ireland	1. 8.1808	arrived from Portugal, no occupation
Comyn, Charles	Paris	1.18.1808	Fr. military service
Comyn, Augustine	Paris	1.10.1808	student of law
O'Farrell	France	1.12.1808	in the corps of guards
Meade, Stanislaus	France	1.10.1808	son of Irish officer in Fr. service
Healy	France	1.12.1808	officer in Fr. service
Burke, Raymond	Bordeaux	27. 3.1809	unknown
Burke, John	Bordeaux	27. 3.1809	unknown
O'Meara, John	Dublin	1.12.1810	son of officer in corps of guards
O'Sullivan, Gratian	Rennes	1. 1.1810	son of pensions official at Rennes
Plunket, Christopher	Brussels	1. 2.1811	son of Baron Plunket
Glashin, Thomas	Paris	1. 2.1811	son of 1798 refugee student of law
Armstrong, Thomas	Bordeaux	1.10.1811	son of Irish merchant at Bx.
Armstrong, Edward	Bordeaux	1.10.1811	idem.
Rogers, John	Dundalk	15. 9.1811	prisoner of war, now prefect of studies
Smith, Edmund	Boulogne	1.10.1811	son of 1798 refugee officer
Moore, Edmund	Paris	1. 6.1812	son of Irish doctor

O'Hegarty, Henry	Paris	1. 7.1811	son of officer in Ir. brigade
O'Meara, William	Dunkerque	1. 9.1813	idem.
Corr, Matthew	Brussels	1.11.1813	son of Irish refugee, shoemaker at Brussels
Collins, Philip	New York	18.10.1814	nephew of M. l'Abbé Collins
O'Connor, Arthur	Kerry	1. 5.1815	nephew of M. L'Abbé O'Connor, student of medicine

Claim : 43,260 frs.

Evidence of alienation of a different kind appears in a document entitled : 'État nominatif des prêtres envoyés de Rome'. In May 1809 Napoleon annexed the papal states including the city of Rome. Some months later British subjects residing in Rome were arrested. Irish priests were obliged to go to Paris. Expenses, lodgings, and maintenance were made a charge on Irish funds. The displaced Irish priests were :

Order of St Francis Matthew Creagh, John Lynch, Bonaventure Kavanagh, Nicholas Walsh, Francis Lanan, Peter Conway.
Order of St Dominic James Ryan, John Murphy.
Order of St Augustine Augustine Cooke, William Walsh, Thomas Condon, Terence Prendergast, William Ready, John Shea, — MacNally, — Keating, — Hayes.

Claim : 58,144.27 frs.

Another form of alienation was the disbursement of Irish funds to Irish émigrés in France. The details of payment are found in a document entitled 'État des donations faites à differentes personnes par ordre de Bonaparte et de Louis XVIII ou de leurs ministres aux dépense des Établissements Britanniques'.[44]

Name	Designation
MacMahon	student of medicine
O'Neill	idem.
MacSheehy[45]	General in the French service in Egypt
Aherne	secretary to General Daendels in Holland

44. MS. calendar no. 45.
45. Bernard Sheehy, native of Dublin, former student of Irish college, Paris; served in French army and organised the Irish legion in 1803.

Kearney[46]	formerly prefect
M. O'Riordan	Irish doctor
M. Gannon	priest refugee
M. Burgess	Irish painter
M. Glenon	Irishman
M. Burke[47]	constitutional priest
M. Cahill	student of medicine
M. Wilkes	former superior of English Benedictines
Widow Forbes	widow of officer in Irish brigade
M. Hickey	Irish priest
M. Murphy	former prefect of studies in Lombard college
M. Jackson	unknown
M. Lanan	Irish priest for his return to Ireland
M. G. Walsh	idem.
M. Plowden	teacher of languages
	Claim : 132,616.27 frs.

3

IRISH BURSES IN FORMER COLLEGES
IN THE BELGIAN NETHERLANDS

With the establishment of independent Belgain sovereignty in 1830 scrupulous regard was paid to capital investments of Irish origin. The Belgian government made a composition whereby current revenues are paid to Maynooth college. The foundations are administered by the provincial commissions of Malines, Hainult, and Brabant.

Founder	Description of burse
Pope Urban VIII	1624, three foundations, value 8000 florins.
Eugene Matthews[48]	1624 for students of the dioceses of Clogher and Dublin.
Maximilian Vilain[49]	1637, two foundations.

---

46. Charles Kearney, superior of Irish college, Paris, 1783-1800.
47. Abbé James Burke, Irish college, Bordeaux.
48. Bishop of Clogher 1609-11, archbishop of Dublin 1611-23.
49. Bishop of Tournai. Vilain drew up the statutes of the college at Lille. In his will he wrote: 'I have always entertained a warm affection for poor Irish students and after my death I would have recommended to the deans' chapter and other notables of Tournai as most deserving youths who have left their country for the faith.' Quoted by Meehan, *The Fate and Fortunes of the Earls of Tyrone and Tyrconnel*, p. 84.

James Normel	1653 for Munster students, preference to be given ot natives of Lismore and Clonmel, 993 fl.
John Sinnich[50]	1666 for natives of Munster, preference to be given to natives of Cork.
Irish Dominicans	1667
Hugh Mauritius	1680 for Connachtmen, preference to be given to natives of Galway, 2372 fl.
Nicholas French[51]	1683 for students of the diocese of Ferns.
Thomas Stapleton[52]	1688, preference to be given to natives of Fethard, Co. Tipperary, 325 francs.
Roger Nottingham	1692 for natives of Dublin, 1000 fl.
Thomas Hurley	1697 for natives of Limerick and Tipperary, 3200 fl.
Arnold O'Connolly	1715 for students of the dioceses of Clogher, 80 francs.
Denis O'Hederman	1715 for students of Munster, preference to be given to natives of Cork and Limerick.
Edmund Trahey[53]	1718, 585 fl.
Paul Roche[54]	1727 for students of the diocese of Ferns, three foundations, 6008 fl.
Michael Hennessy	1730, preference to be given to natives of Fethard, Co. Tipperary.
Raymond Magrath[55]	1734 for founder's kinsmen, 9402 fl.
Florence O'Sullivan[56]	1739 for descendants of O'Sullivans and MacCarthys of Kerry.
John O'Brien[57]	1769, 217 fl.
Helen Duignan	1770, 7848 fl.
Thomas Tyrell	1771, 4800 fl.
Columba Morgan	1777, 7044 fl.
John Kent[58]	1778 for natives of Lismore and Waterford, two foundations, 7002 fl.

50. Sinnich was born in Cork; primarius professor of philosophy in the collège du Porc, Louvain, appointed rector magnificus of the university in 1643. He was involved in the Jansenist controversy and is said to have compiled the index to Jansen's *Augustinus.*
51. Bishop of Ferns 1646-84.
52. Canon of the collegiate church of St Peter, Louvain, died 1694.
53. Doctor of medicine in Antwerp.
54. Parish priest, Forth, Co. Wexford.
55. Doctor in imperial medical services.
56. President of Pastoral college, Louvain.
57. Bishop of Cloyne 1748-67.
58. President of Pastoral college.

BIBLIOGRAPHY

A—Manuscript Materials—see Introduction

SECONDARY DOCUMENTARY SOURCES

B—Irish Manuscripts Commission

Analecta Hibernica, 1, 1930; Rawl. A.20; Thurloe Papers.
Commentarius Rinuccinianus, ed. Kavanagh, 1932-44.
Leabhar Muimhneach, ed. Torna, 1940.
Extents of Irish Monastic Possessions, ed. White, 1943.
Lynch, *Pii Antistitis Icon* (1669), 1952.
—— *De Praesulibus Hiberniae,* ed. O'Doherty, 1944.
Wadding Papers, ed. Jennings, 1953.
Spanish Knights of Irish Origin, ed. Walsh, 1960.
Wild Geese in Spanish Flanders, 1582-1700, ed. Jennings, 1964
Louvain Papers 1606-1827, ed. Jennings, 1968.

C—Catholic Record Society of Ireland, St Patrick's College, Maynooth

Archivium Hibernicum, I, 1912—Archives de le Hte Garonne : Boyle, Toulouse College.
—— II, 1913—Los Archivos del Real Colegio de San Patricio de Nobles Irlandeses Salamanca : Students of Irish College, ed. O'Doherty. Vatican archives : Borghese Papers.
—— III, 1914—Los Archivos *(supra)* continued. Miscellanea Vaticano-Hibernica, ed. Hagan.
—— IV, 1915—Los Archivos *(supra)* continued. Miscellanea Vaticano-Hibernica *(supra)* continued.
—— VI, 1917—Archivio Historica Nacional, Miscellanea Vaticano-Hibernica, continued.
—— VII, 1918-22—Vatican archives : the Nunciatures 1572-85.
—— X, 1943—Archives Générales du Royaume, Brussels : Documents of the Irish colleges at Douai, ed. Jennings.
—— XII, 1946—Archives de Prop. Fid., collegio St Isidore, Rome; archives gen. du Royaume, Brussels; Miscellaneous documents, ed. Jennings.
—— XIV, 1949—Continuation of *Arch. Hib.,* XII; Brit. Museum: *Exhibitio Consolatoria*; arch. de Prop. Fid. : The Irish Colleges in the Low Countries, ed. Brady.
—— XV, 1950—Miscellaneous Documents, ed. Jennings, continued from *Arch. Hib.,* XII; Some Records of the Irish College at Bordeaux, ed. Walsh.

—— XVIII, 1955—Arch. de Prop. Fid. : Letter-Book concerning
Ireland 1672-74, ed. Jennings, MSS. Barberini Latini, ed.
Giblin.
—— XIX, 1956—Arch. de Prop. Fid. : Ireland and Prop. Fide
1672-76.
—— XX, 1957—*Irish Franciscans in Poland,* ed. Jennings.
—— XXII, 1959—Acts S. Cong. de Prop. Fid. 1622-50, ed.
Jennings; Two Reports on the Catholic Church in early
17th century, ed. Corish.
—— XXIII, 1960—Vatican archives : Fondo Borghese I, 1592-
1621, ed. Conway.

D—Collectanea Hibernica, Franciscan House of Celtic Studies, Killiney, Co. Dublin

Collectanea Hibernica, 1, 1958—Vatican archives : *Nunziature di
Fiandra,* catalogue of material of Irish interest 1666-90,
ed. Giblin.
—— 3, 1960—idem.
—— 6 and 7, 1963-64—Arch. de Prop. Fid. : calendar of vol. 1,
1625-68 scritture nei rif. congressi, Irlanda, ed. Millett.
—— 8, 1965—Arch. de Prop. Fid. scritture orig. rif. nelle congreg.
generali, 1629-34, ed. Millett.
—— 9, 1966—Vatican archives : *Nunziatura di Fiandra,* catalogue
of material of Irish interest 1728-36, ed. Giblin.
—— 10, 1967—Arch. de Prop. Fid. : continuation of *Coll. Hib.,*
8, 1634-40; ed. Millet; *Nunziature di Fiandra,* 1737-64,
ed. Giblin.
—— 11, 1968—Arch. de Prop. Fid. : continuation of *Coll, Hib.,*
10, 1627-29, ed. Millet; *Nunziatura di Fiandra,* 1730-31, ed.
Giblin.

E—State Papers

Calendar of State Papers, Ireland (noted *C.S.P.*), 1509-1625.
Calendar of Venetian State Papers, 1603-07.
Calendar of Carew Papers, 1589-1624.
*Sixteenth Report of Deputy Keeper of the Public Records in
Ireland.*

F—Royal Society of Antiquaries of Ireland

Calendar of Archbishop Alen's Register, 1172-1534, ed. McNeill,
1950.

G—Periodicals, etc.
Cox's *Irish Magazine*, 1808.
The Irish Booklover.
Irish Ecclesiastical Record (noted *Ir. Ecc. Rec.*).
Irish Historical Studies.
Journal of the Cork Historical and Archaeological Society (noted *J.C.H.A.S.*).
Revue Catholique de Bordeaux.
Franciscan Round Table of Research, Wisconsin, U.S.A.
Recusant History, Catholic Record Society of England.
The Irish Sword.

H—Pamphlets
Mémoires historiques et chronologiques sur les séminaires établis dans le ville de Toulouse (Toulouse, 1852).
Mémoire sur les fondations Irlandaises en France (Paris, n.d.).
A Brief Statement of the Claims of the Irish College, Paris, on the British Government in virtue of the treaties with France (Paris, n.d.).

GENERAL BIBLIOGRAPHY

Allain, Abbé : *Inventaire sommaire des archives de l'archevêche de Bordeaux* (Bordeaux 1893).
Alzog : *Manual of Universal Church History,* trans. Pabisch and Byrne (Dublin 1880-82).
Anstruther, G. : *The Seminary Priests* (Durham 1969).
Archdall : *Monasticon Hibernicum* (Dublin 1873).
Ashley, M. : *Louis XIV and the Greatness of France* (Eng. Univ. Press 1946).
Bagwell : *Ireland under the Tudors* (London 1885).
Beales, A. C. : *Education under Penalty* (London 1963).
Belloc, H. : *The French Revolution* (London 1911).
—— *Characters of the Reformation* (London 1936).
Bertrand, Abbé : *Histoire des Séminaires de Bordeaux et de Bazas* (Bordeaux 1894).
Biest du : *Notes sur les archives des Capuchins Irlandais ayant en leur siège en France à Charleville, Sedan, Bar-sur-Aube et Vassy* (Reims 1924).
Bouglon de : *Les Réclus de Toulouse* (Toulouse 1912).
Boulenger, J. : *Le Grand Siècle* (Paris 1912).
Boyle : *The Irish College in Paris* (Dublin 1901).

Brady, J. : *Father Christopher Cusack and the Irish College of Douai* in *Measgra Mhichíl Uí Cléirigh,* ed. O'Brien (Dublin 1944).

Brady, M. : *Episcopal Succession* (Rome 1876).

—— *Clerical and Parochial Records of Cork, Cloyne and Ross* (Dublin 1863).

Brenan : *An Ecclesiastical History of Ireland* (Dublin 1864).

Brodrick, J. : *The Origin of the Jesuits* (London 1940).

Burgo, de : *Hibernia Dominicana,* 1762.

Burke, W. : *Irish Priests in Penal Times* (Waterford 1914).

Burke, Edmund : *On Irish Affairs,* ed. Arnold (London 1881).

—— *Correspondence of the Rt. Hon.* (London 1844).

Butler, W. : *Gleanings from Irish History* (London 1925).

Byrne, Miles : *Memoirs of,* ed. Gwynn (Dublin 1907).

Camm, Bede : *William Cardinal Allen* (London 1908).

Campion, Edmund : *Historie of Ireland* (Hibernia Press 1809).

Carlyle : *The French Revolution* (London 1891).

Caulfield, R. : *Council Book of the Cork Corporation* (Guildford 1876).

Clancy, J. : *Funeral Oration at the Obsequies of Dr Timothy O'Hurly* (Cork 1828).

Cogan : *The Diocese of Meath* (Dublin 1874).

Comet, Abbé : *St Loubés* (Bordeaux 1869).

Corish, P. : *The Origins of Catholic Nationalism* (Dublin 1968).

Curtis, ed. : *A History of Ireland* (Dublin 1923).

Cuthbert : *The Capuchins* (Lordon 1928).

Dickens, A. : *The Counter Reformation* (London 1968).

Donlevy, A. : *An Teagasg Críosduidhe* (Paris 1742).

Durengues, Abbé : *La Révolution dans le Lot et Garonne* (Bordeaux n.d.).

—— *Douai College Diaries 1598-1654,* ed. Burton and Williams, in *Catholic Record Society* (London 1911).

—— *Douai College, First and Second Diaries,* ed. Knox (London 1878).

Edwards, D. : *Church and State in Tudor Ireland* (Dublin 1935).

Edgeworth, Abbé : *Letters to his Friends* (London 1818).

—— *Lettres de l'Abbé Edgeworth confesseur de Louis XVI a ses amis* (Paris, 1818).

England, T. : *Life of the Rev. Arthur O'Leary* (London 1822).

Fitzmaurice and Little : *Materials for the History of the Franciscan Province of Ireland* (Manchester 1920).

Fitzgerald : *Cork Remembrancer* (Cork 1783).

Flower, R. : *The Irish Tradition* (Clarendon Press 1947).

Gaillard, Abbé : *La Baronnie de St Magne* (Bordeaux n.d.).

Gerard, J. : *The Autobiography of an Elizabethan,* ed. Caravan (London 1956).

Geyl, P. : *The Revolt of the Netherlands* (London 1932).

Gigot, J.-G. : *Inventaire sommaire des archives communales antérieures à 1815* (Chaumont 1948).

Hayes, R. : *Ireland and Irishmen in the French Revolution* (Dublin 1932).

—— *Irish Swordsmen of France* (Dublin 1934).

—— *Old Irish Links with France* (Dublin 1940).

—— *Biographical Dictionary of Irishmen in France* (Dublin 1949).

Healy, J. : *Centenary History of Maynooth College* (Dublin 1895).

Hogan, ed. : *Ibernia Ignatiana* (Dublin 1872).

—— *Distinguished Irishmen in the Sixteenth Century* (London 1894).

Holland, W. : *History of West Cork and the Diocese of Ross* (Skibbereen 1949).

Hughes, P. : *The Reformation in England* (London 1954).

Janelle, P. : *The Catholic Reformation* (Milwaukee 1951).

Jones, F. : *The Counter Reformation* (Dublin 1967).

Knapp : *Reports of Cases argued and determined before the Judicial Committee of His Majesty's Privy Council* (New York 1963).

Küng, H. : *The Council in Action* (New York 1963).

Lainé, Abbé : *Génealogie de la maison MacCarthy anciennement souveraine des deux Monmonies ou de l'irlande méridionale* (Paris 1839).

Lynch : *Cambrensis Eversus,* trans. Kelly (Dublin 1848).

Lavisse, *Histoire de France,* tom. VI (Paris 1920).

Lecky : *A History of Ireland in the Eighteenth Century* (London 1902).

—— *Lismore Papers,* ed. Grossart, second series 1887.

MacCaffrey, J. : *History of the Catholic Church in the Nineteenth Century* (Dublin 1910).

—— *History of the Catholic Church from the Renaissance to the French Revolution* (Dublin 1915).

MacCarthy, D. : *A Historical Pedigree of the Sliocht Feidhlimidh* (Exeter 1868).

MacCarthy, S. T. : *The MacCarthys of Munster* (Dundalk 1922).

MacCarthy, T. Abbé : *Sermons of* (Dublin 1848).

MacCurtain : *Tudor and Stuart Ireland* (Dublin 1972).

MacGeoghegan, Abbé : *A History of Ireland,* trans. O'Kelly (Dublin 1849).

Maguire, J. F. : *Father Mathew* (Cork 1865).

Manseau, Abbé : *Les prêtres et religieux déportés sur les côtes et dans les îles de la Charente-Inférieure* (Bruges 1886).

Martin, F. X. : *Friar Nugent* (London 1963).

McManners, J. : *The French Revolution and the Church* (London 1969).

Meehan, C. P. : *The Fate and Fortunes of the Earls of Tyrone and Tyrconnel* (Dublin 1886).

Messingham : *Florilegium Sanctorum Insulae Hiberniae* (Paris 1624).

Michelet : *Histoire de France,* tom. XI (Paris 1856).

Millet, B. : *The Irish Franciscans 1651-65* (Rome 1964).

—— *Survival and Reorganisation 1650-95* (Dublin 1968).

Mooney, C. : *The First Impact o fthe Reformation* (Dublin 1967).

Moran, Cardinal : *History of the Archbishops of Dublin* (Dublin 1864).

—— *Spicilegium Ossoriense* (Dublin 1874-84).

Mourett : *The Papacy* (London 1931).

Murphy, D. : *Our Martyrs* (Dublin 1896).

Murphy : *History of Trinity College, Dublin* (Dublin 1951).

Nicolai, Abbé : *Statistique du clergé girondin a Bordeaux au XVIIIe siècle* (Bordeaux 1909).

O'Boyle, J. : *The Irish Colleges on the Continent* (Dublin 1935).

O'Callaghan, J. : *A History of the Irish Brigades* (Glasgow 1870).

O'Connell, Mrs. : *The Last Colonel of the Irish Brigade* (London 1892).

O'Heyne : *Irish Dominicans in the Seventeenth Century,* ed. Coleman (Dublin 1902).

Ó Foghludha, R. : *Cois na Cora* (Baile-atha-Cliath 1937).

O'Sullivan : *Historiae Catholicae Iberniae Compendium 1622,* ed. Kelly (Dublin 1850).

—— *Pacata Hibernia* (Hibernia Press 1810).

Pauly, M.-H. : *Les Voyageurs Français en Irlande au temps du Romantisme* (Paris 1939).

Petrie, C. : *Louis XIV* (London 1938).

—— *The Jacobite Movement, the First Phase* (London 1948).

Prendergast, J. : *The Cromwellian Settlement of Ireland* (Dublin 1922).

Power, P. : *A Bishop of the Penal Times* (Cork 1932).

Renehan-MacCarthy : *Collections on Irish Church History* (Dublin 1861).

Roche, J. : *Essays Miscellaneous and Critical, Memoirs of an Octogenarian* (Cork 1851).

Ronan, M. : *The Reformation in Dublin* (Dublin 1926).

Rothe, D. : *Analecta,* 1619, ed. Moran (Dublin 1884).

Rushe : *Carmel in Ireland* (Dublin 1903).

Simpson, R. : *Edmund Campion* (London 1896).

Smith, C. : *History of Cork,* ed. Day and Coppinger (Cork 1893).

Spenser, ed. : *View of the State of Ireland, 1596* (Hibernia Press 1809).

Stephens, M. : *Revolutionary Europe* (London 1928).

Theiner : *Vetera Monumenta Hibernorum et Scotorum* (rome 1864).

Theiner : *Vetera Monumenta Hibernorum et Scotorum* (Rome

Ussher : *Veterum Epistolarum Sylloge* in *Works,* ed. Elrington.

Wadding, Luke : *Father Luke Wadding,* ed. Mooney (Dublin 1957).

Wakefield : *An Account of Ireland, Statistical and Political* (London 1912).

Walsh, P. : *Gleanings from Irish MSS.* (Three Candle Press 1933).

Wall, M. : *The Penal Laws, 1691-1760* (Dublin 1961).

Ward : *The Eve of Catholic Emancipation* (London 1912).

Ware : *Writers of Ireland* (Dublin 1704).

—— *Works,* ed. Harris (Dublin 1745).

Webster : *The Diocese of Cork* (Cork 1920).

Wilson, P. : *The Beginnings of Modern Ireland* (Dublin 1914).

Windele, J. : *Historical and Descriptive Notices of the City and County of Cork* (Cork 1839).

INDEX